WILLIAM COWPER

WILLIAM COWPER

by

HUGH I'ANSON FAUSSET

'Deprived of joy, I feel I should find cause for deadly feuds with things invisible.'
HERMAN MELVILLE

This is a sight for pity to peruse,
Till she resembles faintly what she views,
Till sympathy contract a kindred pain,
Pierced with the woes that she laments in vain.
WILLIAM COWPER

NEW YORK / RUSSELL & RUSSELL

FIRST PUBLISHED IN 1928
REISSUED, 1968, BY RUSSELL & RUSSELL
A DIVISION OF ATHENEUM HOUSE, INC.
BY ARRANGEMENT WITH THE ESTATE OF HUGH I'ANSON FAUSSET
L. C. CATALOG CARD NO : 68-11325
PRINTED IN THE UNITED STATES OF AMERICA

CONTENTS

PORTRAITS

FOREWORD

Biography bulks larger in this study than in its pre-decessors for two reasons; firstly, because Cowper's life offers more of an adventure of understanding than his poetry; and secondly, because there is no satisfactory biography in existence.

This is not to say that I have neglected his poetry. I have in fact considered it in detail. But its qualities have been well appraised, and little new in this province remains to be discovered. It was, indeed, because certain fundamental needs of his nature, which may be called religious, were not satisfied in his poetry that it remained more of a literary than a vital activity, lacking either complexity or profundity. And even where by an absolute fidelity to concrete experience it embodied life with a sensitive truth, it was truth of a limited and external order.

The religious impulses, however, which failed to find their satisfaction in poetry dictated the pitiful and yet valiant story of his life. Of that life there exist a number of adequate short sketches, of which the best are perhaps Sir J. G. Frazer's and Canon Benham's. But there is no detailed biography which will satisfy a modern reader. Hayley's is too unctuous, Southey's too sententiously and ecclesiastically moral, while Mr. Thomas Wright's is little more than a catalogue of events. And in none of these is any serious attempt made to penetrate beneath the surface and explain Cowper's morbidity in its varying degrees from melancholy to madness in other than conventional terms.

It may be that in trying to explore his personality more deeply, I have allowed too little for the inexplicable element in his mental darkness, and that in combating the complacent religious view of it, enunciated, for example, by Southey, I have exaggerated the destructive part which Evangelical doctrine played in his life. But I have not forgotten Belarius' words –

O melancholy !
Who ever yet could sound thy bottom?

The ultimate pathos of such melancholy lies in the fact that it is beyond rational definition as it is beyond rational control. In Cowper, however, it was never quite irrational, and so never unintelligible. While, therefore, my attempt to explain it may not greatly enhance its reality, it may win a little new ground for human understanding from the meaningless province of mysterious dispensation. As to Evangelicism, I have considered it solely in its relation to his personality and with no desire to slight the undoubtedly great service which it did in stirring the conscience of a complacent and to some extent corrupt age, or the suitability of its doctrines at the time to natures more primitive than his.

Few lives offer a biographer more material, since in Cowper's letters we have an almost daily chronicle of his moods and activities for many years. Upon these I have drawn extensively, not only by specific quotation, but by using his own words, whenever possible, to describe events. My debt, therefore, to Mr. Thomas Wright's edition of the letters is considerable, as it is to Mr. John Bailey's excellent edition of the poems.

Cowper's life was low in tone. A cloud of depression

FOREWORD

hangs over much of it, and delightful and appealing as his personality was, it is not one to excite a very vivid response. I have often had the sensation of an explorer in a dim tunnel haunted by spectres of madness and bigotry. But the endearing humanity of the man is heightened by the darkness in which it shines like a jewel. And while my chief aim has been to throw new light on the darkness which few have tried to penetrate, I have wished, too, to distil something of the companionable virtue of one whose humour played upon the surface of a life, to which he always felt himself to be unequal, like low sunlight on an ebbing sea.

H. I'A. F.

to

LALAGE

¶ PART ONE

THE SEEDS OF MISFORTUNE

THE SEEDS OF MISFORTUNE

§ I

IN the year 1738, in the precincts of a school at Mark-yate Street, a dreary, straggling village between St. Albans and Dunstable, a small boy, slender in build, fresh coloured and with refined features, might have been seen cowering before another nearly ten years his senior, who, with the diabolical taste of the bully for the abnormally sensitive, had singled him out as an object for persistent persecution. The degree of the victim's dread may be gauged from the fact that he was afraid to lift his eyes higher than his tormentor's knees, and in later life his recollection of his suffering centred, not upon a cruel face, but upon a pair of shoe-buckles.

The name of the child so prematurely exposed to the brutality of life was William Cowper. He had been born seven years earlier in the Rectory at Great Berkhamstead. His father combined a talent for writing light ballads with the scrupulous discharge of parish duties. These duties, as interpreted by the typical priest of the period, comprised the preaching of a respectable morality and the argumentative defence of the Established Church against the subversive inroads of the Deists. To the imaginative and experimental side of religion the Reverend John Cowper would seem to have been as insensitive as the majority of his contemporaries; and while he could teach his son morality, in which so inoffensive a boy needed little instruction, he was hardly an ideal guardian for a temperament and a constitution 'delicate in no common degree.'

His father's deficiences, however, would probably have counted for little in William Cowper's life if he had not lost his mother when he was just six years old, and in her lost 'a comfort' which he remembered and regretted so long as he lived. That she should have left such a vivid and persistent impression of tenderness upon him, although the opportunity she had for showing it was so short, is proof both of his intense need for her and of her power to satisfy it. More than fifty years later he could assert that he remembered her perfectly, and that not a week, and often not a day, passed in which she was out of his thoughts.

She was the daughter of Roger Donne, a descendant of the famous Dean of St. Paul's, and Cowper's attachment to her extended later to members of her family with whom he felt a particular kinship. Her death was disastrous to her son's well-being. We may even date from it the sense of homelessness, of isolation from the kindly influences of life, under which he was always to languish. For six years she had stood between him and the power of life to wound, had cherished him as the sun does a tender plant, had been, in his own words, the delight of his heart.

And then inexplicably the smile, the voice, the eyes that chased all fears away, were withdrawn.

> I heard the bell tolled on thy burial day,
> I saw the hearse that bore thee slow away,
> And, turning from my nursery window, drew
> A long, long sigh, and wept a last adieu! . . .

> Thy maidens, grieved themselves at my concern,
> Oft gave me promise of thy quick return.
> What ardently I wished I long believed,
> And, disappointed still, was still deceived.
> By expectation every day beguiled,
> Dupe of *to-morrow* even from a child.
> Thus many a sad to-morrow came and went,
> Till, all my stock of infant sorrow spent,
> I learned at last submission to my lot;
> But, though I less deplored thee, ne'er forgot.

This early experience of being duped by life did more than incline Cowper's nature to melancholy. It laid the foundations in his sensibility of a profound mistrust, a readiness to believe that life had an arbitrary bias against him. And so deeply was it laid that all the acquired rationality of later years could not avail against it. From the cessation of those 'nightly visits'

> That thou mightst know me safe and warmly laid,

he ceased in a very real sense to be 'safe and warmly laid' in the lap of life. There was no one to shield him from the nightmare of his fears and his shyness, or to soften his approach to a world which he was to describe as 'so little to be loved,' because it would give and then callously withdraw a 'constant flow of love, that knew no fall.'

Probably it was from his mother that he inherited the excessive sensibility which she alone might have shielded from premature exposure, from his father the moral temper and good sense so adequate to the demands of normal experience, so ineffectual when a nature is disturbed by

> obstinate questionings
> Of sense and outward things,
> Fallings from us, vanishings;
> Blank misgivings of a Creature
> Moving about in worlds not realised.

Such misgivings were the mark of a kind of sensibility, soon fearlessly to express and so relieve itself in English poetry. But in Cowper it was thwarted and morbidly suppressed, partly through constitutional weakness and the circumstances of his upbringing, partly through the inimical climate of his time, in which the winter of rationalism still lingered, although the spring of romanticism was near. And in the complementary faculties which he inherited from his parents it is perhaps not fanciful to see those also which strove for readjustment in the consciousness of the eighteenth century.

The more we study that century, the less can we accept the verdict usually passed upon it as an age of accomplished sobriety and serene self-sufficiency. For while our knowledge to-day of all the pain and perplexity in which a heightened sensibility was to involve man, of the burden of the mystery which was to lie so heavily upon his shoulders, leads us to appreciate to the full the material advantages of accepting such limits to experience as Pope, for example, did, it also enables us to sympathize intimately with those whose humanity was too warm and vivid to accept them.

And such, in very different degrees, we discover the

majority of Pope's contemporaries and successors to have been. On a near scrutiny the eighteenth century is found to be rather the nursery of modern sensibility than the schoolroom of a prescribed classicism.

Yet the two forces, the rationalism which arbitrarily excluded all experiences that were hard to explain or control, and the desire to enter life more intimately and self-forgetfully by way of feeling and sensation, were seldom positively or profoundly fused, and in many poets they were curiously disconnected.

The morbid element in Cowper's temperament is an example of this disconnection. In one of his letters he commented on his strong head, remarking that wine would never make him drunk, and that an ordinary degree of fever had no effect upon his understanding. And even during the period when later he was paralysed by a fixed delusion, his mind preserved its logical capacity. Indeed, his delusion was so terrible and inescapable because it was served by a ruthless logic while being itself the offspring of a trembling sensibility which his reason could not control.

The good-sense, therefore, the masculine temper which he inherited probably from his father, was actually a condition of his later madness, imposing as it did strict limits on experience, limits against which his sensibility struggled like a bird fluttering frail wings against the bars of its cage. And because his reason could not expand to include and inform experiences which transcended good-sense, there was inevitably a point at which sanity and sensibility became separated.

No subtle analysis, however, is needed to explain Cowper's sufferings as a child. His father, who was apparently as incurious of the ways of boys to boys as of the ways of God to men, sent him within a year of his mother's death to the ill-regulated school at which he experienced the tortures already described. For two years he endured them, suffering as much from the melancholy which persecution induced as from the persecution itself, before the cruelty of his oppressor was discovered and punished with expulsion, while he himself was removed from the school.

It is the tragedy of the tender-minded to be always born into a tough-minded world, and it is doubtful whether Cowper would have fared any better in his upbringing if he had been born fifty or a hundred years later. Fathers, unless they have acquired that psychological understanding which has begun to affect the conduct of our day, are, as Hayley sententiously observed, 'though good men, in general utterly unfit to manage their young and tender orphans.'

Certainly a father who could so carelessly expose an unusually sensitive boy to persecution, or could, a little later, ask him to read and comment on a treatise on suicide, would seem to have justified Hayley's scepticism. And we can hardly doubt that the seeds of Cowper's later delusions were thus already sown before his eighth year, that his later conviction of a God Who could withdraw His love from one of His creatures was rooted in his experience of the sudden withdrawal of his mother's love, while the cruelties of a bully left an ineffaceable impression of a penal power active in the universe, before which man must surrender his will and accept, if necessary, an eternal damnation.

§ 2

Devout biographers, however, have followed Cowper himself in deploring, not so much the misfortune and premature exposure, as the so-called irreligious atmosphere of his early life. They have shared his regret that in his sufferings he could derive only a momentary comfort from remembering the words of the Psalmist, 'I will not be afraid of what man can do unto me.' 'Happy had it been for me,' he wrote in a period of feverish religiosity, 'if this early effort towards a dependence on the blessed God had been frequently repeated by me!'

His unhappiness, however, as his whole later life was to prove, consisted not in his want of a conventional religious faith which would have been unnatural to childhood, but in the fatal sapping by circumstances of a sustaining faith in himself. Indeed, the religion which exploits the despair of childhood for its own ends, instead of curing it by removing its physical causes, can poison human nature at its source.

The Reverend John Cowper's conception of God may have been deficient in vision and depth, and religion may have been 'neither known nor practised' by the majority of those who had the care of his son's education; but at least they honoured human nature enough not to trade upon those instinctive fears which an Evangelicism, tainted with Calvinism, was later so disastrously to excite.

Consequently, from the time Cowper left Dr. Pitman's school at Markyate Street he was tolerably happy. The nervous strain through which he had passed may also explain the inflammation of his eyes which, dating from this time, was to trouble him at intervals throughout his life. It led to his being put under the care of a Mr. Disney, an oculist, who, in spite of his indifference to religion, relieved the weakness of his eyes sufficiently for him to go after two years' treatment to Westminster School.

Thirty years later he was to find comfort in fancying himself once more a schoolboy, and to describe that period as one 'in which if I had never tasted true happiness, I was at least equally unacquainted with its contrary;' and while he severely criticized public-schools in his *Tirocinium* for exploiting the competitive instinct and having more concern for learning than morals, the same poem contains an affectionate reference to 'the play-place of our early days.'

All the admirable influences in Cowper's life were to encourage the free play of his whimsical nature, and Westminster may certainly be numbered among these. He enjoyed the games, he kept a tame mouse until it devoured its own family, and he became a fair classical scholar. He was happy, too, in his friendship with several remarkable boys who shared his tastes, and of whom mention will be made hereafter. And in 'Vinny Bourne,' the fifth-form master, he discovered a nature which, judging by his own account of it, was the very double of his own.

'His humour,' he was to write, 'is entirely original; he

can speak of a magpie or a cat in terms so exquisitely appropriated to the character he draws, that one would suppose him animated by the spirit of the creature he describes. And with all his drollery there is a mixture of rational, and even religious reflection at times; and always an air of pleasantry, good-nature, and humanity that makes him, in my mind, one of the most amiable writers in the world. It is not common to meet with an author who can make you smile, and yet at nobody's expense; who is always entertaining, and yet always harmless; and who, though always elegant, and classical to a degree not always found even in the classics themselves, charms more by the simplicity and playfulness of his ideas than by the neatness and purity of his verse.'

Already too, if we are to believe what he wrote in *The Task*, he had begun to draw upon the two sources of pleasure by which he was to cling later so patiently and precariously to a life inwardly blighted by despair – the love of Nature and of the graces of poetry.

> My very dreams were rural, rural too
> The first born efforts of my youthful muse,
> Sportive, and jingling his poetic bells
> Ere yet her ear was mistress of their powers.
> No bard could please me but whose lyre was tuned
> To Nature's praises. Heroes and their feats
> Fatigued me, never weary of the pipe
> Of Tityrus, assembling, as he sang,
> The rustic throng beneath his favourite beech
> Then Milton had indeed a poet's charms:

New to my taste, his Paradise surpassed
The struggling efforts of my boyish tongue
To speak its excellence; I danced for joy.
I marvelled much that, at so ripe an age
As twice seven years, his beauties had then first
Engaged my wonder, and admiring still,
And still admiring, with regret supposed
The joy half lost because not sooner found.
Thee too, enamoured of the life I loved,
Pathetic in its praise, in its pursuit
Determined, and possessing it at last
With transports, such as favoured lovers feel,
I studied, prized, and wished that I had known,
Ingenious Cowley!

If, then, he 'acquired Latin and Greek at the expense of a knowledge much more important,' it was not at the expense of his sympathies for Nature and Art. The picture of his life at Westminster which he drew later in his harrowing *Memoir* was inevitably distorted by the religious fanaticism which then possessed him. He there deplored the lack of any sentiment of contrition or thought of God during this period except after an attack of sickness. And there could be no better proof of his health, of the fact that the sane and genial elements in his nature were allowed to expand and that no vicious strain was put on his nervous sensibility.

For his was a nature which needed reinforcing rather than chastening. The boy, full of animal arrogance, may profit by being reminded that the pride and lust of the flesh are but foolishness with God, although, even with such, a positive appeal to intelligence and manhood is probably more effective. But Cowper was too little animal either to need or profit by such reminders. So far, therefore, as by religion he implied such chastening, we cannot regret that he left Westminster at the age of eighteen 'tolerably furnished with grammatical knowledge, but as ignorant in all points of religion as the satchel at my back.'

§ 3

On leaving Westminster in 1748 he was apprenticed to the law. He had himself little inclination for the profession and no hopes of success in it, but he was amiable enough to wish to gratify his father's wish, backed as it was by family influence which would favour his advancement. He was articled to a Mr. Chapman, in whose house in Holborn he lived for three years before moving into chambers at the Middle Temple.

The law served Cowper, as it had served his ancestor Donne, as a convenient screen behind which, unvexed by the importunities of relatives, he could indulge in more human activities. But with him, whose nature was neither sensual nor combative, these activities were rather desultory than absorbing. Donne in Lincoln's Inn flung himself hungrily upon life; Cowper, in similar circumstances, played gently and whimsically about her skirts.

But in these whimsical activities he was partnered by a fellow-clerk at Mr. Chapman's, named Thurlow, who possessed sufficient animal energy, ambition and mental force to combine indolence and the frequent drinking of punch with the solid acquisition of the law, by which he rose later to be Lord Chancellor.

Cowper was to owe so much to women that a general impression of him exists as of one destined by nature to spend his life in politely offering his wrists for the winding of wool. But if his sensibility was feminine in its timidity and dependence, the temper of his mind was essentially masculine. And just as later he admired the bold, masculine character of Churchill and tried to force his own milder muse to emulate Churchill's satirical defiance, so in Thurlow's company he came as near to living dangerously, or at least thoughtlessly, as it was ever in his nature to do.

Even with Thurlow, however, he was to be drawn into the net of feminine society. For near at hand, in Southampton Row, there lived a little man whose habit of wearing a white hat lined with yellow led Cowper in later years to suggest that, had the lining been but pink, he might have been gathered by a natural mistake for a mushroom and sent off in a basket. He was his uncle, Ashley Cowper, and his nephew's appreciation of his snug and calm way of living, the neatness of his little person, and the cheerfulness of his spirit, was enhanced by the fact that he was the father of two spirited girls, Harriet and Theodora. Both had beauty; but while Harriet charmed by her vivacity and ready wit, Theodora's nature was more retiring, and in all she thought and felt there was a quality of repose and of quiet integrity.

Cowper met them first when they came with their parents to drink tea at a Dr. Grey's in Norfolk Street,

where he had dined, and so much were he and Thurlow
attracted by them that visits to Southampton Row, which
had at first been confined to Sundays, soon became an
almost daily occurrence, to the subversion of legal studies,
which were exchanged for 'giggling and making giggle'
from morning to night.

Before three years had passed and Cowper had gone
into residence at the Temple, a frivolous relationship had
deepened into a serious attachment for the girl whom her
sister described as having the face and figure of a goddess.
His love for Theodora was never passionate, because he
was incapable of feeling passion. As he was to write later
in *Retirement* –

> Woman indeed, a gift he would bestow
> When he designed a paradise below,
> The richest earthly boon his hands afford,
> Deserves to be beloved, but not adored.

This prudent discrimination of the degree of feeling
justified between the sexes reminds us of Parson Adams'
opinion that 'every man ought to love his wife, no doubt;
we are commanded so to do; but we ought to love her
with moderation and discretion.' But, in fact, Cowper was
only preaching from the text of his own nature, with its
genial passivity, its courteous tenderness, its instinctive
fear of undue excitement and its corresponding appreciation of every relation which soothed and mollified.

Yet such feeling, if less intense than that of passion,
may be (within its own narrower limits) more sincere; nor
can the style and diction of the poems which Cowper

addressed to Theodora be fairly advanced in proof of its artificiality. For not only was a tone of elegant gallantry congenial to his nature, but at this time he was still too preoccupied with the form of poetry to relate it at all intimately to his feeling. Always, indeed, he was to treat his versifying as little more than a diversion, although in later years it became also a necessity.

Certainly the earliest poems addressed to Theodora as *Delia* were composed 'in a trifling butterfly trim,' a trifling equally with love and with the Muse. The lines, for example, in which he begged the favour of a ringlet of her hair were but 'an attempt at the manner of Waller' —

> When you behold it still as sleek
>   As lovely to the view,
> As when it left the snowy neck, —
>   That Eden where it grew, —
>
> Then shall my Delia's self declare
>   That I professed the truth,
> And have preserved my little share
>   In everlasting youth.

He was equally playful when he wrote of the 'little pain of a passing misunderstanding —

> For friendship, like a severed bone,
> Improves and gains a stronger tone
>   When aptly reunited.

But this playfulness did also sincerely reflect the quality of his feeling, which, even when it became more deeply involved in the person of his cousin, never possessed the

whole of his nature to the point of forgetfulness of a
conscious attitude. He could sing in falsetto tones of
those in whom

> copious floods of passion roll,
> By genuine love supplied,

or of the vexations and pollutions of passion –

> These are emotions known to few;
> For where at most a vapoury dew
> Surrounds the tranquil heart,
> There, as the triflers never prove
> The gladness of real love,
> They never prove the smart.

But such lines are themselves proof that, so far as passion
was concerned, he was a trifler himself.

In affection, however, in the quiet devotion of a
nature too delicate to endure a forceful impulse, he was
not a trifler. An inherent passiveness was indeed a
condition of his gentleness. Love to him was

> the shield that guards his heart,
> Or wards the blow or blunts the dart
> That peevish Fortune sends.

Through it he sought to recover the sense of comfort in
life which he had lost with his mother, and when he took
up his residence at the Middle Temple he already believed
that he had found in his cousin one who would thus gently
minister to his needs and be as gently ministered to, had
found his amiable fondness reciprocated, and in an *Ode*,

Supposed To Be Written On The Marriage Of A Friend, approached as near ecstasy as his nature would allow, in hymning the promise of a protective sympathy –

> Ah me! how long bewildered and astray,
>   Lost and benighted, did my footsteps rove,
> Till sent by Heaven to cheer my pathless way,
>   A star arose – the radiant star of love . . .
>
> While vulgar passions, meteors of a day,
>   Expire before the chilling blasts of age,
> Our holy flame with pure and steady ray,
>   Its glooms shall brighten, and its pangs assuage;
> By Virtue (sacred vestal) fed, shall shine,
>   And warm our fainting souls with energy divine.

§ 4

The depth, however, of Cowper's attachment to his cousin is more evident in the verse which he wrote when he could no longer rest upon the hope of her cherishing affection. And he was fated to lose this hope, as he had lost the comfort of a mother, just when he needed it most.

Not long after moving in 1752 from Mr. Chapman's house into the Middle Temple he began to suffer severely from depression. Day and night he was upon the rack, lying down in horror and rising up in despair, losing all relish for the classical studies which before had charmed him, desiring something more salutary than amusement, but lacking the energy to find it.

Once at Westminster he had experienced a similar lowness of spirits, but it had been transitory. Now, however, it persisted for more than a year. Doubtless the seclusion and isolation of his life aggravated such a condition, but it had its roots in an excessive refinement.

Many years later he lamented in a letter the physical degeneracy which civilization entailed, contrasting his nervous weakness with the animal integrity of his primitive ancestors. 'We have reason enough to envy them,' he wrote, 'their tone of nerves, and that flow of spirits which effectually secured them from all uncomfortable impressions of a gloomy atmosphere, and from every shade of melancholy from every other cause. . . . Is it possible, that a creature like myself can be descended from such progenitors, in whom there appears not a single trace of family resemblance? What an alteration have a few ages made! . . . For this difference, however, that has obtained between me and my ancestors, I am indebted to the luxurious practices, and enfeebling self-indulgence, of a long line of grandsires, who from generation to generation have been employed in deteriorating the breed, till at last the collected effects of all their follies have centred in my puny self – a man indeed, but not in the image of those who went before me; a man, who sighs and groans, and who never thinks of the aborigines of the country to which he belongs, without wishing that he had been born among them.'

In a happier mood he could find compensation for his animal degeneracy in the sensibility without which there could be no real happines. But however exquisite the feelings which he owed to it, they were acquired at a grievous cost. He possessed just sufficient animal spirits, if he nursed them, to be pleasantly equable. But he held nothing in reserve. Nor could he have borne the strain of intense feeling, if he had been capable of it. As he was to write – 'That nerve of my imagination that feels the touch of any particular amusement, twangs under the energy of the pressure with so much vehemence, that it soon becomes sensible of weariness and fatigue.'

And just as very small events could give him extravagant pleasure, so a very slight discouragement in his circumstances could plunge him into despair.

Thus the unfamiliar solitude of his rooms in the Temple affected him disastrously at this time, and the tide of life which so precariously sustained his spirits ebbed away. And as it ebbed, he became conscious of the lack of all necessity in his being and his activities. He was not attached to life by a strong animal relish for it, by any compelling intellectual interest, or even by a desire to advance in his profession.

The law meant nothing to him, and literature was no more than a pleasant diversion. He felt himself to be a trifler, stricken with the 'worst of all evils, both in itself and in its consequences – an idle life.'

But though at this time he was conscious only of the distress and vanity of his being, the means by which he tried to relieve the melancholy which was to mar his life were characteristic. He turned to Herbert's poems and their piety touched his heart more effectually than what seemed 'gothic and uncouth' in them shocked his taste. He pored over them all day long, and while he read he ceased to despair.

Yet Herbert's poems were no more than a drug to his distemper. It was not more piety which he needed, but less passivity, as the relative understood who advised him to lay Herbert aside, because he thought such an author more likely to nourish his disorder than to remove it.

Deprived, however, of this consolation, Cowper was once more face to face with his inability either to grasp life purposefully or experience it as a directing force. Yet religion claimed that the devout might realize their identity with life through prayer. And so, convinced of the inefficacy of all human means, he betook himself to God in prayer. 'My hard heart,' he wrote, 'was at length softened, and my stubborn knees brought to bow. I composed a set of prayers, and made frequent use of them.'

There are natures, either very strong or very weak, which can only find peace by such submission. But Cowper's was not one of them. His heart, far from being hard, was all too soft, while his intelligence was too critically detached to share intimately in such an act of prostration and so inform it with real meaning. At best he discovered in prayer only a means of exciting his emotions enough to forget momentarily his rational detachment. Such religious exercises therefore were now, as always, but a passive confession of his morbidity instead of an active solution of it, because he indulged in them one part of his nature at the expense of the other.

A change of scene, however, recommended by his friends, saved him from realizing this immediately. He went with Mr. Hesketh, who was engaged to his cousin

Harriet, to Southampton, where he stayed for some months. Companionship and diversions in the open air at once restored his native geniality. He was pressed into service on 'the good sloop the *Harriet*,' and although he found the confinement of sailing irksome and tedious and was as glad to escape on to dry ground as Noah when he was enlarged from the ark or Jonah when he came out of the fish, the wind that filled the sails swept away the cobwebs of his melancholy.

But it was in walks to Netley Abbey, Redbridge, or Freemantle that he experienced for the first time a vivid sense of the inflowing virtue of Nature. Of one of these experiences he wrote – 'The morning was clear and calm; the sun shone bright upon the sea; and the country on the borders of it was the most beautiful I had ever seen. We sat down upon an eminence, at the end of that arm of the sea, which runs between Southampton and the New Forest. Here it was, that on a sudden, as if another sun had been kindled that instant in the heavens, on purpose to dispel sorrow and vexation of spirit; I felt the weight of all my misery taken off; my heart became light and joyful in a moment; I could have wept with transport had I been alone. I must needs believe that nothing less than the Almighty fiat could have filled me with such inexpressible delight; not by a gradual dawning of peace, but, as it were, with a flash of his life-giving countenance. I think I remember something like a glow of gratitude to the Father of mercies, for this unexpected blessing, and that I ascribed it to his gracious acceptance of my prayers.'

This experience and the interpretation which he put upon it are both very significant, particularly in the light of his later conviction that 'a neglect to improve the mercies of God at Southampton' was 'the sin against the Holy Ghost.'

Throughout his life Cowper's allegiance was disastrously divided between poetry and religion. He lacked the strength to realize the truth which the Romantics were to affirm that for a poet creation is a spiritual adventure transcending creeds as mysticism transcends morality; that the disinterested pursuit of reality involves a truer salvation than the self-interested submission to a creed; and that as theology originated in poets, so every poet must fashion his own.

Cowper was too individual and too much a poet to accept blindly the God of a prescribed dogma. But he was too timid to explore the Universe himself and to realize God in the act of creation. And so poetry remained for him no more than an amusement or a means of forgetting the dark frowns of that Calvinistic God to whose skirts he nevertheless timidly clung.

He was incapable of conceiving of the poet as a dedicated being. At most he could claim that it was 'a noble thing to be a poet, it makes all the world so lively,' and that if he had preached more sermons than even Tillotson did, and better, 'the world would have been still fast asleep; but a volume of verse is a fiddle that puts the universe in motion.'

And this division between poetry as a source of transitory pleasure and established religion as the only approach to

God was reflected in his attitude to Nature. 'O! I could spend whole days and moonlight nights,' he was to write later with a rare ecstasy of self-abandonment, 'in feeding upon a lovely prospect! My eyes drink the rivers as they flow.' But at once he reproved himself. 'I delight in baubles, and know them to be so; for rested in, and viewed without a reference to their Author, what is the earth – what are the planets – what is the sun itself but a bauble? Better for a man never to have seen them, or to see them with the eyes of a brute, stupid and unconscious of what he beholds, than not to be able to say, 'The Maker of all these wonders is my friend.''

The search for an immanent divinity in Nature was indeed the adventure to which poets were more and more to dedicate themselves, and only by such a search could Cowper have discovered a unity in his being and in life. He could not, however, reconcile a joy in Nature with a belief in God as a friend, because he accepted the prevailing dogma of God as a Being outside the Natural world which He had made, and so austerely remote from, and even hostile to, instinctive pleasure that He could only be approached by those who protested the worthlessness of Nature both in and outside themselves.

Cowper was to discover tragically enough how impossible it was for him to believe in the friendliness of such a Maker. For he had a genius for friendship, and knew it as essentially an equal and fearless relationship. But he could not apply his knowledge to the Universe, affirming its friendliness by conceiving God in it, not as an external and exacting Being, but as a spirit intimately informing and progressively realizing itself in the Natural world.

And so on this morning at Southampton he did neglect, in another sense than he gave to the words, 'to improve the mercies of God.' For here he first perhaps intensely realized the inspiration of Nature, and responded to a wider and deeper rhythm than the personal. Here for a moment the classicist and the pietist were resolved in the mystic and his whole being was positively at peace. And it was not the only experience of the kind which he enjoyed. For about this time in a letter to a friend he wrote – 'As for myself . . . the cool hour of contemplation, the evening radiance of the moon, and the illuminated arch of heaven will sufficiently answer my end by drawing my mind nearer to that Source, the Fountain of all hope and the source of all our good.'

It was by virtue of his unconscious loyalty to this experience that he came to sound a new note in English poetry. And if he could have recognized the religious validity of such experience and made it the basis of his faith, instead of subordinating it to Calvinistic dogmas in which he was far too sane and kindly really to believe, and which depressed his physical nature, so prone to droop, he might have mastered his morbidity as Wordsworth was to master his.

But from the beginning his communion with Nature, that fount of sanity and strength, was tainted by religiosity. He attributed his joy at this time, not to the fact that the beauty of the world had stimulated him to a positive act of expression, in which he embraced life on equal terms without either a narrowing pride or a demoralizing humility,

> drinking in a pure
> Organic pleasure

from the Universe of which he was a sentient element, but to the arbitrary intervention of a God, Who chose this moment to signal His appreciation of His servant's prostration in prayer.

This association of Nature with a Magisterial God prevented Cowper from ever discovering in her a real, sustaining 'bond of union between life and joy.' His account of his experience at Southampton resembles on the surface a score of narratives of conversion. But in fact it reveals the timidity, the conventional limitations, which were always to make real conversion impossible. A poet, such as Cowper, cannot lean on the faith or the dogmas of any Church. He must evolve for himself a direct relation to reality. Cowper was prevented from doing this alike by inherent humility and by the superficial conception of poetry common to his time.

And so he compromised, and the compromise was fatal. Years later he was to write – 'Were I permitted to make my choice even now, those hours I spend with poetry I would spend with God.' But the poet realizes the divine in him, as a creator. If his art is not an all-sufficient religion by virtue of its fearless loyalty to experience and its creative faith, his religion must at least be an art, hewn out of experience by himself. Cowper was too humble to realize this, and consequently he failed to unify his nature either in the religion to which he subscribed or the poetry which he practised. The latter, indeed, was seldom anything more than a distraction from the despair generated by his failure to believe in a God Whom his humanity denied.

And so on this morning at Southampton he rehearsed for the first time a part which he was to lack the conviction to play. And piety blinded him to the possibility of a new relation to life through Nature, which would have given a purpose to his being. At the heart of his joy there was a weakness. The shadow of servility lurked beneath the sunlight and the tingling air. It was the shadow of his own timidity projected into the Universe.

§ 5

On his return to the Temple, then, he had recovered enough self-confidence to burn his prayers, but he was still at the mercy of his moods. And in 1754, the year in which he was called to the Bar, he first consciously sought in poetry an antidote to melancholy, writing in *An Epistle of Robert Lloyd*, his old Westminster friend, that his aim in addressing the Muse was

> to divert a fierce banditti
> (Sworn foes to everything that's witty),
> That, with a black infernal train,
> Make cruel inroads in my brain,
> And daily threaten to drive thence
> My little garrison of sense:
> The fierce banditti which I mean,
> Are gloomy thoughts led on by spleen.

This was in two senses the first characteristic poem which he wrote. It was characteristic in the need which it satisfied and in its classically disciplined spontaneity. Here the qualities which were to make him so delightful a letter-writer, the gentle blend of humour and wit, of playfulness and moralizing, are apparent, while Milton's style or 'Mat Prior's easy jingle' are no longer imitated, but subdued to his own domestic uses.

Many of the verses which preceded these foreshadow his own peculiar manner, but it is still entangled in formal imitation. The very first piece, for example, which has survived, the lines written at Bath in his seventeenth year, ends with the characteristic line –

Drags the dull load of disappointment on.

And it reveals also his capacity for deriving from some trivial object a human history and moralizing upon it. The heel of a shoe in these verses serves the same purpose as the sofa on so much larger a scale was to do in *The Task*.

even here
Hints, worthy sage philosophy, are found,
Illustrious hints, to moralize my song.

And the wry step of a peasant, severing 'the strict cohesion' of nails and leather, suggests by analogy the false step of the statesman falling from the heights to which 'the steep road' of proud ambition leads. In the *Ode on Sir Charles Grandison* his sermonizing tendency is even more evident, and also the masculine directness which was always to nerve his elegance.

Again the song 'No more shall hapless Celia's ears' reveals something of the racy humour approaching buffoonery which was to make his wit so genial, while in the lines –

> Grant me the Muse, ye gods! whose humble flight
> Seeks not the mountain-top's pernicious height;
> Who can the tall Parnassian cliff forsake
> To visit oft the still Lethean lake;

he shows already a knowledge of his own unassuming sensibility and its need of quietness and retreat.

But although his early verses are too accomplished to be juvenile, and although he often succeeds in insinuating his own sentiments into them, they are still for the most part formal experiments, strewn with such enamelled poeticisms as,

> The sparkling eye, the mantling cheek,
> The polished front, the snowy neck,
> How seldom we behold in one!

Melancholy, however, enforced a new sincerity. To relieve himself, it was not enough to polish words. He could not feel save in a graceful manner, but his manner became increasingly the expression of his cultivated heart, and of a heart now sadly wounded. For his uncle Ashley refused to sanction an engagement between his nephew and his daughter.

The ground of his refusal was probably their near relationship. Cowper hoped for some time to overcome his uncle's objection. He even wrote, it seems probable, a Latin dissertation, full of classical and Biblical lore, on the theme that marriage between cousins was lawful. But his uncle, confirmed, it may be, in his views by morbid tendencies which he had remarked in his nephew, proved adamant. And before long he forbade the lovers to meet.

Cowper was not the man to rebel against such a veto or to cherish any ill-feeling against his uncle for imposing it. Indeed, he described him at his death as one 'whose heart towards me was ever truly parental, and to whose memory I owe a tenderness and respect that will never leave me.'

Yet it would be wrong to argue from his acquiescence that his feelings were but slightly engaged and that therefore he suffered little. His attachment was of a domestic nature, but to one of his temperament such an attachment was peculiarly binding. He had come to lean upon the hope of Theodora's affection, and her fidelity to him through life (shown later in many anonymous gifts and inquiries), no less than the gentle gaiety which seems to have characterized her as a girl, suggest that she of all women might have saved him from the morass into which he was to sink, by reconciling him with life.

In the poems which he addressed to her, both while hope and fear alternated, and when all hope was at an end, the artificial and the sincere still mingle. But there is enough sincerity of a poignant quality to prove that he was deeply, if not distractedly, moved. In the poem, for example, entitled *On her endeavouring to conceal her grief at parting*, he could indulge in such decorative extravagance as —

Since for my sake each dear translucent drop
　　Breaks forth, best witness of thy truth sincere,
My lips should drink the precious mixture up,
　　And, ere it falls, receive the trembling tear.

But he could write —

Nor think it weakness when we love to feel,
　　Nor think it weakness what we feel to show,

and prove his injunction in the Byronic stanza which
follows —

Bid adieu, my sad heart, bid adieu to thy peace!
Thy pleasure is past, and thy sorrows increase;
See the shadows of evening how far they extend,
And a long night is coming, that never may end;
For the sun is now set that enlivened the scene,
And an age must be past ere it rises again.

How much he looked to love as a reinforcement of his personality, sapped by a sense of insecurity, is felt in the lines —

Love, on whose influence I relied
For all the transports I enjoyed,
Has played the cruel tyrant's part
And turned tormentor to my heart.
But let me hold thee to my breast,
Dear partner of my joy and rest,
And not a pain and not a fear
Or anxious doubt, shall enter there.

Elsewhere he longed, as Shelley was so often to do, that
they might escape to some green island of innocence 'in
the deep, wide sea of Misery,' —

Oh! to some distant scene, a willing exile
From the wild uproar of this busy world,
Were it my fate with Delia to retire;
With her to wander through the sylvan shade,
Each morn, or o'er the moss-imbrownèd turf,
Where, blest as the prime parents of mankind
In their own Eden, we would envy none;
But, greatly pitying whom the world calls happy,
Gently spin out the silken thread of life. . . .

The tone is nearer to that of Coleridge in his days at Clevedon than to Shelley's. It has the same dilating amiability, the same domestic fondness. And the poem, *Written in a Fit of Illness*, although it contains the lines,

There borne aloft on Fancy's wing we fly
Like souls embodied to their native sky,

which approach as near imaginative ecstasy as Cowper could, reminds us also of Coleridge's drooping appeals to love as a narcotic for pain.

Oh! wert thou near me; yet that wish forbear!
'Twere vain, my love, – 'twere vain to wish thee near;
Thy tender heart would heave with anguish too,
And by partaking, but increase my woe.

It was typical of Cowper to refuse to indulge his weakness, as Coleridge would, at his mistress's expense; yet to both of them love was a mollifying influence, which the one could describe as the 'dear Antidote of every pain,' the other as the 'soft Nurse of pain.'

Elsewhere Cowper wrote of 'the thousand soft disquietudes of love,' and the intimate tenderness, pensive melancholy, and affecting dependence which these poems to Theodora reveal had their roots, even more than they had with Coleridge, in a sense of sailing the sea of life upon a raft that shuddered at every wave and might at any moment founder.

Cowper was more stoical and had more self-respect than Coleridge. But for this very reason his morbidity imposed a greater strain upon him, since he refused to indulge it and so gain relief. He suffered inwardly, until his mind could no longer bear the unrelaxed pressure of despair.

And already in three of these early poems, in *The Certainty of Death*, the *Last Stanzas to Delia*, and *On the Death of Sir W. Russell*, he employed the imagery of shipwreck to which he was so often to return, and which he was to use so poignantly in the last poem that he ever wrote, when in truth he was shipwrecked beyond hope of rescue.

Even in the first of these poems the formality of the imagery does not wholly conceal his deep conviction of his own frailty menaced by an ineluctable fate. But in the second, submission to fate has come home to him as a bitter personal necessity, a hell into which he had sunk from the heaven of his hopes –

The seaman thus, his shattered vessel lost,
    Still vainly strives to shun the threatening death;
And while he thinks to gain the friendly coast,
    And drops his feet, and feels the sands beneath,

Borne by the wave steep-sloping from the shore,
  Back to the inclement deep, again he beats
The surge aside, and seems to tread secure;
  And now the refluent wave his baffled toil defeats.

Theodora was the friendly coast to which he had hoped to
cling until the dark tides that threatened him should ebb,
and the loss of her intensified his sense of their impalpable
malevolence.

In all of these verses he preserved his conscious control
over his despair. That, indeed, was his virtue, but he was
to pay for it in periods of utter eclipse. If he could have
abandoned himself, if he had had less concern for his
rational integrity as a man, his reason might never have
been defeated by life.

But in his verses there never sounds that timeless music,
like the surge of wind about a house, which reveals that a
poet has reconciled himself with the dark forces of life
which he fears and resolved their elemental terror by expressing it. Even in the lines *On the Death of Sir W.
Russell* he remains starkly conscious, and to that extent
detached from the shipwreck of his hopes –

Doomed, as I am, in solitude to waste
The present moments, and regret the past;
Deprived of every joy I valued most,
My friend torn from me, and my mistress lost,
Call not this gloom I wear, this anxious mien,
The dull effect of humour, or of spleen!
Still, still I mourn, with each returning day,
Him snatched by fate in early youth away,

And her, through tedious years of doubt and pain,
Fixed in her choice, and faithful, but in vain!
O prone to pity, generous and sincere,
Whose eye ne'er yet refused the wretch a tear;
Whose heart the real claim of friendship knows,
Nor thinks a lover's are but fancied woes;
See me, ere yet my destined course half done,
Cast forth a wanderer on a world unknown!
See me neglected on the world's rude coast,
Each dear companion of my voyage lost,
Nor ask why clouds of sorrow shade my brow,
And ready tears wait only leave to flow,
Why all that soothes a heart from anguish free,
All that delights the happy, palls with me!

Cowper was to find in friendship a shelter from his innate
sense of homelessness. But it was too frail a shelter to turn
the fiercest storms. Such a love as he felt for his cousin
might have availed to do so. It might have been, as he was
to write in *The Doves*, that sustained by her,

> Those ills, that wait on all below,
>   Shall ne'er be felt by me,
> Or gently felt, and only so
>   As being shared with thee.

But he was never to love a woman with his whole being
again. Nearly twenty years after he had parted from
Theodora for ever, and when he was emerging for the
second time from the darkness that was to descend periodically upon him, he was to recall in some Latin Alcaics

this first and only intense devotion of his life, the union which he had so ardently desired, and her

> for whom mine eyes
> Weep sore, more loved than limb or life.

Again, later, in two letters he was to sketch allusively all that he had lost, and he was to remember her at last by the only bequest which he made. Probably nothing could have saved him from eventual shipwreck 'on the world's rude coast,' but it is just possible that in his cousin he might have found not only a shelter from the storm, but a link with life intimate and endearing enough to resist the backwash of his melancholy and the onset of his fears.

§ 6

Cowper was twenty-five when he saw his cousin for the last time, and in the same year he lost his father. He was more moved by parting from his home than his parent, feeling a relation to every tree and gate and stile in the surrounding country. The event must have intensified his sense of homelessness, but for some years the small patrimony which he inherited, together with a meagre stipend derived from an appointment as Commissioner of Bankrupts, enabled him to evade despair by various diversions.

He evaded it by restless movement, by excursions into the country, by visits to Gravesend and Brighton, or to pleasure-resorts such as Vauxhall or Marylebone Gardens, where he enjoyed the performance of plays in the Italian fashion. And he prolonged his illusion of light-heartedness by describing his pleasures in letters in which he affected a philosophical humour and a worldly gallantry.

He wrote, for example, to a friend – 'I look upon you as one of the very best species of libertines, otherwise I should not subscribe myself your affectionate friend.' Or again – 'I could be as splenetic as you, and with more reason, if I thought proper to indulge that humour; but my resolution is (and I would advise you to adopt it), never to be melancholy while I have a hundred pounds in the world to keep up my spirits. God knows how long that will be; but in the meantime *Io Triumphe*! If a great man struggling with misfortunes is a noble object, a little man that despises them is no contemptible one; and that is all the philosophy I have in the world at present. It savours pretty much of the ancient Stoic; but till the Stoics became coxcombs, they were, in my opinion, a very sensible sect.'

Or again, in a letter written in Latin, a fact which further stamps it as a literary diversion, he eulogized the charms and virtues of a young girl whom he had met at Gravesend and who, he averred, 'was at that age, at which every day brings with it some new beauty to her form. No one can be more modest, nor (which seems wonderful in a woman) more silent; but when she speaks, you might believe that a Muse was speaking. Woe is me that so bright a star looks to another region; having risen in the West Indies, whither it is about to return, and will leave me nothing but sighs and tears. You see me tortured with love, I you with lasciviousness.'

Letter-writing was always to be for Cowper a necessary

diversion; but at this time it was still also an affectation. Amiable philandering, for example, was utterly alien to his real nature, which prized sincerity more than most and was paralysed by its own scruple. But he wished to forget his real nature and its quivering sensibility in the pose of a town-wit and a sensible Stoic, to delude himself that an idle life was really a most agreeable one, and that the degree of poverty in which a man enjoys clean linen and good company has a peculiar grace and distinction.

And in this pathetic game of self-deception he was much assisted by the 'good company' which he kept. He had made at Westminster a number of friends between whom literature, and particularly verse-writing, were a bond of union. And seven of these now formed a 'Nonsense Club' and dined together every Thursday. Of these, Cowper was most in sympathy perhaps with Joseph Hill, who combined a solid business capacity with a love of reading upon sunshiny banks and contemplating the clouds as he lay upon his back. Cowper was to describe him later as

> An honest man, close-buttoned to the chin,
> Broadcloth without and a warm heart within,

and although like his fellows he could indulge a playful temper, composing for the Club that truly Græcian line –

> To whom replied the Devil yard-long-tailed,

he differed from them in possessing a greater degree of stability. It was this stability which Cowper lacked, as in different degrees did Bonnell Thornton, George Colman and Robert Lloyd, who were literary triflers like himself.

Addison and Steele had created a demand for the peri-
odical essay, but as the demand increased, it became
less exacting. Addison's humour had had an underlying
moral and educative purpose, but more and more a widening public sought in journalism only amusement.

This demand Thornton and Coleman hoped to satisfy.
They had begun by contributing to *The Student; or Oxford
and Cambridge Monthly Magazine*, and had later founded
both the *Connoisseur* and the *St. James's Chronicle*.

To both of these journals Cowper contributed anony-
mously a few papers, discoursing in a strain of satirical
levity on the indignities received by an old Bachelor from
the ladies or the irrational conversation favoured by
Society. The aim of these periodicals was merely to raise
an innocent laugh, and the desultory style, the cult of
oddity and lack of malevolence appealed to all that was
playful in Cowper's disposition.

But while Thornton and Coleman were quite satisfied
to be humorists, Lloyd, like Cowper himself, indulged
his wit to relieve a sense of inward discontent. He
had returned to Westminster as a master, but soon
wearied of

> labouring with incessant pains
> To cultivate a blockhead's brains,

and so had become a literary adventurer with enough
poetic sensibility and talent to despise the commonplace
world, but with too little to defy it. Lloyd, however, was
the devoted friend of another poet who shared with him
the disease of melancholy, but had the strength of body

and energy of mind to defy the world from which he recoiled.

Cowper was never personally intimate with Charles Churchill, but it was probably Lloyd who brought him prominently to his notice, and Churchill's literary influence upon him was certainly greater than that of any member of the 'Nonsense Club.' Both in a private letter and in his *Table Talk* he was to applaud Churchill's bold masculine character and the force of genius which overrode his carelessness, while he was to flatter him by attempted imitation.

And although the imitation was strained, because Cowper lacked just the robustness which showed in Churchill's stalwart figure and burly face, there was a distinct affinity between them. Both were warm-hearted and sought in satire to relieve an outraged generosity, and while Churchill was apt to bully as a satirist, Cowper was apt to scold. Both fell easily into the prosaic or the artificial when a natural impulse failed, and yet both had a native gusto. In Churchill it was the gusto of a combative virility, in Cowper the milder force of a captivating humour. Both had real insight into character, and both were moralists, the one scourging the objects of his reprobation, the other exhorting them. Churchill's intellectual honesty drove him to deny the religious 'revelation' which he had professed to believe as a clergyman; Cowper tried in an agony of diffidence to accept it, but was too intelligent to do so. And lastly, both had that tenderness of mind and that backward glance, popularized by Rousseau, to an early unspoilt world of Nature, in which the instincts had lost none of their fresh resilience and thought had not yet sullied a primal innocence.

The following lines of Churchill's, for example, are like a verse transcript of Cowper's lately quoted musings upon his own physical degeneracy –

Happy the savage of those early times,
Ere Europe's sons were known, and Europe's aims! . . .
In full content he found the truest wealth;
In toil he found diversion, food, and health;
Stranger to ease and luxury of courts,
His sports were labours, and his labours sports;
His youth was hardy, and his old age green;
Life's morn was vigorous, and her eve serene.

Still closer is the parallel between Churchill's lines –

Can the fond Mother from herself depart?
Can she forget the darling of her heart,
The little darling whom she bore and bred,
Nursed on her knees, and at her bosom fed? . . .
Yes, from herself the Mother may depart,
She may forget the darling of her heart,
But I can not forget. . . .

and Cowper's later hymn –

Can a woman's tender care
Cease towards the child she bare?
Yes, she may forgetful be,
Yet will I remember thee.

Typically enough, Churchill's 'I' referred to himself and

not to the Deity; but we have quoted the two pasages to show that Cowper's relation to Churchill was not merely that of a rather ill-advised disciple in satire, as is generally supposed, but was also one of affinity in sentiment.

Churchill had the strength to play out the part of the 'sensible Stoic.' Dying, he bid his friends not shed a tear, since –

> Whether he's ravish'd in life's early morn,
> Or, in old age drops like an ear of corn,
> Full ripe he falls, on nature's noblest plan,
> Who lives to reason, and who dies a man.

But while his courage enabled him to play the rational Stoic to the end, he, like Cowper and Lloyd, suffered from the inward wretchedness that springs from a negative relation to life, and his wit was the mask, when it was not the snarl, of a profound dissatisfaction.

For nine years, however, Cowper succeeded in keeping this dissatisfaction at bay. Coleman and Thornton were both good scholars and he followed their example in translating some of the Classics, while with another friend named Alston, 'a slothful and forgetful fellow, but of fine classic taste,' he read through the Iliad and Odyssey, comparing the original throughout with Pope's translation and discovering the truth, upon which he was later to act, that 'there is hardly the thing in the world of which Pope was so entirely destitute as a taste for Homer.'

Yet more and more he was burdened with the feeling that there was not one grain of solidity in the many baubles which he possessed, and that the part of the sen-

sible Stoic was one which he was incapable of sustaining.
As he wrote about this time –

> 'Tis woven in the world's great plan,
>   And fixed by Heaven's decree,
> That all the true delights of man
>   Should spring from *Sympathy* . . .
>
> Let no low thought suggest the prayer!
>   Oh! grant, kind Heaven, to me,
> Long as I draw ethereal air,
>   Sweet Sensibility!

But he had no need to pray for a quality which he possessed to such a disabling degree, and which in its demands
for truer delights than the 'Nonsense Club' could offer,
combined with its shy recoil from the bold stare of the
world, was to create a problem beyond his power of solution. The problem was not merely one of inward adjust-
ment. It had its practical aspect, too; and though sooner
or later the desolating sense of having no root in life must
have returned upon him, it was the economic necessity of
finding some stable occupation which forced the crisis.

The financial resources which had enabled him to evade
life were nearly at an end, and it was time to look to that
family influence which had governed his father's choice of
the law as profession. His kinsman, Major Cowper, had
at his disposal the office of Clerk of the Journals of the
House of Lords, an office congenial to his temperament,
since the business connected with it was transacted in
private. In 1763 this office, together with the offices of

Reading Clerk and Clerk of Committees, fell vacant, and Major Cowper satisfied his expectations by immediately offering him the two latter, which were the most lucrative appointments.

It seemed one of those acts of Providence which his Evangelical friends were later to discover in the most discouraging circumstances. He accepted, and for a moment experienced the joy of an assured material security.

§ 7

But his joy was only momentary. From the prospect of outward stability within his grasp he turned inwards, and trembled to discover an alarming incapacity. It has been said that he suffered from some minor physical defect and that an acquaintance, who wished to obtain the post for another, declared that it disqualified him, and threatened to make it public. But no such explanation is necessary for what occurred. Cowper's sensibility was so delicately poised that the slightest burden plunged him into depths of diffidence. And a feeling that he was unequal to life quickly passed into a conviction that life had damned him, that he 'was born to be persecuted with peculiar fury.'

So it happened now. From doubting his ability to perform the office which he had accepted, he came to reproach himself with having wished for the former holder's death. For a week he was torn by indecision, and then he tried to compromise. He begged Major Cowper to give the more lucrative offices to a friend and the poorest, the Clerkship of the Journals, to himself. To this his cousin reluctantly consented, and he obtained temporary relief in the thought that the clerkship would expose him to no severe strain.

But, in fact, his withdrawal in favour of a stranger proved fatal to him. It excited suspicion of a corrupt motive, and a powerful party in the Lords contested Major Cowper's right to nominate and insisted that the new clerk should prove his qualification by being examined at the bar of the House. By his self-denying act Cowper had exposed himself to the very public ordeal from which he shrunk. It mattered not that the examination was of a merely formal nature; it loomed before him like a nightmare, and all the horror of his fears and perplexities returned.

Yet, having asked for the office, he could not withdraw without injuring himself irretrievably in the eyes of his cousin and his friends. He was too sensitive either to flout conventional opinion or to satisfy it. And so he began to attend regularly at the office to qualify himself for examination. But it was all useless. Every time that he set foot in the office he felt like a man arriving at the place of execution. He read the journal books without perception and after many months had really learnt nothing.

That even at this time, however, his humour could hover whimsically, and now devoid of all affectation, above the abyss of his self-distrust is shown by the following letter to his cousin Harriet: – 'I have a pleasure in writing to you at any time, but especially at the present, when my days are spent in reading the Journals, and my nights in dreaming of them. . . . If I succeed in this doubtful piece of promotion, I shall have at least this satisfaction to reflect upon, that the volumes I write will be treasured up with

the utmost care for ages, and will last as long as the English Constitution – a duration which ought to satisfy the
vanity of any author, who has a spark of love for his
country. . . . Oh, my good cousin! if I was to open my
heart to you, I could show you strange sights; nothing, I
flatter myself, that would shock you, but a great deal that
would make you wonder. I am of a very singular temper,
and very unlike all the men that I have ever conversed with.
Certainly I am not an absolute fool; but I have more
weakness than the greatest of all the fools I can recollect
at present. In short, if I was as fit for the next world as
I am unfit for this, and God forbid I should speak it in
vanity, I would not change conditions with any saint in
Christendom. . . . Many years ago, cousin, there was a
possibility that I might prove a very different thing from
what I am at present. My character is now fixed, and
rivetted fast upon me.'

It was just this rational fixity which made it impossible
for him to escape from his weakness. He focused it with
a terrible precision even when the lens of his mind became distorted. And although a change of scene at Margate restored somewhat his spirits, subconsciously anxiety
continued to sap his resolution, and his first reflections on
waking in the morning were horrible and full of wretchedness.

Throughout his life Cowper was to suffer his worst
agonies in sleep or in those early waking hours, when,
isolated from homely human contact, the bewildering
forces which he could only struggle to suppress in the
day-time surged up within him with redoubled virulence

for the restraint that had been imposed upon them. And between his present dread of the peers of the realm and his later dread of a punitive Deity, there was essentially no difference. Each was but the form in which he objectified his terror of his own insufficiency, like a child who clothes his fear of the dark in the white drapery of a ghost.

But it was in the familiar imagery of a man borne away by a rapid torrent into a stormy sea, whence he sees no possibility of returning, and where he knows he cannot subsist, that he dramatized the flight of time which brought his ordeal nearer. And soon every kind of evasion was impossible, and torn between necessity and a conviction of incapacity, between the thought of what he owed to his relatives and the anticipated humiliation of a public disgrace, he came to cry aloud in his chambers, cursing his Maker and the hour of his birth.

And then for the first time the religious delusion which was to make such havoc of his life crept in. A thought would sometimes cross his mind that his sins had perhaps brought this distress upon him, that the hand of divine vengeance was in it. Self-distrust and shyness, if aggravated, inevitably lead on to a sense of sin, a fear of men and a consciousness of isolation developing into a fear of God and a conviction of being separated from Him. But he still possessed enough reason and self-respect to reject the thought, and while he began to look upon madness as the only escape open to him and to desire it earnestly, he was sane enough to doubt the possibility.

And so, too sane to hope for madness and too distraught

to discover self-reliance in his sanity, his thoughts turned to suicide. He remembered the vindication of self-murder which his father had asked him to read and judge, and it seemed easier to be equal to death than to life. Later he attributed this 'grand temptation' to Satan, and still later he interpreted it as the will of God against one peculiarly damned, and henceforth finally damned to an eternity of suffering because he had failed to obey it.

But at this time his panic had not yet clothed itself in the forms of mediæval dæmonology. It was not with a God or a Devil that he strove throughout the weeks before he was required to attend at the bar of the House, but with the positive and negative principles in himself, the will to live and the fear of life. Certainly his mind began to break beneath the strain; his interpretation of a letter in the public Press as a libel or satire upon himself is proof of this. But such a delusion derived from a morbid self-consciousness, and it was this self-consciousness together with his inherent indecision which saved him.

Fortunately, he found it as difficult to abandon himself to death as to life. He approached it in an agony of circumspection. And so neither by laudanum, nor drowning, nor a pen-knife, could he compass his end. Always at the critical moment something seemed to say, 'Think what you are doing.' It was not the voice of an overruling Providence, as he later fancied, but the voice of his own cautious common sense which, in the battle between desire and dread of death, gave victory to the latter.

There are forms of madness which have no rational significance. But Cowper was never mad to this degree.

Even when later he became a victim of a fixed delusion, it was consistent with his nature as a whole, with those qualities which made him at once the most delightful and the most pathetic of men. His limitations as a poet were due, as we shall see, to the barrier which his self-possession raised between him and life, and his exquisite humour as a letter-writer was the fine flower of his humility.

And it was these same qualities, unrelieved by action, which led him now and later to despair of himself. Self-distrust could not have so alienated him from life if it had not been combined with a detached self-possession. He was thus doubly locked within himself, by a sensibility which recoiled from life and a reason which, by narrowly defining his fears, inflamed them.

The inability, therefore, to give himself passionately to life which was to restrict his range as a poet was periodically to paralyse his faith in life as a man. His sensibility, incompletely released and expressed in imaginative action, was to avenge itself upon the mind that inhibited it by filling it with fantastic images of fear.

But if Cowper was thus miserably detached from life, he owed largely to the same detachment his preservation at this time from death. In the prolonged attempt which he made on the morning of the day of his ordeal to hang himself, he was throughout intensely aware of what he was doing. And it was probably to this awareness, even more than to the accident of a breaking garter, that he owed his escape. But the broken garter remained to testify to his attempt and to prove to the relatives and friends, sum-

moned by his alarmed laundress, the distraction which he
had been ashamed to divulge.

And thus ended all his 'connexion with the Parliament
House,' and with it the faint hope which he had cherished
of making a living in the legal profession.

¶ PART TWO

THE HARVEST OF PROVIDENCE

THE HARVEST OF PROVIDENCE

§ I

THE torture of anticipation and divided impulse was over, but it left him maimed for life. It mattered less that his inadequacy was published to the world than that it was impressed with the deep finality of unforgettable anguish upon himself. Such a wound, to a self-esteem which was always fragile, was fatal. Never again could he recover the basic faith in self which is necessary to a faith in life. Neither the domestic haven which he was to reach nor the sheltering arms of Nature in which he was to rest could do more than soothe the smart of an inward defeat. Henceforth through all the recesses of his sensitive being he was 'a stricken deer that left the herd.'

His relatives, however, seem to have been slow to realize the extremity of his condition. Instead of being taken at once to the country and diverted in every possible way from himself, he was allowed to remain in his chambers, where, as he wrote, 'the solitude of my situation left me at full liberty to attend to my spiritual state.'

It was a disastrous liberty; for it led him to interpret his failure henceforth in false theological terms, to try to turn the edge of his lost faith in self by resignation to a God in Whom he could not really believe and Whose penal attributes but aggravated his morbid conviction of sin.

Reviewing his life from the conventionally religious standpoint, he discovered at every stage of it 'a total forgetfulness of God.' He had forgotten Him as a child, at Westminster, and at The Temple. His levity and indolence seemed to him in the light of Biblical admonition 'an uninterrupted course of sinful indulgence,' and he was convinced 'that, if the Gospel were true, such conduct must inevitably end in his destruction.

But did he believe that the Gospel was true? Certainly in the company of Deists he had never failed to assert the truth of it with much vehemence of disputation. Yet in his heart he had to admit that he had 'dared fearfully to doubt,' and this rational dissent, no less than his lack of 'proper' religious feeling, seemed to him now 'an inveterate habit of rebelling against God.'

The falseness of his position is betrayed in the word 'proper.' There is all the difference between a devout life and a devoted one. The former satisfies the needs of un-inquiring piety, but only the latter can satisfy the needs of a poet. Cowper felt the want in himself of a religion which would reinforce his being and invest it with purpose; but the only religion of which he could conceive was that provided by the Churches, and in this, despite all his attempts at self-delusion, he was too critically enlight-ened to believe.

Later he was to write of his generation that 'the exercise of reason, enlightened by philosophy, has cured them of the misery of an abased understanding,' and he was to remark the melancholy fact that 'the Gospel, whose direct tendency is to promote the happiness of mankind in the present life, as well as in the life to come . . . should through the ignorance, the bigotry, the superstition of its professors . . . have produced incidentally so much mis-chief . . . the Prince of Peace Himself comes to confirm and establish it, and war, hatred, and desolation are the consequences. Thousands quarrel about the interpretation of a book which none of them understand.'

When he wrote thus, he was himself 'cured of the misery of an abased understanding,' and yet through timidity he thought it necessary to humble himself to the very bigotry and supersitition which he had rationally out-grown. This was the 'lamentable inconsistency' of his position and not, as he argued, 'that of a convinced judg-ment with an unsanctified heart.' His heart, his quailing nerves, desired the support of a conventional creed which his judgment refused. And so, perversely and ironically enough, he clung for comfort to a creed which guaranteed him only the punishment of unbelief. For too critical to benefit by its sensational promise of salvation, he was not critical enough to reject its sensational assurance of damnation.

It is difficult in these comparatively emancipated days to realize the oppressive idea of God accepted by the religious in the eighteenth century. The God of the Old Testament is now regarded as a tribal Deity and a symbol of the sterner workings of natural law, while our idea of God is becoming more and more purged of the primitive Jewish and other pagan conceptions of Him. But to Cowper's devout contemporaries He was still a very palpable potentate, with the arbitrary power to interfere in human lives, either to punish any lack of proper respect to His Person, or to preserve those who grovelled before Him from the risks which are now generally covered by insurance.

It was in such a God that Cowper supposed himself required to believe. He was, of course, far too sane to believe in Him. Rationally he would have agreed with Goethe when he said – 'What sort of a God would it be who only pushed from outside?' But he was also far too timid and dependent to admit consciously his scepticism. And so he shuddered at the thought of His vengeance without the compensation of a real belief in His Providence. Far better had it been for him to shudder, like Pascal, before the bleak immensities of space. For they at least were too large to be accredited with a capacity for petty persecution. But his imagination could never extend itself to the infinite. When he conceived of God's vengeance against him as boundless, he thought of it as a life-sentence imposed by a magnified oriental despot and indefinitely prolonged.

And this 'sense of God's wrath, and a deep despair of escaping it' now took possession of him. He no longer suffered simply from a sense of desertion by God. His amiable weakness and indecision, culminating in the agonized attempt at suicide, appeared to him a depravity which an outraged Deity would ruthlessly punish. The frowns of this Deity were even more terrible than those which he had anticipated in the House of Lords. He could now bear neither the eyes of men nor of God. In every book which he opened he found something that struck him to the heart. In the Bible itself, Christ, cursing the barren fig-tree, pointed the curse directly at him, and in every street he heard a mocking laugh.

These familiar symptoms of persecution mania were

accompanied by others of a more purely physical nature – loss of memory, a frequent flashing, like that of fire, before his eyes, and an excessive pressure upon his brain. He felt a sense of burning in his heart and concluded it was an earnest of those eternal flames which would soon receive him.

The doctor whom he consulted assured him that these were all delusions, and his brother, who was a cleric, but one who respected human nature too much to subscribe to the fetiches of popular theology, being 'a man of letters and of manners too,' tried to convince him that his reference of all his ills to 'supernatural interposition' was as unfair to the Deity as to himself. But his despair, inflamed by religious terrorism, now obsessed him. He could only walk to and fro in his chambers, saying – 'Oh! Brother, I am damned! think of eternity, and then think what it is to be damned!'

And so from his brother he turned to one who shared his belief in the possibility of damnation, to his cousin Martin Madan, chaplain of the Lock Hospital and a strong Calvinist. Madan was the first of the 'benevolent Divines' who, with the best intentions, were to prescribe the worst possible treatment. He was one of the leaders of the Evangelical party and, like many of them, he had a robust constitution. His powerful voice, his height and imposing looks must have in themselves overawed Cowper, and when he began by speaking of 'original sin, and the corruption of the world, whereby every one is a child of wrath,' he must have confirmed in his listener all the terrors of the religious melodrama in which he believed himself cast for the villain's part.

It was useless after this to insist on the 'all-atoning efficacy of the blood of Jesus' and to assure Cowper, when he deplored the want of such a faith, that 'it was the gift of God, which he trusted He would bestow upon him.' Cowper could only reply, 'I wish He would,' with as little hope of his wish being realized as any child would have in a father of so spiteful a temper and primitive a morality.

Martin Madan failed in his treatment of Cowper, as John Newton was later to fail, because he was blind to the fact that the religious needs of people differ. To a Jonathan Edwards the idea of a God arbitrarily dealing out salvation and damnation to selected individuals was 'a delightful conviction,' as of a doctrine 'exceeding pleasant, bright, and sweet,' since he was agreeably sure which treatment would fall to him. But to Cowper, unsustained by such pious self-satisfaction and too timid to challenge the meanness and cruelty of such a sovereign power, or to argue that 'retributive justice' was not in any true ethical sense justice at all, it was a desolating conviction.

To him William James' words are peculiarly applicable: – 'Ought all men to have the same religion? Ought they to approve the same fruits and follow the same leadings? Are they so like in their inner needs that, for hard and soft, for proud and humble, for strenuous and lazy, for healthy-minded and despairing, exactly the same religious incentives are required? Or are different functions in the organism of humanity allotted to different types of man, so that some may really be the better for a religion of consolation and reassurance, whilst others are better for one of terror and reproof?'

Cowper of all men needed a religion of reassurance, a religion which would reinforce his self-respect and convince him that a degree of intelligent scepticism, far from being an offence against God, was a proof of the divine in man eliminating the superstitions of savagery. But he was fated to fall into the hands of those who needed a religion of terror and reproof to subdue their animal nature, who, masterful and aggressive themselves, created a God in their own image at once to satisfy and to chasten their egotism, and who tried, as in a revival meeting, to compel him to the 'mercy-seat' by a crude appeal to fear. And they succeeded only in deepening his conviction that from so unintelligent and irascible a God he could expect no mercy.

Inevitably, then, soon after Martin Madan's visit, Cowper 'awoke with ten times a stronger alienation from God than ever,' while yet clinging pathetically to the delusion that these were 'the efficacious means which Infinite Wisdom thought meet to make use of' for the purpose of 'humbling the natural vainglory and pride' of his heart.

Yet above all the delirium of his despair his mind preserved its masculine grip and shaped these terrible sapphics –

Hatred and vengeance, my eternal portion,
Scarce can endure delay of execution,
Wait with impatient readiness to seize my
        Soul in a moment.

Damned below Judas; more abhorred than he was,
Who for a few pence sold his holy Master!

Twice-betrayed Jesus me, the last delinquent,
  Deems the profanest.

Man disavows, and Deity disowns me,
Hell might afford my miseries a shelter;
Therefore Hell keeps her ever-hungry mouths all
  Bolted against me.

Hard lot! encompassed with a thousand dangers;
Weary, faint, trembling with a thousand terrors,
I'm called, if vanquished, to receive a sentence
  Worse than Abiram's.

Him the vindictive rod of angry Justice
Sent quick and howling to the centre headlong;
I, fed with judgment, in a fleshly tomb, am
  Buried above ground.

Such were the fruits of having full liberty to attend to his
spiritual state in the lurid light of the Old Testament as
directed by the stern hand of Martin Madan. Barred
from Hell by his lack of positive vice, and from Heaven
by his lack of positive virtue, he crouched on an Earth,
from which he seemed an outcast too, imprisoned in a
body dead to all sensation, and expecting from moment to
moment the vindictive onslaught of an infuriated Deity.

He was mad, although, as we have shown, there was a
clear logic in his madness, and after consultation between
his brother and other members of the family, he was removed in December, 1763, to an asylum at St. Albans.
Indifferent as he was to the fate of all his belongings, with
a characteristic humanity which would surely have put the

God he feared to shame, if He had existed, he remembered, even in this crisis, his cat which he entrusted to his friend Hill. Of the presence of his cousin Harriet, now Lady Hesketh, and her husband, who called on him shortly before he left, he was almost insensible, sitting speechless and only saying in his heart as they were going out of the door – 'Farewell! there will be no more intercourse between us for ever.'

But in this, as in his conviction of an imminent doom, he was fortunately mistaken.

§ 2

The proprietor of the 'Collegium Insanorum' at St. Albans was an elderly doctor who combined the tact of a physician with the sentiment of a minor poet, and grounded both in a conviction that Christianity was a system able as no other 'to sustain the soul amidst all the distresses and difficulties of life.'

Benevolent himself, he created God in his own helpful image, and gradually his genial influence had its effect. Instead of discussing original sin and the curse of the law, he told humorous stories and encouraged Cowper to cap them. He appealed, in short, to the human in his patient, and soon the large Elizabethan house began to appear as a comfortable sanctuary against the inroads of celestial rage and the expectation of the bottomless pit.

In six months Cowper's taste for food and for life began to revive, and he was less haunted by awful visions and sounds. His nature had so far recovered its tone that it needed only a slight impulsion to pass from a negative into a positive phase of being. And this impulsion he received in July, 1764, from his brother, who, appealing as he always did to the rational in him, encouraged him to assert his judgment against the tyranny of a fixed and a false idea.

And this gave a new direction to his emotional nature. A tremor of hope passed through him and he awoke next day, for the first time, with a sensation of delight. And turning in this mood to the Bible, he inevitably found passages to confirm his delight. The benevolence, mercy, goodness and sympathy of Christ gathered force and became for the time a conviction. 'In a moment,' he wrote, 'I believed,. and received the Gospel.' And he added truly enough – 'Thus may the terror of the Lord make a Pharisee; but only the sweet voice of mercy in the Gospel can make a Christian.'

Yet the tone of yielding pietism which sounded in the refrain of the *Song of Mercy and Judgment*, with which he celebrated his recovery –

> Sweet the sound of grace Divine,
> Sweet the grace which makes me Thine,

might have warned his friends, if they had been critical enough to appreciate its significance, that his conviction was indeed only 'for the time.'

Passive devoutness, as William James has remarked, is usually associated with intellectual feebleness, and no devoutness, with those who are not intellectually feeble, can prove stable which does not satisfy the rational as well as the emotional nature. Cowper's mind was, indeed, at the moment enfeebled by the terrible ordeal through which it had passed, and so in the lines just quoted, as in most of the hymns which he was soon to write, he did not express his whole nature. They are of secondary value as poetry because his mind is not really in them. However touching, therefore, their unction, they lack creative necessity. They did not carry meaning to Cowper's mind, and so they do not carry it to ours. Rather they persuade us of the truth that devoutness unsustained by intellectual effort is a form of self-indulgence, and is as such inferior both to true poetry and true science, which are disinterested activities.

And of this Cowper's future history was a melancholy proof. The attainment of faith in which he now read a final conversion, and which lifted as by magic the weight of his madness and melancholy, was only the positive extreme of which his conviction of sinfulness was the negative. Both were delusions, were, to quote William James' phrase, 'theopathic conditions,' in which the Cowper whom we know and love, whimsical, sympathetic, sane, the foe of all extremes and the humanist, had little, if any, share.

In writing thus we do not, of course, question the reality and the value of a true conversion, in which the whole personality is vitally changed, discovering a new centre and orientation of energy and consequently an immense enhancement of life and power. Yet sudden conversions, when they are not mere convulsions of fear, are possible only to simple, if not primitive, natures. More complex and highly developed natures may date their conversion from a given moment, but such a moment must be the culmination of a long preparatory process. For a reflective nature cannot resolve its inhibitions by a sudden emotional storm. It demands, to quote Mr. Julian Huxley, 'that its religious life shall be a whole. It must be a whole intellectually, strung together upon a consistent theology; a whole morally, based upon a coherent moral philosophy . . . and a whole emotionally, related to an æsthetic sense which demands the fullest beauty.'

This triple demand cannot be satisfied by a melodramatic act of self-abandonment, in which the intellect is isolated, 'driven back upon itself and led into a mood of permanent and unsatisfied questioning.' Cowper's intellect was thus isolated, and so inevitably in due time disproved his 'conversion.' He never, indeed, succeeded in reconciling his mind with his emotions, yet within limits he realized such a unity in his poetry. It is even possible that if he had not been diverted from a wholesome line of development by the claims and conventions of religion, he might have found in poetry, not merely a harmonizing diversion, but the ultimate harmony of creative experience. For he possessed potentially what Goethe defined as the poet's divine endowment 'the right enjoyment of the world, the feeling of himself in others, the harmonious conjunction of many things that will seldom exist together.'

But the dogmatic religion which fear tempted him to embrace forbade him to enjoy the world rightly. It taught him to consider as worthless, from the point of view of salvation, the poetical activity which, at its highest, was more truly religious than itself, and in which he might have discovered a real equilibrium. The faith which he now possessed merely perpetuated his unbalance, although for others more primitive than himself it might and did offer a means of balancing an arrogant self-assurance with self-abasement. But there were no dark passions in him for an angry God to counterbalance: there was only a too delicate sensibility which an angry God either depressed or inflamed.

It was merely the nervous and emotional man, then, in him that was temporarily released. His conversion was not really a rebirth into a new life and a new consciousness, but only a transformation of his rigid fear into melting acquiescence.

For many succeeding weeks tears were ready to flow, if he did 'but speak of the Gospel or mention the name of Jesus,' and if, as he believed, the Lord had enlarged his heart and he ran in the way of His commandments, his mind had not come to terms with the despot Who haunted the background of his consciousness.

His relation to God was, in fact, still servile and fatalistic, and his was not a slave mentality. Only by affirming the divinity in himself, by disproving the God he feared with all his humane faculties, could he have realized an inner freedom beyond the reach of any theological menace.

For he was a poet, whose sin, in the sense of separation, consisted not of moral vices, but of creative indecision, of an imperfect contact with reality. The deep sorrow and contrition, therefore, which he continued to feel on account of fantastic sins which he had never committed were not necessary, as has been argued, to an effectual cure, but merely symptoms of the persistence of disease, while his delirious conviction of faith was only an intoxicant which enabled him to forget for the time the listlessness that was a symptom of creative frustration.

And so, whenever 'the ardour of his first love' should fail, whenever the abnormal emotional tide should cease to flow, and those 'lifeless and unhallowed hours,' which he feared so much, return to drag out their dreary length, once again the spectre of an angry Deity would emerge to denounce a failure of spirits as an unforgivable sin.

Then, indeed, the Paradise which he had emotionally found would be mentally and irretrievably lost. Yet his fate turned so much upon the chance of a kindly environment and one which put no strain upon his fragile sensibility, that even now, if another 'benevolent Divine' had not soon fanned the flame of his fanaticism, he might have enjoyed his 'naturally easy and quiet disposition' with no more than occasional periods of dejection, such occasions as Mark Rutherford, another victim of Methodism and of a kindred temperament, knew all his life, when he was suddenly plunged in the Valley of the Shadow and no outlet seemed possible, but which he contrived to traverse, or wait in calmness for access of strength.

§ 3

Dreading a relapse and still shrinking from a world of which weak piety exaggerated the pollution, Cowper remained with Dr. Cotton for a year after his recovery. To re-enter the world which he had known was indeed un-

thinkable, and like so many of the poets of his century,
if by a deeper necessity, he turned in thought to the countryside, not only as an asylum from the restless glitter of
the town, but as a source of refreshment to jaded nerves
and a corrective to the troubled, because too self-conscious, mind.

That Cowper's spirit best communed 'with her God'
directly through Nature rather than by the channel of
religious devoutness was to be proved by the quality of
the poetry in which he expressed that communion. In the
hymn *Retirement*, however, in which, shortly before his
removal from St. Albans, he voiced his longing for quiet
places, Nature was still for him the handmaid of scriptural
redemption –

> Far from the world, O Lord, I flee,
>   From strife and tumult far;
> From scenes where Satan wages still
>   His most successful war.
>
> The calm retreat, the silent shade,
>   With prayer and praise agree;
> And seem by thy sweet bounty made
>   For those who follow thee.

Of all the hymns which Cowper wrote, we shall find that
those come nearest to pure poetry in which God is invoked
through Nature. And the feeling, even in this hymn, is
sincere enough to inform the conventional idiom with a
degree of personal meaning.

The calm retreat which he first chose was at Hunting-

don, by reason of its nearness to Cambridge, where his
brother was a Fellow of Benet (now Corpus Christi)
College. He left St. Albans on June 17, 1765, at four
in the morning, and after spending a few days with his
brother moved into the lodgings which had been taken
for him. He was now wholly dependent upon relations
for his support, and possibly his sense of indebtedness to
them increased his concern that they 'might be made
partakers of the same mercy which it had pleased God
to vouchsafe to himself.'

Later he was to write apologetically to one of them –
'When I left St. Albans I left it under impressions of the
existence of God, and of the truth of Scripture, that I had
never felt before. I had unspeakable delight in the discovery, and was impatient to communicate a pleasure to
others that I found so superior to everything that bears the
name. This eagerness of spirit, natural to persons newly
informed, and the less to be wondered at in one who had
just emerged from the horrors of despair, made me im-
prudent, and, I doubt not, troublesome to many.'

Certainly his relatives showed no great eagerness to
share in his rapture. Even his clerical brother John became very reserved when Cowper took care at once to
show that he had received, 'not merely a set of notions,
but a real impression of the truths of the Gospel.' His
brother was sceptical of such feverish impressionism, but
he wisely discouraged the excitement involved in discus-
sions of 'Gospel truths,' and it was only when he himself
was on his death-bed that Cowper had the satisfaction of
making a convert, and published an account of his triumph

as a proof of the virtues of Evangelicism and a pleasant testimonial to the 'benevolent Divine' who was then unduly exciting his nerves.

Chief among the friends and relatives, however, whom he now wished to be 'not almost but altogether Christians' was his cousin Lady Hesketh. And for two years he used his experience as a text upon which to hang a persistently edifying correspondence. Terrible as had been his chastisement, he assured her that he acknowledged in it the hand of an infinite justice, that, without hypocrisy, he esteemed it the greatest blessing, next to life itself, which he had ever received. The ways of Providence, he had to admit, were very mysterious, but he begged his dear cousin to believe that a firm persuasion of the superintendence of Providence over all our concerns was absolutely necessary to our happiness, and that without it we could not be said to believe in the Scripture, or practise anything like resignation to His Will. The fact that 'a convert made in Bedlam was more likely to be a stumbling-block to others than to advance their faith' only led him to redouble his efforts.

Doubtless the impulse behind these efforts was not so much an altruisitic concern for others as a desire to increase, by constantly affirming the pleasure which he derived for the time from the sanctification of his worldly failure, the surrender of his will, and the reduction of the whole Earth to something 'too poor and trifling to furnish us with one moment's peace.'

At first Lady Hesketh tried to respond, and Cowper rejoiced to have a friend to whom he could open his heart upon these subjects; but she soon grew weary of being prayed for in letter after letter of which the pietistical tone was as wearisome as it was uncharacteristic. She knew her cousin too well and was too healthy-minded herself to applaud so unintelligent an enthusiasm or to believe that the faith which he professed with such abject excess was 'a principle of virtue.' And so there came a time when Cowper could no longer doubt that she belonged to that one half of the world which 'would call this madness, fanaticism, and folly,' and their correspondence ceased.

Fortunately, however, before this occurred, he had discovered reliable substitutes. Huntingdon was then little more than a single street, and although it boasted 'a card-assembly, and a dancing-assembly, and a horse-race, and a club, and a bowling-green,' these amenities were hardly calculated to lessen his feeling of being 'like a traveller in the midst of an inhospitable desert.'

He depended on the countryside and the Church. In the summer he enjoyed bathing beneath the blue willows of the Ouse, and walking to the little village of Hertford, which lay about a mile and a half away on rising ground above the river; but in the winter he often found the country flat and insipid and complained of the flooded meadows. The evil of his situation lay, of course, in the fact that he had nothing to do but what was most agreeable to himself. For if 'the spectator at a play,' as he remarked, 'is more entertained than the actor,' he is also more dependent on the merits of the play.

The monotony, however, was somewhat relieved by weekly visits on horseback to and from his brother, by the acquaintance of three or four social men who 'suited his temper to a hair,' and by the emotional satisfaction which he derived from the church services and often carried thence into the surrounding countryside, where he would fall on his knees and pray.

The most important result of his church-going was, however, the friendship to which it led, a friendship which at a critical moment transformed Huntingdon into the one place in all England where he would have chosen to live, and himself from a derelict on a sluggish stream into 'a Thames wherry in a snug creek.'

§ 4

Among the families of Huntingdon who discussed the habits and appearance of the new resident was one of the name of Unwin. It consisted of an elderly clergyman, 'a man of learning and good sense and as simple as parson Adams,' his wife who was much younger than her husband, and a son and daughter.

The son, William Cawthorne Unwin, who was reading for holy orders at Cambridge, had wished to call upon Cowper, being attracted by his appearance, at once genially refined and curiously abstracted, but had been dissuaded by his mother, who understood that the stranger was averse to society. One morning, however, as he followed Cowper out of church, he saw him taking a solitary walk under a row of trees and introduced himself. His nature was one of engaging frankness and it immediately disarmed Cowper's shyness. He was 'known almost as soon as seen,' and without more delay they 'opened their hearts to each other.' On the next Sunday Cowper dined with the family. He found 'a house full of peace and cordiality in all its parts,' and in Mrs. Unwin, with whom he had much delightful talk, what seemed to be a faith like his own.

Mary Cawthorne Unwin was only seven years his senior. She was devout, but she was very far from grave. On the contrary, she was cheerful and laughed upon the smallest occasion. In speaking upon grave subjects she adopted a pietistical tone, but on all others she revealed a nature with a fund of gaiety. In addition she had read much to excellent purpose, and was more polite than a duchess.

A woman who could thus combine piety with humour satisfied to a peculiar degree the needs of Cowper's nature at this time. Merely to meet her in the street and walk home with her relieved his sense of isolation. 'That woman,' he said, soon after making her acquaintance, 'is a blessing to me, and I never see her without being the better for her company;' and it is safe to say that he derived as much comfort from her human sympathy as from the 'great piety' of which he considered her one of the most remarkable instances within his experience.

He was soon treated by the family like a near relation, and acclaimed his happiness as a gracious finishing given to those means which the Almighty had been pleased to make use of for his conversion. And Providence was to prove equally kind in solving the problem of his improvidence. Absorbed in heavenly matters, he had come near to bankruptcy. On leaving St. Albans he had taken into his service Dr. Cotton's factotum, Sam Roberts, and assumed the guardianship of a poor boy, Richard Coleman, who was to reward his benevolence in rescuing him from a drunken father by becoming a drunkard himself. In this and other ways, by 'the help of good management and a clear notion of economical matters,' he had contrived to spend in four months the income of a twelvemonth, and his relatives were no more likely to appreciate a humorous attitude towards financial embarrassment as the sign of grace which it was than a humourless attitude towards the Almighty.

He wrote jestingly to his friend Hill – 'I never knew how to pity poor housekeepers before; but now I cease to wonder at that politic cast which their occupation usually gives to their countenance, for it is really a matter full of perplexity.' And his perplexity might have lost its comic aspect if Mr. Unwin had not chanced to lose the pupil who lodged with him and so been able to offer Cowper his place.

It was all decided in a few days, and on November 5, 1765, he became an inmate of the large red-brick, gabled residence that looked on the High Street, and could announce that he was happier than the day was long and that sunshine and candle-light saw him perfectly contented. The inward peace which he owed so precariously to his professed conversion was now reinforced by simple human contacts. He was no longer

> Unmoved with all the world beside
> A solitary thing.

He had found a home, 'a place of rest,' as it seemed, 'prepared for me by God's own hand, where He has blessed me with a thousand mercies,' and the unquiet waters, which still at times murmured a menace of shipwreck in his inward ear, were hushed. Mrs. Unwin could not enrich life for him as his cousin Theodora might have done, but the more intimately he came to know her, the more 'excellent a person' did she appear. So 'truly Christian' was the friendship with which she regarded him that he could almost fancy his own mother restored to life again. And if her affection for him was almost maternal, he had something very like a filial one for her. Soon she was knitting all his stockings, 'and would knit my hats too,' he gleefully wrote, 'if that were possible.'

Something, then, of that 'constant flow of love, that knew no fall,' so lamentably stemmed in childhood, was restored to him in this cheerful household, and walking in the garden which extended at the back of the house to the Common or beneath the row of lime trees that connected the two, he realized fully for the first time that Retirement was his passion and delight, that in still life alone we look for that measure of happiness we can rationally expect below. He thought of Rousseau and his description of an English morning, and it seemed a picture of the mornings which he spent with these good people; and the evenings differed from them in nothing, except that they were still more snug and quiet.

And while piety was woven into the routine of his day, it was not yet the oppressive or exacting duty which it was soon to become. The family breakfasted commonly between eight and nine, after which they read the

Bible or sermons until eleven, when they attended Divine Service. From twelve to three they separated, and Cowper walked, rode, or worked in the garden. After dinner, if the weather allowed, he sauntered in the garden with Mrs. Unwin and her son and enjoyed 'religious conversation' till tea-time. If it rained or was too windy for walking, they passed the time similarly within doors or sang hymns to Mrs. Unwin's accompaniment on the harpsichord. After tea they sallied forth to walk in good earnest and seldom returned home without covering four miles. At night they read and talked, commonly finishing the day with hymns or a sermon and family prayers.

Assuredly religion was not neglected in such a day's programme, but it was cultivated in its most soothing form, and so long as the Reverend Morley Unwin lived it was leavened with a quite unfanatical cheerfulness. And in this atmosphere of pious geniality Cowper began to feel that 'to live comfortably while we do live is a great matter, and comprehends in it everything that can be wished for on this side the curtain, that hangs between Time and Eternity.'

It is true that he still considered it his duty to proselytize; he even thought anxiously of taking Orders, but wisely interpreted his dread of publicity as a divine assurance of the propriety of declining. In his desire, however, to be 'an instrument of turning many to the truth in a private way,' he may actually have tried to persuade the Unwin family to a stricter piety. His own conversion was at once so excessive and precarious an experience, that any piety which fell short of feverish self-

abandonment approached for him too near the mood of
cool rationality, of which he dared not contemplate the
return, while any indulgence in social amusement reminded him too painfully of his past.

It may be, therefore, that the polite inhabitants of
Huntingdon had some ground for their complaint that
Mr. Cowper was converting the Unwin family into
unsocial Methodists. But if Mrs. Unwin entered into
his religious views to the extent of curtailing some of her
social engagements, she retained the gaiety and vivacity
for which she had been noted in public for private con-
sumption; and since Cowper was convinced that she shared
his faith, it followed that she helped to combat its morbid
tendencies.

How much he needed such an antidote of human
cheerfulness is proved by the painful Memoir in which
he traced at this time the history of his conversion, contrasting the fictitious beatitude of the present with the
fictitious depravity of the past. Martin Madan, too, was
in the habit of conducting preaching tours in the neigh-
bourhood, and most unwisely Cowper accompanied him;
while he discovered in Madan's mother a correspondent
who encouraged him to indulge in an orgy of revivalistic
self-depreciation.

The cheerful sanity of the Unwin household, however,
set a limit to the possibilities of such religious dissipation, and when, shortly after he had settled with them,
his family complained of the expenses which he had
incurred and one of them threatened to withdraw his
contribution, he was further cheered by an anonymous

letter from a person who 'loved him tenderly and approved his conduct,' begged him not to distress himself, and promised to make up any loss of income which he might incur.

He may not have guessed that the writer was his cousin Theodora, but at least he could take pleasure in the thought that some one loved him, without inquiring whether he or she were 'clearly and strongly persuaded of Evangelical truth.' He had begun, too, to discover in gardening a refuge from himself, and so incidentally a refuge from religious preoccupation, announcing that he was become a great florist and shrub-doctor, studying the art of pruning, sowing and planting and enterprising everything in that way from melons down to cabbages.

And so for eighteen months the days slipped peacefully and piously by. He was occasionally indisposed, and though stout enough in appearance, a little illness, he had to confess, demolished him. Yet physically his life did not hang by the slender thread which he thought it right to believe, in order to emphasize his attitude of dependence. And mentally he was well placed to recover gradually his stability.

And then on July 2, 1767, Mr. Unwin was flung from his horse and fatally fractured his skull. His death was indeed to prove, for Cowper at least, 'an awful dispensation.' For although Mr. Unwin had expressed a wish that Cowper should continue to live with his widow, she alone was not able, even if she had wished it, to guard him from the excesses into which a misguided Evangelical enthusiasm now led him.

But it was not only because Huntingdon was 'an unevangelical pasture' that he wished to leave it. Already their neighbours, with 'a gross ignorance of the principles of Christian friendship,' had amused themselves with 'casting black and shocking aspersions' upon the names of Mrs. Unwin and himself. And now the scandal-mongers would inevitably wax bolder.

Both of them therefore wished to be 'with the Lord's People,' who would, presumably, be too busy 'hearing the glad tidings of salvation' to discuss the domestic affairs of their neighbours. And when, soon after Mr. Unwin's death, they received a visit from the Reverend John Newton, it seemed to have 'pleased God, who always drops comfort into the bitterest cup,' to open a door of escape both from gossip and godlessness.

Mr. Newton was the curate-in-charge of Olney, a little town in the north of Buckinghamshire, which was to earn the apt title of 'The Evangelical Mecca.' In Cowper and Mrs. Unwin he promised himself a very desirable accession to the numbers and strength of the devout, and with little delay engaged for them a house called 'Orchard Side.' It was not ready for occupation until December, but so anxious was Cowper to be 'nourished by the sincere milk of the Word' that he and Mrs. Unwin moved to Olney in October and shared the vicarage with Mr. and Mrs. Newton.

Of the benevolence of their new friend and his wife they could not doubt. But so ardent and exacting a benevolence as John Newton's was in truth to prove for Cowper an 'afflictive Providence.' Religious enthusiasts are often fundamentally selfish. They have little respect, in their proselytizing self-satisfaction, for the rights and needs of personalities that differ from their own. And Cowper, indeed, was ripe for victimization. His religious fever had been reasonably tempered at Huntingdon, but it had not been cured. At Olney, under the ministration of John Newton, it was to burn itself out.

Possibly Cowper would never have justified himself as a poet if circumstances had allowed him the satisfaction of a tranquil piety. Possibly his faith was too neurotic ever to come to terms with sanity. Yet if his nerves could have been spared the strain which was now imposed upon them by evangelical enthusiasm, he might have in time adapted his faith to the rational as well as the emotional needs of his nature, and so never acquired, through a return of madness, the delusion which was to darken the rest of his days – that he was abandoned by the God Whom he had failed to propitiate.

§ 5

Cowper was driven to embrace an extreme form of Evangelicism not only by chance and inward necessity, but by the climate of his age. The two forces which he could not reconcile in himself were also reflected in the conflict of the Established Church and the Deists. And although the Deists were too limited and narrowly self-sufficient in their championing of reason and of natural knowledge, their attempt to raise the dignity of man and challenge the tyranny of a traditional and still essentially tribal God ranges them far more definitely than the

Church which stooped to defame them on the side of the forces of light.

Professor Whitehead has written of the French philosophers and encyclopædists – 'The commonsense of the eighteenth century, its grasp of the obvious facts of human suffering, and of the obvious demands of human nature, acted on the world like a bath of moral cleansing.' And although the English Deists, with the possible exception of Shaftesbury and Bolingbroke, expressed a more provincial enlightenment than the pioneers of the Enlightenment, they played an early and by no means negligible part in the emancipation of the human mind from the intolerant and intolerable visionaries to whom Europe for a thousand years had been a prey. And if their attitude was to a large extent negative, and occasionally even flippantly sceptical, it had its constructive aspect.

For a morality of rewards and punishments, for example, rooted in fear and self-interest, they wished to substitute a morality of human decency, independent of any selfish motive, and they denied the false view of man's depravity because they believed in his potential virtue. They appealed consistently to human intelligence against every kind of enslaving superstition, and to the individual against authority.

There were two authorities which then perpetuated superstition and refused the freedom of mind which was becoming a necessity of human growth. They were the Scriptures and the Church, which claimed that its traditional interpretation of the Scriptures was final. The Deists insisted that the Scriptures should be criticized like any other book, and they refused to accept the Church's interpretation of them as a final revelation from God. And time has fully justified their demand.

The 'Reason,' however, which they opposed to Biblical revelation was too superficial to satisfy the needs of men or to criticize adequately the external 'revelation' which they opposed. Coolly rational themselves, they did not realize that religion might imply super-rational as well as irrational experiences; that a decent and logical morality, however admirable in itself, made no allowance for certain organic cravings in human nature which traditional religion, despite its fetiches, had recognized. They neglected, in short, the mystical impulse, the desire in man to merge and fulfil himself in life, not merely through his 'natural power of mind,' but through the spiritual unity of his whole being.

The Evangelicals were to confuse the sensational with the spiritual, but the Deists circumscribed, and even sterilized, the spiritual in the rational. Human thought, as it moved onward through the next hundred and fifty years, was to confirm more and more boldly the contention of the Deists that the religion which transgresses reason is both false and degrading. But it was also to enlarge the meaning of 'reason,' to realize it not as a mere critical faculty, but as the directing and correcting principle in creative ventures of faith.

The Deists, however, by detaching 'reason' from sensational impulse, cut its roots with life, and so with all that imaginative activity which is the essential concern of poetry and religion, and which it is the part of reason to inform and purify. They were right to deny all that was arbitrary and fantastic in man's supernatural beliefs, but they were wrong to restrict men's natural belief to the narrow province of dispassionate good-sense.

Most of the pulpit-divines, however, who opposed them were equally devoid of imaginative depth, while they lacked the intellectual courage and faith in human nature which linked the Deists, despite their shallowness, with the life and thought of the future. The sane, unfanatical clergy of Cowper's day preached as one man of the world speaking to another. They were conventionally correct, when they were not conventionally dissolute, and the religion which they professed was little more than a manual of conduct or a reproof of licence or free-thought.

The religious instinct, then, of the age was satisfied neither by the rationalism of the Deists nor the correctness of the Established Church. And it was this need which Methodism without the Church and Evangelicism within it sought to satisfy. Like the Deists, the Evangelicals reasserted the importance of the individual; not, however, as a critical and enquiring being, but as an emotional one. They did, indeed, make a show of rational argument, but essentially they retained the irrational basis of doctrine against which the whole rationalistic movement was directed.

And they not only retained it, but by their very enthusiasm imposed it with a new and melodramatic force upon the individual. If they questioned the authority of the Church, they reasserted that of the Scriptures, and in particular that of the Old Testament. They allowed religion to be experimental only within these Biblical boundaries, and they exploited the emotional reactions in the individual which would incline him to accept these boundaries instead of appealing to his rational faculty which was outgrowing them. They excited especially that fear of an all-powerful arbitrary tyrant behind the unknown forces of Nature, which had survived in man from savage times with all its ritual of propitiatory sacrifice, its terrors of everlasting torment, its perverted contempt for the body, and its interested enslavement of the mind.

In short, the tyrant God of Evangelicism, as later the mechanic God of Scientific Materialism, was a conception which confined those who accepted it in a fatalistic prison. And it overshadows all the generous fervour and intensity of faith which the movement expressed.

To some extent it was dictated by the admitted, though exaggerated, licence of the times. The appeal to fear seemed still a more potent weapon against immorality than the appeal to reason, because the Evangelicals themselves were deficient in reason. The instincts of the savage still possessed them, and they confused bodily sensations with spiritual insight. The 'reason' of their age was formal and prosaic, and in their demand for life they abandoned themselves to primitive feeling and claimed for it Divine sanction.

This 'misconceit of inspiration' was fatal to the growth of a humane spirit. And if Butler was a little severe when he said to Wesley – 'Sir, the pretending to extraordinary revelation and gifts of the Holy Ghost is a horrid thing, a very horrid thing,' he was right to condemn an arrogance of which the fruit has invariably been bigotry, persecution, and obscurantism. It is by criticizing his feelings that man has purified them, and by informing them with reason that he has achieved spiritual insight.

This the Evangelicals failed to do, and so they lacked any criterion by which to distinguish subjective inclination from truth apprehended by a creative act of thought. They claimed to be partaking in the Divine nature even when they were indulging a disordered imagination, and instead of fostering the supersensual faculties of the soul, they invested with a supernatural authority the sensuous and emotional reactions of the body. For if religion preserves its reality by the activity of its non-rational elements, it is only by being steeped in reason that it avoids sinking into fanaticism and can prove a really civilizing force in human affairs.

This digression into the religious movements of the time has a direct and intimate bearing upon Cowper's dilemma. All the sane, positive, and cultivated elements in his temperament would have inclined him to the side of the Deists. But the Deists were tough-minded and he was tender-minded; they were self-assured and he was profoundly self-distrustful; they stood firmly in an egocentric universe while he drifted upon a tide of life that incalculably ebbed and flowed; they were content to strip the world of mystery and to affirm its reason, while darkness welled about him from some abyss of non-being, and sensation, trembling along his nerves, threatened his reason with imminent collapse.

The rational self-assurance of the Deists could not re-assure such a nature as his, because it offered nothing to his emotional sensibility; but the emotional self-assurance of the Evangelicals not only failed to satisfy, but distorted his reason.

Nevertheless, it was inevitable that, for want of any religious faith in his day capable of satisfying and har-monizing the two sides of his nature, he should be drawn into the Enthusiasts' Camp. The Evangelical movement was in some way a crude anticipation of the Romantic Movement. It preached the doctrine that 'feeling is all,' although it narrowly prescribed the feelings which might be indulged. And Cowper, worn out by mental distress, welcomed such an organized and sanctified emotional licence.

He was too weak to assume the responsibility of real liberty, of hewing and chiselling Christianity for himself into an intelligible human faith; but Evangelicism spoke to him as an individual and in a way which cultivated Churchmen failed to do, and its particular solicitude for sick souls and the emphasis which it laid upon conversion by supernatural means seemed exactly suited to his needs. For he was at this time one of those in whom, to quote Locke's words, 'melancholy was mixed with devotion, so that they flatter themselves with a persuasion of an im-mediate intercourse with the Deity. Their minds being thus prepared, whatever groundless opinion comes to settle itself strongly upon their fancies is an illumination from the Spirit of God, and presently of Divine authority.'

Evangelicism confirmed in him most fatally this false, because uncriticized, persuasion. For when he could no longer interpret an emotional satisfaction as proof of Divine approval, he continued to hear in every mood of depression the voice of an angry God. Only buoyant natures, in fact, or those unmenaced by the canker of self-conscious thought, can afford to indulge in such dangerous self-flattery.

But Evangelicals were not in the habit of adapting their treatment to the needs of their patients. For them the technique of the art of spiritual health, which is the concern of religion, was fixed and final. It was that which effectively gratified themselves, based, indeed, upon the traditional textbook of the Bible, but little tempered by any informed respect for human psychology. As Newton wrote – 'The vast satisfaction of mind I possess makes me generally desirous to impart the same to everyone,' and he was far too engrossed in his own experiences to consider their relevance to others.

Cowper, however, was not a primitive convert. His nature was precariously poised and his mind finely cultivated. A religion which respected these facts might possibly have reinforced his sanity. The religion of John Newton only excited him to madness.

§ 6

'I am a wonder unto many,' was the motto which Newton inscribed over his Autobiography, and the events of

his life gave him some excuse. Like Cowper, he had lost his mother, an earnest Dissenter, at an early age and had been savagely treated at a boarding-school, but he was not unduly sensitive and had survived these misfortunes unscathed. As a boy he passed through a precocious religious phase, during which he fasted, abstained from animal food, and prayed for the greater part of the day. But of this he was cured by Shaftesbury's *Characteristics*. He also fell precociously in love, and it is a proof of the staunch fidelity of his nature that this early love survived every vicissitude of fortune which fell upon him, and sustained him through all 'the scenes of misery and wickedness' which he afterwards experienced. In this, too, he was more fortunate than Cowper.

At the age of seventeen, following the profession of his father, he went to sea, and for the next seven years, now on a man-of-war, now on a Guinea ship trading in slaves, and eventually in the service of a slave-dealer on one of the Plantain Islands, endured every sort of rough treatment and privation, was kept in irons, flogged and degraded, contemplated killing his captain and drowning himself, was persecuted by the black wife of the slave-dealer, was compelled to eat raw roots, kept in chains, exposed to wind and rain, and nearly died of fever.

Only a very strong man could have survived such a seven years' ordeal, and even after his rescue from the Plantain Islands, the ship on which he was returning was nearly sunk in a storm and he narrowly escaped killing himself with a gun. But by this time his suppressed religious instinct had reawakened and he reviewed his whole life as 'a course of most horrid impiety and profaneness,' although one in which, he congratulated himself, Providence had shown particular concern for his safety.

Whether, in fact, he had been the infidel, blasphemer, sensualist and corrupter of others which he described himself is doubtful. Certainly in the violence of his revulsion he exaggerated. He had become a free-thinker, had indulged his passions, and lived recklessly, but he equally indulged himself when he claimed that the grossest of profligates found in him one who had sunk to a lower depth than themselves, and tendered to God a foul, blotted and corrupt heart.

The conversion, however, of such a nature is effective in proportion to the primitive force which is turned into a new channel. Newton derived an immense satisfaction from it and embraced religion with the same headlong violence with which he had spurned it, while his lurid experiences rather heightened by contrast his sense of salvation than tortured him with remorse.

And having saved his own soul, he was eager to save others and to heighten the relish which they derived from salvation by attributing to them the same inherent viciousness with which he credited himself. His marriage and subsequent abandonment of the sea enabled him to prepare for the missionary vocation to which he felt so compellingly called. He was long undecided whether to enter the Established Church, whose preachers disappointed him, or to join the Dissenters and contribute to the 'great work of revival' begun by Wesley and Whitefield.

But the offer of the living of Olney decided him, and he

accepted it with an enthusiastic determination to repair the mischief which he had done in his unregenerate days and wage unceasing war upon the infidelity which he had once in his unhappy folly encouraged.

Such was the 'spiritual warrior' into whose hands Cowper, a man of peace with no passionate past to invert, surrendered himself. Newton was a downright, homely man, with a warm heart, a genial humour and an ardent sensibility. But he was also a man with strong animal energies which now demanded chastening as forcefully as they had once demanded indulging. He admitted that he was 'what they call a Calvinist,' but in a modified sense. And those who have agreed that his influence on Cowper was beneficent have accepted his claim to moderation. A few typical quotations, however, from his letters will be enough to controvert them.

'I believe,' he wrote, 'that sin is the most hateful thing in the world; that I and all men are by nature in a state of wrath and depravity, utterly unable to sustain the penalty, or to fulfil the commands of God's holy law; and that we have no sufficiency of ourselves to think a good thought.' Or – 'We find depravity so deep-rooted in our nature, that, like the leprous house, the whole fabric must be taken down before we can be freed from its defilement.' Or – 'I would not wish you to be less affected with a sense of indwelling sin. It becomes us to be humbled into the dust.' Or – 'But let him look and talk as he list, he is Satan's still; and those who are experienced and watchful may discern his cloven hoof hanging below his fine garment of light.' Or again – 'My soul is like a besieged city: a legion of enemies without the gates, and a nest of restless traitors within.'

And in the same style he wrote of Providence – 'We have then no more to do but to attend His prescriptions, to be satisfied with His methods, and to wait His time. . . . As to daily occurrences, it is best to believe that . . . each one the most suitable to our case, is adjusted and appointed by the hand which was once nailed to the Cross for us. . . . It is not in man that walketh to direct his steps. . . . The Scripture itself, and the spirit of God are the best and only sufficient expositors of Scripture. . . . I beg you to be on your guard against a reasoning spirit. . . . The Gospel, my dear Sir, is a salvation appointed for those who are ready to perish, and is not designed to put them in a way to save themselves by their own works. It speaks to us as condemned already, and calls upon us to believe in a crucified Saviour, that we may receive redemption through His blood.'

These rabid sentiments are not exceptional. They dominate all Newton's writings, because they completely satisfied his own needs. He could balance his aggressive egotism by believing that all events were beyond its power to influence, while exerting his influence in every direction. He had tried both ways, and found that religion 'does not destroy but greatly heightens the relish of temporal things . . . that we may, like David, be satisfied in our souls as with marrow and fatness.'

To oppose and deny the senses can afford a man of strong appetites a gratification which is both physical and moral. And it was thus that Newton gratified himself, whether he denounced the theatres as 'fountains and means of vice' or his own heart as 'deceitful and desperately wicked,' or wrote – 'While we have such a depraved nature, and live in such a polluted world; while the roots of pride, vanity, self-dependence, self-seeking, are so strong within us, we need a variety of sharp dispensations to keep us from forgetting ourselves, and from cleaving to the dust.'

Newton could flourish upon so coarse and animal a diet, but it was poison to Cowper. Later, indeed, even Newton learnt the necessity of some discretion, but by that time the evil had been done; and how irresponsible he was, as a ruthless zealot, is shown by the letter in which he wrote of a member of his congregation whose mind had become disordered – 'I believe my name is up about the country for preaching people mad. . . . I suppose we have near a dozen, in different degrees disordered in their heads, and most of them I believe truly gracious people. This has been no small trial to me. . . . But if He (the Lord) brings them through fire and water safe to His kingdom, whatever they may suffer by the way, they are less to be pitied than the mad people of the world, who think themselves in their senses, and take occasion to scoff at the Gospel, as if it was only fit to drive people out of their senses. Perhaps the Lord permits these things, in judgement, that they who seek occasion for stumbling and cavilling may have what they want. I trust there is nothing in my preaching that tends to cast those down who ought to be comforted.'

Newton was far too much of a God-assured egotist to appreciate the effect of his words on others. In this very

letter he attributed to God his own readiness to drive the
devout mad, if by that means the undevout might be more
effectively exposed to judgment. And he did not realize
that so Machiavellian a God could be equally credited by
disciples more consistent and less confident than himself
with a cynical cruelty. When Cowper later came to believe that God had cast him off, Newton was shocked and
amazed, failing to understand how little reliance a timid
and reasonable man could place on the love of a God
capable of such malice and partiality.

Evangelicism, in short, could not adapt itself to higher
types. It tried to reimpose doctrines which had once had a
natural origin in the necessities of human nature, but
which advanced human natures had outgrown. Its God
was but little removed from the Jehovah whose mouth
watered at the smell of charred cattle, and was less true to
the facts of life than impartial Nemesis treading upon the
heels of Hubris. Its dogma was adapted only to primitive
natures, but it claimed that 'the sin of nature is equal in
all.' And to sensitive and diffident natures this indis-
criminate emphasizing of inherent depravity, no less than
its literal assumption of an overruling Providence, was
wholly demoralizing.

There are, indeed, simple and uninquiring natures
which can turn the edge of life's brutality by imputing to
every evil and every accident a divinely benevolent purpose. But no thinking man can evade the problem so
facilely. Far nobler, far more human, honest and astrin-
gent is even the imperfect solution which Richard Jefferies
propounded when he wrote – 'How can I adequately

express my contempt for the assertion that all things occur for the best, for a wise and beneficent end, and are ordered by a humane intelligence? It is the most utter falsehood and a crime against the human race. Even in my brief time I have been contemporary with events of the most horrible character. . . . It is the duty of all rational beings to acknowledge the truth. There is not the least trace of directing intelligence in human affairs. There is a foundation of hope, because, if the present condition of things were ordered by a superior power, there would be no possibility of improving it for the better in the spite of that power. Acknowledging that no such direction exists, all things become at once plastic to our will. . . . That which is thoughtlessly credited to a non-existent intelligence should really be claimed and exercised by the human race.'

Jefferies, in his recoil from the pain of the world, under-estimated perhaps the latent constructive intelligence in Nature, with which man can co-operate. But he was right in his contention that man could only realize God by asserting his human dignity, by a constant effort and application of understanding.

It is this need of human dignity and understanding, realized at a deeper level, which Katherine Mansfield affirmed when she wrote in her 'Journal' – 'I do not want to die without leaving a record of my belief that suffering can be overcome. For I do believe it. What must one do? There is no question of what is called 'passing beyond it.' This is false. One must *submit*. Do not resist. Take it. Be overwhelmed. Accept it fully. Make it *part of life*.

Everything in life that we really accept undergoes a change. So suffering must become Love. This is the mystery. This is what I must do. I must pass from personal Love to greater love.'

There is no grovelling in such submission. Humanity is not cramped or distorted by it, but extended to its utmost capacity. The cravings of egotism are transcended by an all inclusive understanding. Man accepts not as a slave, but as an equal.

But in Newton's creed the cravings of egotism were either indulged or inverted, and two aspects of God were fatally confused. To write, as Mr. Santayana has done, that 'the spirit of God . . . means simply the genius of men,' is possibly to over-simplify the problem. But certainly the problem of religion is to bring the God in man, which is his personality, into true relation with the God outside man, which is an impersonal force.

Newton, however, endowed God with a personality very like his own, and also gave to that arbitrary Being the ruthlessness of an impersonal force. His God therefore combined the calculating self-interest of an imperfect human being with the unconcern of the elements. The combination, to anyone who was too timid to realize its egotistic absurdity and yet too intelligent to prostrate the mind before it, was indeed terrifying.

For a time Cowper succeeded in sacrificing his intelligence upon the altar of Newton's God. But it was a demoralizing and agitating experience, and when at last his nerves, tried also in another direction, broke beneath the double strain, his intelligence had become permanently warped. For Newton's belief that there was only one way of having 'the heart right with God' inevitably put the head of a more sensitive and intelligent man than himself in the wrong.

§ 7

The solid, red-brick house into which Cowper and Mrs. Unwin moved in December, 1767, had at first sight, with its imitation embattlements, something of the look of a prison. It stood on the south side of Olney market-place, close to the poorer quarter of the town with its public-houses and wailing infants. But if at its front it was exposed to the mud-splashing of unruly urchins, its back overlooked a garden threaded by a gravel path, which led through a doorway into another garden in which a summer-house stood. Between this garden and the Vicarage lay only an orchard, and to facilitate communication Newton made a doorway in his garden wall.

Like Huntingdon, Olney consisted of one street, but it was a long and broad one widening into the spacious market-place where 'Orchard Side' stood. Here, too, the river Ouse continued its turns and twinings through level meadows about the town, while over it hung the tall steeple of the church with its bulging sides.

To one so detached as Cowper from the bustle of the world, and yet so interested in and observant of humanity, there was a real advantage in being placed in the midst of a little town where he could follow the course of local events without participating in them. To that fortunate circumstance we owe some of the most delightful passages in his letters. And the domestic comfort of the town extended to the countryside. Whether he walked by the 'pack house bridge' which bestrode with its quaint irregular arches the valley between Olney and Emberton, or by the footpath to Weston, or by the northern road to the Poplar Field at Lavendon Mill, he moved through a landscape varied enough in its undulations and unfolding distances to interest, but quiescent enough to soothe.

The country took its tone from the leisurely Ouse that watered it. Even the Clifton uplands and the distant spinneys of Bedfordshire seemed, like the willows and aspens, loaded hawthorn hedges and lush meadows, to owe their character to this placid stream. As Cowper was later to write —

> Here Ouse, slow winding through a level plain
> Of spacious meads with cattle sprinkled o'er,
> Conducts the eye along his sinuous course
> Delighted. There, fast rooted in their bank,
> Stand, never overlooked, our favourite elms,
> That screen the herdsman's solitary hut;
> While far beyond, and overthwart the stream,
> That, as with molten glass, inlays the vale,
> The sloping land recedes into the clouds;
> Displaying on its varied side the grace
> Of hedge-row beauties numberless, square tower,
> Tall spire, from which the sound of cheerful bells
> Just undulates upon the listening ear;
> Groves, heaths, and smoking villages remote.

Not yet, however, was Cowper to be allowed to bathe

his being in this flowing landscape. For Newton was constantly at his side, and so strenuous an Evangelist, even
when walking by the river banks or under the shade of
poplars, was unlikely to encourage Nature-worship. To
him the dissatisfaction of a contrite soul afforded more
pleasure than natural contentment. And Cowper, agitated
soon after moving into 'Orchard Side' by the circumstance
that Mrs. Unwin, whom he now regarded as 'the chief of
blessings' and his 'dearest comfort,' fell ill, was in a condition to please him.

Already, indeed, if we are to believe the hymn which he
now wrote, the reaction from emotional abandonment had
begun. For although he prayed for 'a closer walk with
God,' he asked regretfully –

> Where is the blessedness I knew
> When first I saw the Lord?
> Where is the soul-refreshing view
> Of Jesus and his word?
>
> What peaceful hours I then enjoyed!
> How sweet their memory still!
> But they have left an aching void
> The world can never fill.

This 'aching void,' however, Newton, with his 'frame of
adamant and soul of fire,' filled with an incessant round of
Evangelical activities. To him Cowper was not a poet
with a nervous system that required the most careful
cherishing, but 'an astonishing instance of grace' ordained
to further his own work of revivalism. He not only per-

suaded him to visit the poor and minister to the sick and
dying, but he swept him into prayer-meetings in the
crowded cottage of a certain Molly Mole, or to the Great
House, an unoccupied mansion, to which before day on
Sunday mornings in winter he trudged with Mrs. Unwin,
often through snow and rain, by the light of a lantern.

But it was not the physical so much as the nervous
strain involved in 'these social labours of the Poet with an
Exemplary Man of God' which was fatal to Cowper's well-
being. For Newton demanded that he should engage in
prayer at these meetings; and although his extemporary
prayers were generally admired and brought him relief,
it was relief from an agitation experienced, as he confessed, for some hours previously, which should never
have been incurred.

Later Lady Hesketh, with her lively and sympathetic
good-sense, summed up the situation admirably when she
wrote to her sister – 'Mr. Newton is an excellent man, I
make no doubt, and to a strong minded man like himself
might have been of great use: but to such a mind . . .
such a tender mind, and to such a wounded, yet lively
imagination as our cousin's, I am persuaded that eternal
praying and preaching were too much. Nor could it, I
think, be otherwise. One only proof of this I will give
you, which our cousin mentioned a few days ago in casual
conversation. The case was this. He was mentioning that
for one or two summers he had found himself under the
necessity of taking his walk in the middle of the day,
which he thought had hurt him a good deal; "but," continued he, "I could not help it, for it was when Mr. New-

ton was here, and we made it a rule to pass four days in the week together. We dined at one, and it was Mr. Newton's rule for tea to be on table at four o'clock, for at six we broke up." "Well, then," said I, "if you had your time to yourself after six, you could have good time for an evening's walk, I should have thought." "No," said he; "after six we had service or lecture, or something of that kind, which lasted till supper." I made no reply, but could not and cannot help thinking, they might have made a better use of a fine summer's evening than by shutting themselves up to make long prayers.'

But no adverse comment by undevout relatives could temper Newton's influence at this time. Cowper was so deeply wallowing in a pool of unction that even in writing to his bluff friend Hill on the occasion of his marriage he took the opportunity of emphasizing the fact that all bonds but that between Christ and His Church should be dissolved. And when his clerical brother visited him he continually engaged him, much to his embarrassment, 'in conversation of a spiritual kind.'

John Cowper preserved a civil reticence, but he was not allowed to officiate even at family prayers when Newton was present, and Cowper himself wrote to Mrs. Madan with 'an aching heart upon my poor brother's account. . . . He is with us, and his presence necessarily gives a turn to the conversation that we have not been used to. So much said about nothing, and so little said about Jesus, is very painful to us, but what can be done?'

Providence, however, was to gratify the revivalists even in this unhopeful case. For John Cowper's health had been undermined by the sedentary life of a scholar, and in the autumn of 1769 he took a fever and had a hæmorrhage. Cowper was shocked, on visiting him, to find his bed strewed with volumes of plays, to which he had frequent recourse for amusement, and that 'he seemed to have no more concern about his spiritual interests than when in perfeĉt health.'

He recovered quickly, but, to quote from the edifying 'Sketch of the Charaĉter and Account of the Last Illness' of his brother which Cowper wrote later, 'it is probable that, though his recovery seemed perfeĉt, this illness was the means which God had appointed to bring down his strength in the midst of his journey, and to hasten on the malady which proved his last.'

In short, he fell ill again in the following February. Cowper hurried once more to his side and was horrified to see once again on his bed, not a Bible, but a book of plays. Moreover, he did not seem to lay his illness at all to heart, and whenever Cowper tried to give an Evangelical turn to the discourse, he received what he said with a kindly, but clearly unconcerned, affeĉtion.

The disease, however, played into Cowper's hands. His brother had a violent fit of asthma which left him weak and miserable. On that day, as he wrote, 'the Lord was very present with me, and enabled me, as I sat by the poor sufferer's side, to wrestle for a blessing upon him.' And he noted significantly that 'if at any time, I find liberty to speak to him, it is when his sufferings are greatest; for when his pains are abated, he is cheerful in spirits and exaĉtly the man he always was.'

As his brother grew worse these occasions increased, and in the weakness and hysteria induced by pain Cowper saw with exultation 'the Spirit of God, gradually preparing him, in a way of true humiliation, for that bright display of Gospel Grace which he was soon after pleased to afford him.' He redoubled his efforts to convince him that he was 'asleep upon the brink of ruin,' and at last he succeeded.

The exhausted patient abandoned his will to live and accepted the theological interpretation which his brother put upon it. He admitted that 'the evil I suffer is the consequence of my descent from the corrupt original stock, and of my own personal transgressions;' he saw himself 'odiously vile and wicked' and confessed his own utter insufficiency. To Cowper's inquiry as to whether he did not feel comfort flowing to his heart from a sense of his acceptance with God, he replied that 'sometimes I do, but sometimes I am left in desperation;' but he died peacefully, having satisfied his brother that he had not only accepted, but experienced, 'salvation by grace.'

We have quoted at length from this document because it reveals so clearly the morbid aspect of Evangelicism and its readiness to exploit physical and mental sickness. Cowper believed sincerely that he was saving his brother's soul from Hell-fire. 'My thoughts,' he wrote, 'are interested in his condition all day long, and at night I pray for him in my dreams.' He thought it his duty to terrify him, to make him despise the learning which he once valued, and to belittle all his efforts to perfect his mind or assume a personal responsibility for his actions.

The death-beds of the weak and fearful may be eased by a denial of everything which gives dignity to human life and endeavour. But John Cowper was both an intelligent and a highly moral man. His was not a 'dark and Christless condition,' full of self-interest and contempt for 'the doctrines of the Cross.' He was, as Cowper was to write in less feverish days,

> A man of letters, and of manners, too;
> Of manners sweet as virtue always wears
> When gay good-nature dresses her in smiles. . . .
> Some minds are tempered happily, and mixed
> With such ingredients of good sense and taste
> Of what is excellent in man, they thirst
> With such a zeal to be what they approve,
> That no restraints can circumscribe them more
> Than they themselves by choice, for wisdom's sake.

Such a man could have been trusted to die as equably and wisely as he had lived, and in working upon his weakness Cowper was acting the same part towards him as Newton was acting towards himself.

His brother died at the age of thirty-three, and Cowper, with the strange self-consolatory callousness of the devout, could safely interpret his death as a signal manifestation of the grace of God. But he himself was to live for another thirty-three years, and he was soon to discover what Leonardo discovered in a stricken moment, that 'when I thought I was learning to live I was but learning how to die.' Evangelicism might enslave the dimming faculties of a death-bed, but it could not indefinitely enslave an active intelligence.

Newton, however, was too overjoyed by the news of John Cowper's conversion to consider the tragic aspect of his approaching death, and he turned it at once to pastoral uses. 'When we shall meet on Tuesday evening,' he wrote with a glee that strikes the modern mind as almost indecent, 'I propose to impart it (the good news) to the people in a body by reading your letter. My heart jumps at representing to myself how they will look, how they will feel, how they will pray and give thanks, when they hear what God has wrought.' And he commended Cowper's later painful narrative as a 'striking display of the power and mercy of God,' as a counterblast to 'the boasted spirit of refinement, the stress laid upon unassisted human reason and the consequent scepticism to which they lead,' and above all as a convincing example of 'vital experimental religion.'

If the living John Cowper had been too suspect to officiate at family prayers in Newton's presence, he had qualified himself by dying to admonish 'many unstable persons . . . misled and perverted by the fine words and fair speeches of those who lie in wait to deceive.'

§ 8

The strain, however, was beginning to tell upon Cowper, and a God Who frowned so darkly upon human reason was hardly a support to sanity. Late in 1771 he was depressed, and Newton, alarmed by the symptoms, suggested the writing of hymns in the hope that 'concen-

tration of mind on holy themes would afford relief.'
Cowper had already composed several hymns for use at
Newton's prayer-meetings, and it was proposed that the
two of them should now collaborate in producing and
publishing a volume of them.

During the next year, therefore, the little secular leisure
which Cowper allowed himself was further curtailed, and
although the writing of hymns may have brought him
some relief, it was, like the relief experienced after his
extempore prayers, the sequel to an unnecessary and morbid agitation. The hymns were not published until some
years later, but since the majority of them express the
self-lacerating moods of this time, it will be well to consider them now. Later, in his *Table Talk*, Cowper was to
write –

> Pity religion has so seldom found
> A skilful guide into poetic ground!

and Evangelical hymnology on the whole fully justifies
his complaint and proves the deep gulf which lies in
modern times between poetry and theology.

St. Augustine of Hippo defined a hymn as 'singing
with the praise of God,' and in such a generous definition
poetry might indeed be reconciled with religion. It was
so reconciled in many mediæval hymns or in the devo-
tional verse of Herbert or Traherne, who in their self-
abasement affirmed the lyrical beauty and sanctity of life.
Moreover, Newman and Keble proved later that it is
possible to combine singing with a certain degree at least
of sensitive and personal contemplation. Two factors,

however, militated against such a reconciliation in Evangelical hymns: the narrowness and damnatory nature of the doctrine and the interested purpose for which they were written.

A poet is, in any case, somewhat restricted by the congregation for which he is writing. He must simplify his experience and avoid subtleties, whether of idiom or of rhythm. But if he is not tied to a narrow theology, he may yet express his faith, his moral aspiration or conflict, in vivid, if simple, personal terms. He may derive his images direct from Nature instead of borrowing the Biblical symbolism, which has lost its immediate pregnancy by becoming generalized in use. It is true that such a hymn-writer as Watts can, by his intense force of conviction, pour new reality into Biblical idiom and a primitive theology, but few Evangelical hymn-writers could thus recreate the symbols which they borrowed. The 'Hound of Heaven' was a real equivalent of Francis Thompson's religious experience; he could not have related it to the 'Lamb of God.'

But Cowper, in writing for the simple rustics who gathered in Molly Mole's cottage or the Great House, was required to graft his experience not only on to a Biblical idiom with which they were familiar but which remained for him a convention that at best he could only emotionalize, but also on to a doctrine which was alien to his true poetic impulse. He was a partner, too, with Newton in a Salvationist mission, and no true poetry is written with a particular design upon people. He was required, in short, to express a creed first and a faith second, and the creed was a negation of any enlightened poetic faith.

Evangelicism suspected and hated the æsthetic instinct as it did the material world. It considered, for example, that a congregation assembled to honour the memory of Handel was guilty of 'folly and wickedness.' It sacrificed the beauty and virtue that is in the world on the altar of Judah's tribal God. There could be no true relation between poetry and such warped sectarianism, and where Evangelical hymn-writers did achieve poetry of a kind, they did so either by passing beyond theology and doctrine to a direct and elemental apprehension of the terror of the world and of God above it, an experience that may excite the imagination as potently as that of the beauty of the world and God in it, or by a pure surrender of self to the mystery of life.

Between these two moods Cowper alternated in writing his hymns, but only in the second, and then at rare moments, did he rise above emotional piety to an imaginative level. The classical discipline which he had already cultivated in the writing of secular verse preserved him from sentimental transports and crudities, but his mind for the most part only exerted a formal discipline. It did not inform his emotions and so generate a metaphysical reality. The same valueless feeling therefore characterized his claim to salvation by Christ and his terror of the wrath of God. The latter, however, was far the more real as feeling.

The emotional argument that runs through the whole collection is that peace and happiness in the world are irrevocably lost, that a criminal sin has occasioned the loss, and that the only hope of comfort lies in complete surrender to an unreal formula, entitled 'The Lamb.' How little Cowper really believed in the kind of salvation which he commended to others, may be gathered from such conventional jingles as –

> The saints should never be dismayed,
>   Nor sink in hopeless fear;
> For when they least expect his aid,
>   The Saviour will appear.

This, however, is an extreme example. More often, in what may be called his affirmative hymns, he plainly sings, not out of conviction, but in an attempt to convince himself. The conflict of faith and distrust, personal feeling and conventional diction, is apparent even in such lines as these –

> I will praise thee every day
> Now thine anger's turned away;
> Comfortable thoughts arise
> From the bleeding sacrifice . . .

> Jesus is become at length
> My salvation and my strength;
> And his praises shall prolong,
> While I live, my pleasant song.

Occasionally he professes faith with more reality and almost forgets his fear –

A cheerful confidence I feel,
My well-placed hopes with joy I see;
My bosom glows with heavenly zeal,
To worship him Who died for me.

As man he pities my complaint,
his power and truth are all divine;
he will not fail, he cannot faint;
Salvation's sure, and must be mine.

But even here we feel him to be arguing against an inward doubt and laying claim to a 'heavenly zeal' which is not his. And when he thanks God for preparing

a blood-bought, free reward,
A golden harp for me,

or asserts that He has

breathed upon a worm
And sent me from above
Wings such as clothe an angel's form,
The wings of joy and love,

the unreality is obvious, and proves only the truth of the lines –

Thy saints are comforted, I know,
And love thy house of prayer;
I therefore go where others go,
But find no comfort there.

Far less artificial, however, are the hymns in which he cries out of a heart stricken with terror that he is 'forsaken

and alone' and hears 'the lion roar.' Here the Evangelical
idiom does correspond with an hysterical conviction, –

> My former hopes are fled,
>   My terror now begins;
> I feel, alas! that I am dead
>   In trespasses and sins.
>
> Ah! whither shall I fly?
>   I hear the thunder roar;
> The law proclaims destruction nigh,
>   And vengeance at the door.
>
> When I review my ways,
>   I dread impending doom:
> But sure a friendly whisper says,
>   "Flee from the wrath to come."

The absurdity of the epithet 'friendly' does not need
emphasizing, and Cowper's hymns are strewed with all
the barbarous concomitants of sacrificial suffering judici-
ously inflicted by the God of Evangelicism for the purpose
of redemption. There is the notorious

> fountain filled with blood
> Drawn from Emmanuel's veins;

he writes of Jerusalem that

> Jehovah founded it in blood,
>   The blood of his incarnate Son;

from which we turn with relief to Blake's 'Sweet Zion's
ways.' He cries of 'the legions of God's foes,'

> See from the ever-burning lake
> How like a smoky cloud they rise!

and comforts the devout with the thought of

> How light thy troubles here, if weighed
> With everlasting pain.

He is, of course, morbidly preoccupied with sin and luxuri-ates in self-abasement. Sin, he remarks, 'has undone our wretched race'; and he warns those who 'contented lick their native dust' that

> We see, though you perceive it not,
> The approaching awful doom;
> Oh tremble at the solemn thought,
> And flee the wrath to come!

and he prays, with a grotesque association of metaphors –

> Now, Lord, thy feeble worm prepare!
> For strife with earth and hell begins;

All such writing has, of course, no poetical value, blending, as it does, hysteria with a sectarian idiom; yet the hysteria throughout the collection far outweighs the professions of faith and has a greater individual intensity.

There are, however, a few hymns in which Cowper transcended a morbid religiosity and conceived God for himself as a divine natural principle. There is, for example, the hymn, entitled *Wisdom*, which begins –

> Ere God had built the mountains,
> Or raised the fruitful hills,

or the more familiar 'God moves in a mysterious way.'
The spirit of awe and reverence which animates these
hymns is wholly distinct from the base fear which Evangelicism did so much to excite. It is instinct with wonder
and admiration, with human strength calling to the
strength which upholds the universe. Cowper accepts
here the mystery and the immensity of life, but he draws
power from it. His personality is not contracted and
turned inward on itself, but extends to the limits of the
material world and beyond them. And when he writes
that God

> plants his footsteps in the sea,
> And rides upon the storm,

or that

> like a tent to dwell in,
> He spread the skies abroad,

we are conscious of a large sense of Nature and its creative
power, of a rhythm that rolls round, like Wordsworth's,

> in earth's diurnal course,
> With rocks, and stones, and trees,

and of a moral valiancy that compares with Emily Brontë's
'No Coward Soul is mine.' Such hymns disprove Cowper's plaintive cry – 'My fears are great, my strength is
small,' and they suggest that a religion which had emphasized his strength and belittled his fears might have
saved him from madness.

There are other hymns which approach poetry by the

appealing quality of their sentiment. 'Hark, my soul! it is the Lord' is one of these, although the cloying tune to which it is usually set has debased it for most of us. 'God of my life, to Thee I call' is another, and 'Peace After Storm,' with its gentle resignation masquerading as faith —

> Oh! let me, then, at length be taught
> What I am so slow to learn;
> That God is Love, and changes not,
> Nor knows the shadow of a turn.

Even nearer to pure poetry are those in which his theme is not specifically religious, but blends, as in 'Winter has a joy for me,' with his love of Nature, in which, as he had written before Newton had restricted his religion to prayer-meetings —

> The calm retreat, the silent shade,
> With prayer and praise agree;
> And seem by thy sweet bounty made
> For those who follow thee.

§ 9

The little relief, then, which the writing of these hymns afforded Cowper was far outweighed by the dangerous introspection which they encouraged. For in his inability to express a religious faith, he must have grown more conscious of his disillusionment, while the rabid religious idiom in which he did indulge must have aggravated his terrors. Few activities, indeed, could have been worse for one who was in course of waking from a religious intoxication. He could still 'wait with patient hope' for a return of rapture, but he had to confess that hope delayed fatigues the mind,

> And drinks the spirit up.

And as Evangelicism ceased to intoxicate him, as the flood of emotion which had carried him to an abnormal level turned back upon itself, the negative pains and perversities of Evangelical dogma more and more fastened upon his mind. And it was at this critical moment that a domestic event occurred which renewed in him that hopeless feeling of inadequacy which, ten years earlier, had distorted his mind.

In 1772 Mrs. Unwin's daughter became engaged to a clergyman, and since her absence would tend still further to compromise Cowper in the eyes and on the tongues of local gossips, it was arranged that he should marry Mrs. Unwin early in 1773. Of the sincerity of his attachment to her there is, of course, no doubt. Two years before he had written from his brother's death-bed – 'Let nothing I have said distress you; your peace is as dear to me as my own, and I cannot grieve you without suffering myself.' But it was expediency, and not any emotional necessity, which urged him to contract an engagement.

Mrs. Unwin was at this time forty-eight, and Cowper, besides being seven years younger, was more fitted to play the part of a son than a husband. Instead, therefore, of being sustained and animated by the prospect of realizing his desires, the marriage which he now contemplated was forced upon him by circumstances and opposed to his inclination.

Consequently the prospect of keeping this private engagement soon weighed upon his spirits, already enervated by religious dissipation, as severely as had the public engagement in the House of Lords. His native shyness and the stigma of sin which had become attached to it completely unmanned him. Late in January, 1773, he experienced for a day and night such melancholy as made him almost an infant. But the cloud as suddenly lifted. His agitation, however, remained and he tried to relieve it in poetry, invoking peace in the lines —

> Come, peace of mind, delightful guest!
> Return and make thy downy nest
>   Once more in this sad heart:
> Nor riches I nor power pursue,
> Nor hold forbidden joys in view;
>   We therefore need not part. . . .
>
> For thee I panted, thee I prized,
> For thee I gladly sacrificed
>   Whate'er I loved before,
> And shall I see thee start away,
> And helpless, hopeless, hear thee say,
>   "Farewell! we meet no more"?

But the peace of nature could not soothe a mind feverish with anxiety. The glassy stream, the alders quivering in the breeze, did but reflect his mood, while the memory of their beauty, no longer felt, deepened his sadness, telling 'of enjoyments past' and 'sorrows yet to come.' Less and less did life flow into him from outside; increasingly he felt the presence of his own solitude. And the more he tried to possess himself, the more dispossessed he became.

And then towards the end of February the self-distrust, composed of so many elements, took form in a dreadful dream in which he heard the words, 'Actum est de te, periisti' (It is all over with thee, thou art lost). And to him it was no nightmare. It was the Almighty delivering sentence of death in the Latin tongue, and a sentence from which there was no appeal.

Before this dream 'all consolation vanished;' despair became 'an inveterate habit.' For he never recovered from his delusion that God had forsaken him for ever, that He had erased him with an infuriated scrawl of His pen from the 'Book of Life.'

§ 10

To this tragic delusion Cowper was brought by a fatalistic religion. For it was a false theology that bound his despair to his mind with knots that no restoration of spirits could untie. The idea of damnation was not only enforced by Evangelicism with a wealth of melodramatic imagery, but with a show of perverse logic. It enslaved the mind to fear as well as the body.

Cowper's mind was not diseased. He had, in fact, the marked sanity which so often seems to balance, as it did, for example, in the persons of Samuel Johnson and Charles Lamb, a neurotic tendency. And of his experience at this time he wrote – 'I did not indeed lose my senses, but I lost the power to exercise them. I could return a rational answer even to a difficult question, but a question was necessary, or I never spoke at all.'

The depression from which he periodically suffered was at root physical. It was an efflux of vitality, common to the sensitive either in reaction from unusual excitement or in consequence of some prolonged anxiety which isolates the individual and at the same time consumes his nervous energy. Both these conditions preceded Cowper's depression at this time, and it was proportionately acute and prolonged. But later its onset was often seasonal, and since the first two months of the year, which prove particularly fatal to the old and ailing, were those which invariably weighed most heavily on him, the cause was perhaps climatic.

To trace mental depression back to possible physical causes is not, of course, to explain it away, but at least it tends to make it more intelligible even to the victim. He may continue to experience a nameless dread, 'the ghostly haunting horror,' which Mark Rutherford described as being so nearly akin to madness. He may still tremble to feel how thin a floor separates his own emptiness from some gaping abyss. But he can take comfort from the thought that as life flows back into him, the abyss will close, and form, colour and taste return.

Evangelicism, however, explained such a state in theological terms which were at once intelligible and subversive of all intelligence. For nearly ten years it had repeated to Cowper that his heart was 'desperately wicked,' and that a God overstrode him Who punished wicked-

ness with the utmost severity and Who could only be pro-
pitiated by utter self-abasement. He had been taught to
accept the most trivial and adventitious events as direct expressions of His will. Inevitably, therefore, he interpreted
his depression as a judgment, his apathy as a desertion by a
God so incensed with him as to spurn even his humility.
And it was not much more irrational to attribute divine
purpose to the chance words which had emerged from the
subconscious in sleep than to attribute it, as Evangelicism did, to a street accident, or to typhoid caused by bad
sanitation.

In the very impotence, however, which, carried to an
extreme, resulted in such insane fatalism Newton found
cause for religious satisfaction. 'In the beginning of his
disorder,' he wrote, 'how often have I heard him adore and
submit to the sovereignty of God, and declare, though in
the most agonizing and inconceivable distress, he was so
perfectly satisfied of the wisdom and rectitude of the
Lord's appointments, that if he was sure of relieving himself only by stretching out his hand, he would not do it,
unless he was equally sure it was agreeable to His will that
he should do it.'

Certainly he added, 'I hope I shall never have so
striking a proof of the integrity of any other friend, –
because I hope I shall never see any other in so dreadful
a state of trial.' But he approved such impotence as in the
highest degree edifying and described as integrity what
proclaimed itself as disintegration.

It may be, as Meredith wrote, that 'there is nothing the
body suffers that the soul may not profit by;' but Mere-

dith's words were a summons to action, Newton's were a sanctification of paralysis.

And Mrs. Unwin shared his views. Dr. Cotton was not called in for five months because she was anxious that 'the Lord Jehovah' should 'be alone exalted when the day of deliverance comes.' And when Cowper tried to take his life, in the belief that it was God's will that, 'after the example of Abraham,' he should 'perform an expensive act of obedience, and offer, not a son, but himself,' Newton approved 'the same perfect spirit of submission,' and read in his failure to do so 'such evident proofs of the Lord's care and goodness.'

Cowper, however, thought, with almost equal justice, otherwise. He believed that God had meant him to commit suicide, had given him power to accomplish this act of obedience, and that his failure to use it was his culminating and unforgivable sin against his Maker. And neither from this delusion nor from his dream did he ever wholly recover.

For a year and five months, then, he remained in this condition of melancholy impotence and, fittingly enough, he spent most of the time at the Vicarage. Unwilling at first even to enter Newton's door, he was prevailed upon in March, 1773, to do so and to remain a night to avoid the noise of an annual Fair. He was then equally unable to leave, and although Newton consoled himself by reflecting that 'the Lord's hand was concerned,' he had to admit that 'the cross was a heavy one to bear.' That he bore it nobly is proof at least of the efficacy of his religion so far as it concerned himself.

In the eclipse of his personality Cowper was convinced that he was hated not only by God, but by every one including even Mrs. Unwin, who devoted herself to him untiringly; but in May, 1774, the tide which had so long ebbed began to turn. He had worked incessantly in the garden, and while he worked he was tolerably easy. For the concrete drew him out from himself; even clods of earth were something to cling to in a void of fear and insensibility. And one morning as he was feeding the chickens, some little incident provoked the first smile for more than sixteen months. His personality had returned to him and with it his power to sympathize with things outside himself. Newton's inhuman God still remained, a firmly figured menace for ever impressed now upon the yielding surface of his mind. But he had smiled at a chicken and affirmed his humanity.

He returned to Orchard Side the same month, and the return implied something more than a change of residence. He continued to the end of his life to regard Newton with an uneasy affection; for some time too he sought his approval as a poet. But he no longer regarded him as a spiritual adviser. He ceased from public worship and from private prayer, 'apprehending that for *him* to implore mercy, would be opposing the determinate counsel of God.'

Certainly his abandonment of religion was as irrational as his participation in it had been, but at least it came to emancipate the poet in him. In religion he had both indulged his weakness and dissipated his strength. His weakness remained, defined for the rest of his life in the delusion of damnation which Evangelicism had done so much to fix and foster. But his strength was his own to cultivate.

'My mind,' he was shortly to write, 'has always a melancholy cast, and is like some pools I have seen, which, though filled with a black and putrid water, will nevertheless, in a bright day, reflect the sunbeams from the surface.' And again, – 'Alas! what can I do with my wit? I have not enough to do great things with. . . . I must do with it as I do with my linnet; I keep him for the most part in a cage, but now and then set open the door, that he may whisk about the room a little, and shut him up again.'

More and more frequently was the door to be set open, and not only for the whisking of his wit. At first in his letters and then, with a deepening confidence, in his poetry, the sensibility which had cowered beneath a tyrant God discovered beauty, kindness and humour in life. Newton may have deplored the fact that his friend was no longer a 'burning and a shining light' to many. But it was better for Cowper to feel himself deserted by such a God as Newton's than enslaved. At least it left him free to be as happy and human as his temperament allowed, and to become a poet in whom Nature lived again.

WINTER GROWTH

WINTER GROWTH

§ 1

Cowper drew near to Nature by way of the garden. In this he was like many of his contemporaries, but while they sought in garden-craft an opportunity for cultivating the picturesque or experimenting in pseudo-classical design, he devoted himself to it in the humblest way as a kind of activity which engaged both the body and the mind without overtaxing either. And he discovered in it something more. His distinctive characteristic as a poet of Nature was to be his mastery of detail. Unlike Thomson he was never to write of anything in Nature with which he had not had an immediate personal relation. And as a gardener he was continually experiencing this intimate contact with life. He feared life in the large, but he could love it in the small, and by tending its growth partake of its virtue.

It is true that in *The Task* he was to deprecate the work that asks 'robust tough sinews bred to toil' and to write that —

> strength may wield the ponderous spade,
> May turn the clod, and wheel the compost home,
> But elegance, chief grace the garden shows,
> And most attractive, is the fair result
> Of thought, the creature of a polished mind.

But although the graces of the garden were as dear as the graces of poetry to one who shrunk from the rude and prolific forces of Nature, the manual toil was at least as important to him as the mental preoccupation.

He began with lettuces and cauliflowers, from them proceeded to cucumbers; next to melons for which he had to make frames and glaze them. He then bought an orange tree, to which in due time he added two or three myrtles. This served him day and night with employment during a whole severe winter. To defend them from the frost he contrived to give them a fire-heat, and waded night after night through the snow, with the bellows under his arm, just before going to bed, to give the latest possible puff to the embers. Then he built himself a greenhouse, so small that 'Lord Bute's gardener could take it upon his back and walk away with it,' but an invaluable resort when the season or the weather kept him from the soil. To wade through the snow to his myrtles was as helpful to him as to wade through it to Newton's prayer-meetings had been harmful, and for the next twenty years gardening was his perpetual resource and one which, in the summer at least, was to mean almost more to him than the practice of poetry.

And in animal life as well as vegetable he found a healing virtue. Years later he was to write – 'All the notice that we lords of Creation vouchsafe to bestow on the creatures, is generally to abuse them; it is well therefore that here and there a man should be found a little womanish, or perhaps a little childish in this matter, who will make some amends, by kissing and coaxing, and laying them in one's bosom.'

Many a one wounded in the stress of life or recoiling from man's inhumanity to man has turned for comfort to the birds, forgetting his own frailty and timidity in ministering to theirs. Cowper had eight pairs of tame pigeons which he fed every morning as they perched on the garden wall, and among his pets were a linnet, a magpie, a jay, a starling, and several robins, gold-finches and canary birds. And birds served him in his poetry as well as in his life. For he used them often in his Fables either to preach or to adorn a moral.

But it was another creature, seldom domesticated before or since, that diverted him most. A neighbour gave him a leveret, and as soon as it was known that the present pleased him, he had as many leverets offered him as would have stocked a paddock. He undertook the care of three whom he named Puss, Tiney and Bess. They were allowed in the hall in the day-time and in the parlour sometimes in the evening, while they slept in a house which he built for them. He spent much time in studying their peculiarities of character and temper, and as two of them lived to a good old age, they were objects of interest and affection for more than ten years.

How closely he studied them is proved by the paper which he contributed in 1784 to the *Gentleman's Magazine*. Puss, he there recorded, who survived the longest, at once grew familiar, would be carried out in his arms, more than once fell asleep on his knee, and after recovering from a sickness, signified his gratitude for the kindness shown him by licking his master's hand, 'first the back of it, then the palm, then every finger separately, then between all the fingers, as if anxious to leave no part unsaluted.' Tiney refused to be tamed even by sickness, but his very surliness and the air of gravity which he preserved, even in his play, were vastly entertaining. 'I kept him,' Cowper was to write –

> for his humour's sake
> For he would oft beguile
> My heart of thoughts that made it ache,
> And force me to a smile.

Bess 'had a courage and confidence that made him tame from the beginning.'

Cowper's affection for his hares, as for all shy creatures, had its poetic as well as its personal aspect. The impulse which drew him to them was kindred to Whitman's, when he exclaimed that he could turn and live with animals, or to Wordsworth's when he embodied in 'Peter Bell's' ass or the White Doe of Rylstone an unexacting fidelity to life that reproved the agitations of men. This appreciation of natural integrity, whether in the animal or in the child, was typical of the romantic reaction against the meaner aspects of human self-sufficiency and its rationalized brutality.

Cowper himself was later to inveigh against –

> Detested sport,
> That owes its pleasures to another's pain,
> That feeds upon the sobs and dying shrieks
> Of harmless nature, dumb, but yet endued
> With eloquence that agonies inspire,
> Of silent tears and heart-distending sighs!

And, while admitting man's rational superiority, he was to recognize –

That man's attainments in his own concerns,
Matched with the expertness of the brutes in theirs,
Are ofttimes vanquished and thrown far behind,

while in moral qualities —

       learn we might, if not too proud to stoop
To quadruped instructors, many a good
And useful quality, and virtue too,
Rarely exemplified among ourselves:
Attachment never to be weaned or changed
By any change of fortune, proof alike
Against unkindness, absence, and neglect;
Fidelity that neither bribe nor threat
Can move or warp; and gratitude for small
And trivial favours, lasting as the life
And glistening even in the dying eye.

In gaining Puss's confidence then and pledging all that
was human in him to protect his 'unsuspecting gratitude
and love,' Cowper was quite unconsciously practising a
religion which was to supersede the restricted rationalism
of the Deists and the pagan theology of the Evangelicals.
It was the religion of humanity in which Nature and man
were reconciled, and he was to be among the first of its
poets.

By these diversions, which included also the making of
squirrel-houses, hutches for rabbits, bird-cages and cab-
bage nets, he superimposed a conscious life of industry and
interest upon his subconscious despair. He took lessons,
too, in drawing from an Olney painter, whom he named

his 'Michael Angelo,' found it 'a most amusing art,' and for nearly a year was 'unwearied' in his application. 'I draw mountains,' he wrote, 'valleys, woods, and streams, and ducks, and dab-chicks. I admire them myself, and Mrs. Unwin admires them; and her praise, and my praise put together, are fame enough for me.'

Although it was only the necessity of amusement which made him dabble in art, the careful study of nature which it involved may have had some influence upon his later pictorial exactitude as a poet. Nature, however, was not yet a subject for verse-making. Still stricken with the remembrance of the abyss into which feeling had plunged him, he was cautious of expressing it even in the unfanatical medium of poetry. We shall see how gradually he acquired courage to give himself cautiously to life with a consequent growth of inward experience in his poetry. But for the time he drew in his verse, as he did in everything else, only upon the surface of his being.

Thus late in 1779, he sent William Unwin a set of verses, entitled *The Yearly Distress*, in which he painted with a drollery that foreshadows 'John Gilpin' itself, the embarrassment of a country clergyman on the day appointed for receiving tithes, the arrival of the farmers and their entertainment at dinner, and their disinclination to part with their money. To Unwin also, he sent a little fable entitled *The Nightingale and Glow-worm* and three stanzas, provoked by the cruelty of a neighbour whose goldfinch had been starved to death in his cage, in which pity and indignation were at once pointed and tempered by wit.

It is perhaps significant too of his emancipation from Newton that he wrote in *The Nightingale and Glow-worm* –

> Hence jarring sectaries may learn
> Their real interest to discern;
> That brother should not war with brother,
> And worry and devour each other;
> But sing and shine by sweet consent,
> Till life's poor transient night is spent,
> Respecting, in each other's case,
> The gifts of nature and of grace.
> Those Christians best deserve the name
> Who studiously make peace their aim;
> Peace both the duty and the prize
> Of him that creeps and him that flies.

And in the following year Newton was to carry his spiritual warfare elsewhere. Alarmed by a disastrous fire which had occurred in Olney, he had provoked the hostility of the undevout by suggesting that November 5th should not be celebrated with fireworks. His house had consequently been threatened by a mob, and although he had the satisfaction of comparing Olney in his next sermon to a Sodom, saved only from total destruction by 'the believers,' whose prayers had contributed more to stopping the fire than water, he was deeply hurt by the treatment which he had received and welcomed, two years later, the offer of a cure in London.

His successor, the Reverend William Bull, was also a preacher of 'heart religion,' but of a kind tempered by delicate health. 'My heart,' he wrote, 'is formed for grati-

tude, and my head for vapours,' and since an attack of
brain fever had, in his own words, 'brought him to his
senses,' leaving him, however, henceforth subject to
depression which he countered as much by exercising his
comic powers as by invoking higher ones, Cowper found
in him a kindred spirit.

'Dear Taureau,' as he came to call him, soon dined
regularly once a fortnight at Orchard Side, smoked his
pipe and let his imagination run away with him into fields
of amusing and enlivening speculation. He described his
sermons as 'at best a sort of rant,' and although as a
pastor he strove to emulate Newton's dominating zeal,
he had far too much tact to preach to Cowper. The verses
which his visits provoked are themselves proof of his tran-
quillizing influence and the unexacting affection which
he inspired, notably the charming little domestic fable,
entitled *The Doves,* and the rhyming letter sent with a box
of 'Orinoco' tobacco and the wish –

> may smoke-inhaling Bull
> Be always filling, never full.

In the year also in which Newton left Olney, the other
Evangelical who had dominated Cowper committed a
Biblical indiscretion which made him, much to his surprise, an outcast among his Evangelical brethren. With
more consistency than they, Martin Madan published a
book entitled *Thelyphthora; or a Treatise on Female Ruin,*
in which he argued, on the evidence of the Scriptures and
particularly the Pentateuch, that polygamy was allowed by
the Most High to the Jews and indefinitely sanctioned.

Madan was probably influenced by his experience of the fallen women who came under his charge at the Lock Hospital, and who, he thought, might have been happy wives and mothers under another social system. And the Biblical justification which he found for this humanitarian sentiment differed in no essentials from that which Newton found for his conviction of a 'vengeful God.' One who accepted the Old Testament as an absolute instead of a relative revelation of God had an equal right to attribute a permanently Divine sanction to the polygamy of the Jews as to their sacrificial theology.

Newton, however, was outraged by such a ruthless application of his own Judaism to modern society, and, still blind to the harm which he had done to Cowper, was anxious to brief him as counsel for the defence of Evangelical respectability. Cowper, however, was no longer at his call. 'If I had strength of mind,' he wrote, 'I have not strength of body for the task which, you say, some would impose upon me. I cannot bear much thinking. The meshes of that fine net-work, the brain, are composed of such mere spinner's threads in me, that when a long thought finds its way into them, it buzzes, and twangs, and bustles about at such a rate as seemed to threaten the whole contexture. – No. – I must needs refer it again to you.'

Cowper, in fact, was at first more amused than disgusted by the affair. He only read a chapter of the treatise, but he remarked that if he had a wife of whom he was weary and wished to be indulged with the liberty of taking another, he would certainly read it all and study it too.

With a wit, too, that was at once legal and shrewd, he wrote that 'an officer of a regiment, part of which is quartered here, gave one of his soldiers leave to be drunk six weeks, in hopes of curing him by satiety; – he *was* drunk six weeks and is so still, as often as he can find an opportunity. One vice may swallow up another, but no coroner in the Sate of Ethics ever brought in his verdict, when a vice died, that it was *felo de se.*'

He was witty also in verse, remarking that –

It has always been reckoned a just cause of strife
For a man to make free with another man's wife;
But the strife is the strangest that ever was known,
If a man must be scolded for loving his own.

But when he had exhausted the humorous aspect of the subject, he began to view it as an outrage, not on any religious faith, but on human decency, on 'the rusty and old-fashioned bonds of fidelity, friendship, and love.' He even saw it as the fruit of a mind 'Evangelically enlightened' and wrote with a discrimination which might earlier have saved him from fanaticism, 'the question is not "was polygamy lawful to a Jew?" which nobody will dispute; but "Is it lawful to a Christian?" '

The affair, however, is chiefly of importance because it provoked the first long poem in which he exercised his satirical powers and incidentally wrote of nature in something approaching the style which he was to make his own. *Anti-Thelyphthora* has been condemned as 'a coarse and vulgar effusion,' but although Cowper revolted so violently from the suggestion that a 'faithful English husband' should be 'converted into a Turkish stallion,' as to lose something of his cultivated poise, his ridicule, under the form of a Spenserian allegory, of the victims of the enchantress Hypothesis is never rank and is often bluntly effective, as in the lines in which he pictures Madan, the 'Sir Airy' of the poem, dreaming of –

> Large population on a liberal plan
> And woman trembling at the foot of man;
> How simple wedlock fornication works,
> And Christians marrying may convert the Turks.

Cowper was too gentle and humane to be a satirical pugilist like Churchill. And in this poem he had not yet acquired the more delicate foil or learnt the passes which were to take the place in his satire of the more thrusting and defiant sword-play of his satirical predecessors. It was uncongenial to him also to attack persons even under an allegorical disguise. Just as he was morbidly shy with strangers, so the thought of a direct and aggressive relation towards individuals, even in verse, made him nervously self-conscious and tempted him to simulate an uncharacteristic violence.

Anti-Thelyphthora, however, is characteristic enough to be interesting as his first extended effort in satire and doubtless he learnt from its very crudities that it suited his mild and moral temperament better to satirize types by a direct method than persons by an indirect and fantastic one. In the short descriptive passage too, the first of its kind, that occurs in this poem, he was not yet distinctly himself because he was still too chary of feeling.

The details chosen for description are typical and finely selected, but his relation to them lacks the later intimacy —

> 'Twas on the noon of an autumnal day,
> October hight, but mild and fair as May;
> When scarlet fruits the russet hedge adorn,
> And floating films envelop every thorn;
> When gently as in June the rivers glide,
> And only miss the flowers that graced their side;
> The linnet twittered out his parting song,
> With many a chorister the woods among;
> On southern banks the ruminating sheep
> Lay snug and warm; — 'twas Summer's farewell peep.

With Madan then in disgrace, Newton in London, and Bull puffing a philosophic pipe in his place, Cowper was under no temptation, even if he had desired it, to desert literature again for Evangelicism, Humanism for Hebraism. He was never a great reader, chiefly perhaps because he had few books, but he read Grey at this time and considered him 'the only poet since Shakespeare entitled to the character of the sublime,' while Johnson's treatment of Milton in his *Lives of the Poets* drew from him the impulsive remark — 'Oh! I could thresh his old jacket till I made his pension jingle in his pocket.' 'He has plucked,' he wrote, 'one or two of the most beautiful feathers out of his Muse's wing, and trampled them under his great foot . . . was there ever anything so delightful as the music of the *Paradise Lost?* It is like that of a fine organ; has the fullest and the deepest tones of majesty, with all the softness and elegance of the Dorian flute.'

Like all his contemporaries Cowper held Johnson in some awe for his 'good sense and strong intellect,' but the degree to which he had recovered his power of independent judgment is shown equally by his description of Johnson as 'that literary Cossack' and his appreciation of Milton's style apart from his ethic.

He had begun, too, those walks about the countryside, of which he was to write –

> For I have loved the rural walk through lanes
> Of grassy swarth, close cropped by nibbling sheep
> And skirted thick with intertexture firm
> Of thorny boughs; have loved the rural walk
> O'er hills, through valleys, and by rivers' brink. . . .

And slowly a landscape in which there was nothing to terrify or unduly excite eased his self-constraint. Here amid pastoral uplands or river meadows he could yield his being to life and find a kindliness and a sympathy which matched his own. Here he could project an intelligence, so long self-centred and self-consuming, into the lines of a hillside or a waving branch. And sometimes for a change he would drive over in a post-chaise to Gayhurst, a country seat about four miles away, to admire the 'elegantly disposed' gardens or appraise with a specialist's eye, the hot-houses and orange-trees.

The poverty of his humble neighbours in Olney, who were suffering much from a decline in the lace-trade upon which they depended, offered him also a practical outlet for his sympathy. Never a year passed during his residence at Olney when he failed to plead the necessities

of the lace-makers with influential friends. Later he was
happy in being able to distribute the gifts of a Mr. Smith
who wished to remain an anonymous benefactor, and no
better channel for charity could have been found.

Cowper's sketches in verse and prose of Olney worthies
reveal the same qualities which inspired his charitable
activities. He neither patronized the poor nor used them
as a text for any moral or economic doctrine. He could
write indeed in words with which Tolstoy would have
agreed that 'almost all the real virtue there is in the world
is to be found living and dying in a state of neglected
obscurity.' But this did not prevent him from viewing
the poor, as he viewed the rich, with the poet's disinterested eye, respecting equally the truth of their virtues
and their vices.

And so his charity was at once wholly human and self-
respecting; because he really stood, by virtue of his
sympathy, on the level of suffering, he had no need to
accuse himself, although the insensitiveness of the privi-
leged to it, came home to him as a personal affront. 'Oh,
what things pass in cottages and hovels,' he was to write,
'which the great never dream of!' And, – 'when ministers
talk of resources, that word never fails to send my
imagination into the mud-wall cottages of our poor at
Olney.' Of a peer, too, who disregarded an appeal for
charity, he remarked with whimsical irony, – 'I do not
know that the eye of a nobleman was ever dissected. I
cannot help supposing however, that, were that organ, as
it exists in the head of such a personage, to be accurately
examined, it would be found to differ materially in its

construction from the eye of a commoner; so very different is the view that men in an elevated, and in an humble station, have of the same object. What appears great, sublime, beautiful, and important to you and to me, when submitted to the notice of my lord, or his grace, and submitted, too, with the utmost humility, is either too minute to be visible at all, or, if seen, seems trivial, or of no account!'

Cowper's attitude to the poor, like his relation to nature, lacked the emotional and imaginative intensity of a Wordsworth or a Tolstoy; but it lacked also any tendency to sentimentalize them or exploit them either philosophically or ethically. 'The poor,' he was to write with a blunt sincerity reminiscent of Crabbe –

> inured to drudgery and distress,
> Act without aim, think little, and feel less,
> And nowhere, but in feigned Arcadian scenes,
> Taste happiness, or know what pleasure is.

But his attitude was human enough too to be humorous, and of their application to him for legal advice he remarked that the 'cheapness of a gratuitous counsel has advanced my credit to a degree I never expected to attain in the capacity of a lawyer.'

After six years then, thus variously occupied, Olney had become for him something more comfortable than an 'Evangelical Mecca.' If clouds still hung upon the horizon and the sun was fitful or subdued, the thunder of an angry deity no longer rolled across the sky. Already indeed he might have written –

O blest seclusion from a jarring world,
Which he, thus occupied, enjoys! Retreat
Cannot indeed to guilty man restore
Lost innocence, or cancel follies past;
But it has peace, and much secures the mind
From all assaults of evil.

§ 2

But the sense of guilt remained. The dreadful words were not unsaid. Mrs. Unwin and her son might be perfectly sure of his deliverance. But he did not share their confidence. Certainly he had recovered sufficient spirits to visualize the possibility of a withdrawal of the penal sentence, but he was still as far from realizing that it lay with him and him only to rescind it.

Newton tried to cheer him by bringing to his notice the case of one Simon Browne who had recovered from a delusion that God had deserted him. But Cowper considered his own case too singular to take hope from any other, while he wrote that 'there is no encouragement in the Scriptures so comprehensive as to include my case, nor any consolation so effectual as to reach it. You will think me mad; but I am not mad, most noble Festus, I am only in despair.'

How much his despair was a nervous obsession is shown by the liberality of his religious views when he himself was not concerned. He could write, for example, of another – 'The forgiveness of God is large and absolute; so large that, though in general He calls for confession

of our sins, He sometimes dispenses with that preliminary.'

But his sense of being unfit for life, of being disqualified
by an inherent nervous weakness from being useful either
to himself or others, convinced him that something dis-
criminated his story from that of every other man; his
virtues, he felt, counted less in the eyes of God than the
vices of a criminal, because his roots in life were less
secure. And so behind all his diversions he continued to
suffer from a fundamental want of purpose. He longed
to live inevitably, to surrender his self-consciousness to
an overruling force, and he could not. 'My days,' he
wrote, 'steal away silently, and march on (as poor mad
King Lear would have made his soldiers march) as if they
were shod with felt; not so silently but that I hear them.'

But he had one other resource, which availed him,
before poetry became a daily routine, even more than all
those which have been mentioned, the resource of letter-
writing. 'This occupation,' he confessed, 'above all others
assists me in that self-deception to which I am indebted
for all the little comfort I enjoy.' And he explained its
peculiar virtue when he wrote – 'There is a pleasure
annexed to the communication of one's ideas, whether
by word of mouth or by letter, which nothing earthly can
supply the place of, and it is the delight we find in this
mutual intercourse that not only proves us to be creatures
intended for social life, but more than anything else fits
us for it.' And again – 'The happiness we cannot call our
own, we yet seem to possess, while we sympathize with
our friends who can.'

Through letter-writing Cowper achieved that intimate contact with human life which he experienced by other means with vegetable and animal life. The nervous qualms and inhibitions which were always liable to cripple his relation with all but most intimate friends, never troubled him as a letter-writer. Rather the act of writing made him self-possessed, enabling him to concentrate on paper all his faculties, and with them that 'generosity of soul, and a brotherly attachment to our kind,' to which he was often too timid to give full play in immediate intercourse. 'Nothing is necessary,' he wrote, 'but to put pen to paper, and go on, in order to conquer all difficulties. . . . I now begin with a most assured persuasion, that sooner or later, one idea naturally suggesting another, I shall come to a most prosperous conclusion.'

His letters indeed were not only works of art, but natural growths, and it was in them that he first experienced the satisfaction of surrendering himself, as he did later in poetry, to the flow of impulse. 'Thus it is with my thoughts,' he wrote: – 'when you shake a crab-tree the fruit falls.' And although his later letters to Lady Hesketh were to abound more in that affection of which he claimed the gift when he wrote – 'Whatever else I want, I have, at least, this quality in common with publicans and sinners that I love those that love me,' the earlier letters, and particularly those to William Unwin, are more generally characteristic.

His correspondence with Newton, as he later admitted, was not seldom a burden, because he felt constrained to adopt a serious and even rather sanctimonious tone, and to refer to his spiritual condition. But even these letters are full of felicities of humour, anecdote and general observation. And the fact that little of his energy was yet going into poetry makes this a fitting moment to consider his qualities in a humbler, if no less endearing art.

§ 3

Letter-writing, as an art, is subject to the same conditions as any other art. Ideally a letter must in every phrase and sentence express a personality: it must convey an illusion of spontaneity, but it must not reflect an unorganized impulse. Its language must be conversational (as Cowper wrote to Lady Hesketh – 'When I read your letters I hear you talk, and I love talking letters dearly'), but its conversation must be so choice as to be keyed up above the level of the accidental. It must speak directly and even casually to its reader, but with a distinction which is at once personal and memorable. And finally it must be a unity, the expression through all its parts, however delicately interlinked or unconsciously associated, of a single mood.

The best of Cowper's letters satisfy all these conditions. 'I do not write,' he remarked, 'without thinking, but always without premeditation.' And this distinction goes to the root of the matter. Premeditation would have stemmed the flow of impulse, but by thinking he imposed form on it and made it completely his own.

Cowper was not consciously practising an art when he wrote, but he was artist enough to guard against artifice. Sensible people, as he of all men was of a nature to know, 'are best pleased with what is natural and unaffected,' and when Unwin praised his gifts as a letter-writer he was concerned lest it should make him self-conscious and so tempt him into artifice.

'Now this foolish vanity,' he wrote, 'would have spoiled me quite, and would have made me as disgusting a letter-writer as Pope, who seems to have thought that unless a sentence was well turned, and every period pointed with some conceit, it was not worth the carriage. Accordingly he is to me, except in very few instances, the most disagreeable maker of epistles that ever I met with. I was willing, therefore, to wait till the impression your commendation had made upon the foolish part of me was worn off, that I might scribble away as usual, and write my uppermost thoughts, and those only.'

But although it was essential to him, both as an artist and as a man, to write self-forgetfully, although to begin a letter might seem always 'a sort of forlorn hope,' so undetermined was he of what, if anything, he was going to communicate, his very expectant passivity brought his faculties into perfect fusion. He opened himself, 'gently and gradually as men of polite behaviour do,' and gathered with an elegance in which was no mannerism because it expressed inevitably his own innate cultivation –

> all the floating thoughts we find
> Upon the surface of the mind.

Cowper was fortunate in having the leisure to cultivate the art of letter-writing, but no amount of leisure would have enabled him to distil his personality in his letters, to

squeeze out the humorous essence of a situation, to
develop an idea or an argument with an inevitable and
wholly individual propriety, if he had not found in this
activity an ideal means of harmonizing all his faculties.

He lived in his letters as the being, at once sympathetic
and self-possessed, which he wished to be. He obeyed
an impulse that life itself seemed to dictate, and he
ordered it as an individual. The experience was not profound, but it was organic. His letters at once satisfied
the literary craftsman in him and grew by the law of their
own being. Although never aiming 'at anything above
the pitch of every day's scribble,' it was a scrupulous
pitch. 'I did not perceive till this moment,' he wrote for
example in one letter, 'that I had tacked two similes
together; a practice which, though warranted by the
example of Homer, and allowable in an epic poem, is
rather luxurious and licentious in a letter.'

But his literary conscience never stayed his easy
advance. His style was implicit, and the fact that his
letters were uniformly written in a beautiful hand and
almost without an erasure is an additional proof of the
equable manner in which he exemplified his own dictum
that 'a letter is written as a conversation is maintained, or
a journey performed; not by preconcerted or premedi-
tated means . . . but merely by maintaining a progress.'

The fact throws further light on his nervous constitution. 'When I am in the best health,' he wrote, 'my tide
of animal sprightliness flows with great equality, so that
I am never, at any time, exalted in proportion as I am
sometimes depressed.' That he was never troubled by an

excess of animal energy even in his most vigorous moments saved him from that struggle to master a chaos of ideas which is the agonizing lot of most creative writers, but it also meant that he had little reserve of energy to draw upon, so that when, for any reason, his energy sank below the normal level, he experienced what seemed to him a cessation of life or, as he now interpreted it, a desertion by God.

His equableness was, however, the quality from which all his virtues as a letter-writer derived. It dictated not only his style but his perspective. 'Every scene of life,' he wrote to Bull, 'has two sides, a dark and a bright one, and the mind which has an equal mixture of melancholy and vivacity is best of all qualified for the contemplation of either; it can be lively without levity and pensive without dejection.'

Both his humour and his moralizing or the blend of the two which was most typical of him were conditioned by his sensitiveness to the equal mixture in the world of the lementable and the ridiculous, a sensitiveness which corresponded superficially with what in natures more passionate and penetrating than his was to become a dual vision of the positive and negative forces in life so hard to reconcile.

In profound insight his letters were as deficient as his poetry. He viewed what was uppermost, but with an exquisite appreciation of its contrasted aspects, truly comparing his mind to 'a board that is under the carpenter's plane . . . the shavings are my uppermost thoughts; after a few strokes of the tool, it acquires a new surface; this again, upon a repetition of the task, he takes off, and a new surface still succeeds.'

What he wrote was thus always fresh and always consistent. His personality pervaded every sentence, but he was never tediously self-engrossed, never over-subtle or picturesque. He unfolded his impressions or described his own moods with the same unassertive but perceptive naturalness, in which thought and illustrative simile reinforced each other, not merely aptly and ingeniously, but by an inevitable association.

For example he wrote – 'I have heard (for I never made the experiment) that if a man grasp a red-hot iron with his naked hand, it will stick to him, so that he cannot presently disengage himself from it. Such are the [American] Colonies in the hands of administration. While they hold them they burn their fingers, and yet they must not quit them.' Or again – 'But you think Margate more lively. So is a Cheshire cheese full of mites more lively than a sound one; but that very liveliness only proves its rottenness.' Or – 'Whatever is short, should be nervous, masculine and compact. Little men are so; and little poems should be so.' Or – 'A critic of the present day serves a poem as a cook does a dead turkey, when she fastens the legs of it to a post and draws out all the sinews.'

Or he began a letter to Unwin thus – 'My dear Friend – 'As two men sit silent, after having exhausted all their topics of conversation, one says, "It is very fine weather"; and the other says, "Yes;" – one blows his nose and the other rubs his eyebrows (by the way, this is very much in Homer's manner); such seems to be the case between you and me.'

Or, for a final example, he wrote thus of the slow labour and delay of correcting proofs – 'So the wild goose in the meadow flaps her wings and flaps them, but yet she mounts not; she stands on tiptoe on the banks of Ouse, she meditates an ascent, she stretches her long neck, she flaps her wings again; the successful repetition of her efforts at last bears her above the ground; she mounts into the heavenly regions exulting, and who then shall describe her song? – to herself at least it makes ample recompense for her laborious exertions.'

His similes, as these examples show, were taken directly from his own experience, and because that experience was restricted he disdained nothing as being too lowly to be interesting. 'The mind,' he wrote, 'long wearied with the sameness of a dull dreary prospect, will gladly fix its eye on anything that may make a little variety in its contemplations, though it were but a kitten playing with her tail.'

And how interesting he could make such an incident, how completely he could concentrate his being on it, at once dispassionately observing and humorously commenting, is proved by his description of his own kitten – 'I have a kitten, my dear, the drollest of all creatures that ever wore a cat's skin. Her gambols are not to be described, and would be incredible if they could. She tumbles head over heels several times together, she lays her cheek to the ground and presents her rump at you with an air of most supreme disdain; from this posture she rises to dance on her hind feet, an exercise that she performs with all the grace imaginable, and she closes these various exhibitions with a loud smack of her lips, which, for want of greater propriety of expression, we call spitting. But though all cats spit, no cat ever produced such a sound as she does . . . no wisdom that she may gain hereafter, will compensate the loss of her present hilarity.'

This devotion to small details was to be one of the chief characteristics of his poetry, and we may compare the manner in which he was to trace, at the beginning of *The Task*, the stages of transition from the stool to the arm-chair and from the settee to the couch with the account, that filled nearly half of one of his letters, of the card-table at which he was writing for the first time. The reason for the change, the condition of the round-table which had been superseded, the inadequacy of the fly-table, the too ponderous dimensions of the dining-table, and finally the humble virtues of the card-table and its one flaw – a sharp splinter that tore Mrs. Unwin's dress – are all described with such an engrossed fidelity to detail that the humble card-table acquires something of the personal significance which Van Gogh gives to a kitchen chair.

And with the abstract no less than the concrete he achieved a personal relation. With the latter it was a relation of loving fidelity, with the former of whimsical reflection. One of the excitements which Olney provided was exhibition ascents in a balloon. And upon this early effort of science to master the elements his wit played in this manner, – 'How happy in comparison with myself, does the sagacious investigator of nature seem, whose fancy is ever employed in the invention of *hypotheses*, and his reason in the support of them. While he is accounting for the origin of the winds, he has no leisure to attend to their influence upon himself; and while he considers what the sun is made of, forgets that he has not shone for a month. . . . One generation blows bubbles, and the next breaks them. But in the meantime your philosopher is a happy man.'

These views are not original, but how well they are put and from what a personal angle! And from the reflective he rose with quickening pulse and fancy to the droll. 'By the way,' he continued, 'what is your opinion of these air-balloons? I am quite charmed with the discovery. Is it not possible (do you suppose) to convey such a quantity of inflammable air into the stomach and abdomen, that the philosopher, no longer gravitating to a centre, shall ascend by his own comparative levity, and never stop till he has reached the medium exactly in equilibrio with himself? May he not by the help of a pasteboard rudder, attached to his posteriors, steer himself in that purer element with ease; and again by slow and gradual dis-charge of his aerial contents, recover his former tendency to the earth, and descend without the smallest danger or inconvenience? These things are worth enquiry.'

So beautifully mock-solemn is his tone throughout, that a humorless person might almost take his speculations seriously. The degree of humour and seriousness in his reflections depended entirely on his mood. He accepted everything which entered his mind and played upon it according to the mood of the moment. Unlike Newton he did not complain 'of that crowd of trifling thoughts that pesters you without ceasing,' nor did he have 'a serious thought standing at the door of his imagination, like a justice of peace, with the riot-act in his hand, ready to read it, and disperse the mob.' On the contrary, trifling thoughts or incidents were to him unexacting enough to allow of an attitude of fertile self-possession. He was at his ease with them, while 'the serious thought' of a Newton would have destroyed the free-play of his nature.

That free-play was as often serious as sportive. But the moralizing which occurred so frequently in his letters was itself a kind of humour, the whimsical comment of a sensitive sanity upon the follies and extravagances of the world rather than the scolding of a partisan piety.

In this his letters differed for the most part from his poetry, in which, to justify himself in the eyes of his Evangelical friends who could not conceive of poetry as a disinterested activity, he too often adopted the preacher's tone. He did not scold the young, however, when he wrote – 'I am an old fellow, but I had once my dancing days, as you have now; yet I could never find that I had learned half so much of a woman's real character by dancing with her, as by conversing with her at home, where I could observe her behaviour at the table, at the fireside, and in all the trying circumstances of domestic life. We are all good when we are pleased; but she is the good woman, who wants not a fiddle to sweeten her. If I am wrong, the young ladies will set me right. . . .'

No uncle could reprove youth's frivolity more endearingly, and the same persuasive good-sense is well illustrated elsewhere in his reflections upon 'fashion' – 'While the world lasts, fashion will continue to lead it by the nose. And, after all, what can fashion do for its most obsequious followers? It can ring the changes upon the same things, and it can do no more. Whether our hats be white or black, our caps high or low – whether we wear two watches or one, is of little consequence. There is indeed an appearance of variety; but the folly and vanity that dictates and adopts the change, are invariably the same. When the fashions of a particular period appear more reasonable than those of the preceding, it is not because the world is grown more reasonable than it was; but because in a course of perpetual changes, some of them must sometimes happen to be for the better. Neither do I suppose the preposterous customs that prevail at present, a proof of its greater folly. In a few years, perhaps next year, the fine gentleman will shut up his umbrella, and give it to his sister, filling his hand with a crab-tree cudgel instead of it: and when he has done so, will he be wiser than now? By no means. The love of change will have betrayed him into a propriety, which, in reality, he has no taste for, all his merit on the occasion amounting to no more than this, – that, being weary of one plaything, he has taken up another.'

That he himself was capable of agreeable little vanities, as when he asked Unwin to buy him a more fashionable stock than he possessed, and a handsome stock-buckle 'that will make a figure at Olney,' qualified him to be particularly disinterested on the subject of 'fashions.' But a humorous common sense was typical of all his moralizing, apart from that contained in letters to Newton. His comment upon the text, 'If a man smite one cheek, turn the other,' that 'though a Christian is not to be quarrelsome, he is not to be crushed,' was characteristic of the equal appeal which generosity and justice made to his temperament.

He revealed the same blend of sanity and sympathy in his literary judgments, considering perspicacity in writing as 'always more than half the battle' and the want of it as 'the ruin of more than half the poetry that is published,' but elsewhere criticizing Blair for being 'a critic very little animated by what he reads, who rather reasons about the beauties of an author, than really tastes them; and who finds that a passage is praiseworthy, not because it charms him, but because it is accommodated to the laws of criticism in that case made and provided.'

It was, however, in his accounts of local incidents that he most delightfully combined a judicial detachment with a self-forgetful response to the humours of a situation. We cannot forbear to quote two of these. In the first he was writing of a youth who had committed a theft during one of the local fires. 'Being convicted, he was ordered to be whipt, which operation he underwent at the cart's tail, from the stone house to the high arch, and back again. He seemed to show great fortitude, but it was all a great imposition upon the public. The beadle, who performed it, had filled his left hand with red ochre, through which, after every stroke, he drew the lash of his whip, leaving the appearance of a wound upon the skin, but in reality not hurting him at all. This being perceived by Mr. Constable Handscomb, who followed the beadle, he applied his cane, without any such management or precaution, to the shoulders of the too merciful executioner. The scene immediately became more interesting. The beadle could by no means be prevailed upon to strike hard, which provoked the constable to strike harder; and this double flogging continued, till a lass of Silver-end, pitying the pitiful beadle thus suffering under the hands of the pitiless constable, joined the procession, and placing herself immediately behind the latter, seized him by his capillary club, and pulling him backwards by the same, slapt his face with a most Amazonian fury. This concatenation of events has taken up more of my paper than I intended it should, but I could not forbear to inform you how the beadle threshed the thief, the constable the beadle, and the lady the constable, and how the thief was the only person concerned who suffered nothing.'

This description is not only exquisitely ridiculous, but exquisitely composed. It has both a logical continuity and an admirably controlled dramatic movement. And the style of mock-gravity concentrated in the phrase – 'the scene immediately became more interesting' – which may be compared with a similar phrase in his account of the vocal contest between a loud-voiced visitor and the birds in the parlour – heightens our appreciation of the actual absurdity.

The second example is even more Dickensian, but it, too, has a classical quality in its composition. It describes a candidate's visit during a Parliamentary election. 'We were sitting yesterday after dinner, the two ladies and myself, very composedly, and without the least apprehension of any such intrusion in our snug parlour, one lady knitting, the other netting, and the gentleman winding worsted, when, to our unspeakable surprise, a mob appeared before the window; a smart rap was heard at the door, the boys hallooed, and the maid announced Mr. Grenville. Puss was unfortunately let out of her box, so that the candidate, with all his good friends at his back, was refused admittance at the grand entry, and referred to the back door as the only possible way of approach. Candidates are creatures not very susceptible of affronts, and would rather, I suppose, climb in at a window than be absolutely excluded. In a minute the yard, the kitchen, and the parlour were filled. Mr. Grenville, advancing towards me, shook me by the hand with a degree of cordiality that was extremely seducing. As soon as he and as many more as could find chairs were seated, he began to open the intent of his visit. I told him I had no vote, for which he readily gave me credit. I assured him I had no influence, which he was not equally inclined to believe, and the less, no doubt, because Mr. Ashburner, addressing himself to me at that moment, informed me that I had a great deal. Supposing I could not be possessed of such a treasure without knowing it, I ventured to confirm the assertion by saying that if I had any, I was utterly at a loss to imagine where it could be or wherein it consisted. Mr. Grenville squeezed me by the hand again, kissed the ladies and withdrew. He kissed likewise the maid in the kitchen, and seemed on the whole a most loving, kissing, kind-hearted gentleman. He is very young, genteel, and handsome. He has a pair of very good eyes in his head, which not being sufficient, as it should seem, for the many nice and difficult purposes of a senator, he has a third also, which he wore suspended by a riband from his button-hole. The boys hallooed, the dogs barked, Puss scampered, the hero, with his long train of obsequious followers, withdrew.'

Here again the composition is perfect, both in phrasing and in its inward pulse. The candidate with his motley supporters rolls like a wave upon the calm sea of domestic industry, breaks in a foam of flattery and kisses, and ebbs with as inevitable a rhythm. And within this tidal movement are the cross-currents and ripples of comic comment. And Cowper's after-comment was equally characteristic. 'It is comfortable,' he wrote, 'to be of no consequence in a world where one cannot exercise any without disobliging somebody. . . . Mr. Ashburner, perhaps was a little mortified, because it was evident that I owed the honour of the visit to his misrepresentation of my importance. But had he thought proper to assure Mr. Grenville that I had three heads, I should not, I suppose, have been bound to produce them.'

The self-depreciation which had such disastrous consequences in his religious experience was indeed one of the most fertile elements in his humour, because here it was balanced by the self-content which he derived from exercising his own admirable judgment. His very modesty enabled him to turn the tables more effectively upon pretentiousness of all sorts, to emphasize his own worth by pretending to deny it.

Often, indeed, his humility was not assumed, but even then it was self-respecting. He wrote, for example, much as Wordsworth was to write, on the irregularities of genius – 'I never knew a poet, except myself, who was punctual in anything, or to be depended on for the due discharge of any duty, except what he thought he owed to the Muses. The moment a man takes it into his foolish head that he has what the world calls Genius, he gives himself a discharge from the servile drudgery of all friendly offices, and becomes good for nothing. But I am not yet vain enough to think myself entitled to such self-conferred honours.'

Occasionally in his later letters his humility deepened into despair. But to reflect upon your own sadness and express your reflections is a sure way of relieving it, and in this, too, letter-writing served Cowper well. 'A yellow shower of leaves,' he wrote in a passage typical of his musing in a minor key, 'is falling continually from all the trees in the country. A few moments only seem to have passed since they were buds; and in a few moments more, they will have disappeared. It is one advantage of a rural situation, that it affords many hints of the rapidity with which life flies, that do not occur in towns and cities. It is impossible for a man, conversant with such scenes as surround me, not to advert daily to the shortness of his existence here, admonished of it, as he must be, by ten thousand objects. There was a time when I could contemplate my present state, and consider myself as a thing of a day with pleasure; when I numbered the seasons as they passed in swift rotation, as a schoolboy numbers the days that interpose between the next vacation, when he shall see his parents and enjoy his home again. But to make so just an estimate of a life like this, is no longer in my power. The consideration of my short continuance here, which was once grateful to me, now fills me with regret.'

The very sobriety of such writing was an antidote to morbid excess and a confirmation of self-respect.

The charm, however, of Cowper's letters can be but imperfectly conveyed by isolated passages. He revealed himself in a continual interplay of fancy, sentiment, humour, and good sense. Never assertive, he was yet always wholly and distinctively himself; never excited, he wrote always with a gentle animation which was sober in its sprightliness and sprightly in its sobriety. And he affords us the continual satisfaction of an elegance which is native to himself. With what tact, for example, did he reprove by condoning an impoliteness, when he wrote to Newton – 'About three weeks since Mrs. Unwin sent you a couple of fowls, and about ten days since a spare rib from her own pig. We do not wish you to thank us for such matters, nor do we even imagine that any are due; every idea of that sort vanishes before the recollection of the many obligations under which you have laid us; but it is always satisfactory to us to know that they have reached you.'

But it was in the pointing of humble comedy by a gravity and rotundity of speech that he excelled. 'We hope,' he wrote, 'that Patty has been falsely accused. But, however that may be, we see great cause to admire either the cogency of her arguments, or her husband's openness to conviction, who, by a single box on the ear, was so effectively assured of the innocence of his wife, as to become more attached to her than ever.' Or he wrote of Bull's attempts to combat melancholy – 'He showed me a nook, in which he had placed a bench, and where he said he found it very refreshing to smoke his pipe and meditate. Here he sits with his back against one brick wall and his big nose against another, which must, you know, be very refreshing and greatly assist meditation.'

Or again, he described thus Mr. Ashburner in his rôle of undertaker – 'He might be truly said to march; for his step was heroic, his figure athletic, and his countenance as firm and confident as if he had been born to bury others, and was sure never to be buried himself.' That the majestic undertaker was dead within a week of the writing of this letter was an apt demonstration of the tragi-comedy in life to which Cowper was so finely sensitive.

The same association of grave logic with the ridiculous is illustrated in the passage – 'I thank you for the snip of cloth, commonly called a pattern. At present I have two coats, and but one back. If at any time hereafter I should find myself possessed of fewer coats, or more backs, it will be of use to me.' Or again, in a letter urging Unwin to let nothing prevent a promised visit – 'As to the masons you expect, bring them with you; bring brick, bring mortar, bring everything that would oppose itself to your journey; all shall be welcome. I have a greenhouse that is too small, come and enlarge it; build me a pinery; repair the garden wall, that has great need of your assistance; do anything; you cannot do too much. . . .'

The essence of all such humour lies in its blend of a gay impulse with logical solemnity. And it was because Cowper satisfied in letter-writing both his heart and his head, his classical temper and his human sympathy, each correcting any tendency to excess in the other, that he derived such comfort from it. In this activity he possessed his world and so possessed himself.

His letters, however, must be read in their continuity to be properly appreciated. They are a mirror of his life from day to day, and they offer us an unconditional intimacy with one of the most amiable and cultivated of men. Grounded in good-sense, they abound in constant drolleries and endearing idiosyncracies. Wise or wistful, mildly malicious or humorously affectionate, they always breathe a perfect sincerity, if we except the 'perfectly scriptural' passages, usually addressed to Newton, on Christian hope and Christian consolation.

Yet even these passages have their pathos, in so far as they are attempts at self-delusion. For it is against a remembered background of despair that his letters should be read, as they were written. Beneath all their sallies and whimsies is a moral valiancy, that 'heroism of a passive kind' which is perhaps the hardest of all to sustain. Every moment of gaiety in them is a triumph of faith, or at least forgetfulness, over experience, a challenge to the dread sense of personal nullity which gnawed at his heart.

'We are strange creatures,' he wrote, 'everything that we do is in reality important, though half that we do seems to be push-pin.' In his letters he did but play at push-pin, but he played on the edge of an abyss. The game so engrossed him that he often forgot the hazard of his position. He looked out from himself at life, and his heart that felt so sensitively and his head that appraised so justly no longer distorted each other. 'Human affairs,' he remarked in a phrase which was the forerunner of a more famous one of Horace Walpole's, 'are a tragedy seen on one side, and a comedy on the other.' And he relieved his own melancholy by sympathizing with both aspects. For the tragic in human affairs, no less than the comic, is an expression of life, and to appreciate either is to partake of life.

Letter-writing was to Cowper a means of such vital association, a precarious defence against that loss of personal identity which was his haunting disability.

§ 4

Cowper entered his fiftieth year, then, with tolerable cheerfulness. It is true that he was now buried in Olney and had no business with the world on the outside of his sepulchre. He had accepted his disabilities as incurable and all his efforts were directed towards forgetting them. Much of his success in this he owed to Mrs. Unwin's happy and sympathetic temper. Sitting with her in the winter evenings, as she worked at her needle-work and listened to his reading, often from books of travel, with Puss gambolling at his feet, a kettle singing on the hob, and his cup full of the beverage 'which cheers but not inebriates,' he experienced a comfortable inner glow. The world which he had deserted and the God Who had deserted him were both forgotten. The besiegers drew back from the domestic citadel which they encircled.

But each morning, when he awoke to cold daylight, they had closed in again, and it was essential that he should be too busy to regard them closely. And in the winter both the countryside and the garden had less to give; the fields were often too sodden to traverse and the soil too heavy to work. In him, too, life was apt to ebb at this dark season, while, assiduously as he might write his letters, his correspondents were still few. Something else was necessary to diversify the 'dull rotation' of the days, and he remembered that he was a poet.

'While I am in pursuit of pretty images, or a pretty way of expressing them,' he wrote to Newton in December 1780, 'I forget everything that is irksome, and, like a boy that plays truant, determine to avail myself of the present opportunity to be amused, and to put by the disagreeable recollection that I must, after all, go home to be whipped again.'

Three months before he had asked William Unwin for a second-hand *Iliad* and *Odyssey* and had contemplated translating them, but Mrs. Unwin, upon whose critical intuition he had come to rely, encouraged him to attempt original work; and so the translation of Homer was deferred until after he had discovered and thoroughly worked a vein of poetry of unsuspected richness in himself.

He began to compose without any preconception or plan apart from that of composing himself. And as one sentence added itself to another in his letters, so one line followed another in his poetry. The winter of 1780 passed imperceptibly into the spring of 1781, and still he wrote. In February, indeed, he had a mind to hang up his harp for the remainder of the year, but by that time the habit of verse-making had acquired an insistent momentum, although he was careful to inform Newton that he rode Pegasus with a curb and would never be run away with again. Possibly the fact that he had collaborated with Newton in hymn-writing explains his choice of him as a confidante, and it is significant that as he became more of a poet and less of a moralist he ceased to confide in one who attributed merit to poetry as he did happiness to man only so far as they helped to further his own particular kind of religious enthusiasm.

To some extent a consciousness of Newton's censorship must have influenced Cowper's tone as a poet at this time. In his letters he anxiously forestalled with explanations the frowns which he feared. 'If my Muse,' he wrote, 'was to go forth clad in Quaker colour, without one bit of riband to enliven her appearance, she might walk from one end of London to the other, as little noticed as if she were one of the sisterhood indeed.' And in his account of *Table Talk*, he at once described and apologized for the characteristics of the poems which preceded and succeeded it. 'It is a medley of many things, some that may be useful, and some that, for aught I know, may be very diverting. I am merry that I may decoy people into my company, and grave that they may be the better for it. Now and then I put on the garb of a philosopher, and take the opportunity that disguise procures me, to drop a word in favour of religion. . . . A poet in my circumstances has a difficult part to act: one minute obliged to bridle his humour, if he has any, and the next to clap a spur to the sides of it: now ready to weep from a sense of the importance of his subject, and on a sudden constrained to laugh, lest his gravity should be mistaken for dullness.'

It would be foolish, of course, to suggest that Newton was responsible for the mixture of didacticism and satire in which Cowper now indulged. He had not yet realized, even to the extent which he did later, that poetry might be a self-sufficient activity which needed no justification before the bar of conventional morality. He never did consciously realize this truth, but as he came to draw more on inward experience and on that personal relation with Nature which was wholly his own, he came unconsciously to practise it.

But at this time he needed two things: to divert his mind and to reinforce his self-respect by engaging in an activity which he conceived to be of use to others. In humour he satisfied the one need, in moral seriousness the other. And so when he wrote a poem entitled *Truth*, he was careful to announce that his subject was 'religious truth,' and he excused a 'too light and trifling tone' by claiming to have 'endeavoured to deliver religious thought from doctrinal dryness by as many pretty things, in the way of trinket and plaything, as I could muster upon the subject.' But, in fact, he derived more benefit from the playthings than the religious thought.

And so, 'in hope to do good' both to himself and others, he embarked, later in 1780, on a poem entitled *The Progress of Error*. It was natural, perhaps, that the world which had wounded him should be his theme, and for style, Churchill, as in *Anti-Thelyphthora*, was still his model. But he aspired now as a satirist to something more personal and direct.

'Truths,' he announced,

> that the theorist could never reach
> And observation taught me, I would teach.

Unfortunately, Cowper's observation of the world which he chastised was both vague and warped by moral preconception. Satire to be effective must cling with a biting necessity to a particular object, although in the particular it must expose the universal. Cowper, however, was qualified neither by worldly experience nor by passion for such a personal relation with the objects of his attack. As he was to write in *Expostulation* –

> Far be the thought from any verse of mine,
> And farther still the formed and fixed design,
> To thrust the charge of deeds that I detest
> Against an innocent, unconscious breast:

> The man that dares traduce, because he can
> With safety to himself, is not a man;
> An individual is a sacred mark,
> Not to be pierced in play or in the dark . . .

Such scruple redounds to his credit as a man; but it disabled him as a satirist, compelling him to moralize in the air, to sermonize over certain personified foibles and vices instead of portraying individuals who were guilty of them with a damaging penetration that expressed at once his own moral judgment and their moral infamy. He generalized, in fact, about types rather than universalized individuals.

This defect was necessarily aggravated when the morality which he preached was not so much his own as of a kind to please Newton, while the invective which he interspersed in a valiant effort to emulate Churchill betrayed by its falsetto tone his complete inability to hate.

The pungent invective of true satire is, of course, something more than an expression of personal hatred. It rises above the personal by virtue of the ecstatic wit which informs it. Nevertheless, it has its roots in a passionate personal antipathy. When Cowper, however, wrote —

> Of manners rough, and coarse athletic cast,
> The rank debauch suits Clodio's filthy taste.
> Rufullus, exquisitely formed by rule,
> Not of the moral but the dancing school,
> Wonders at Clodio's follies, in a tone
> As tragical as others at his own.

> He cannot drink five bottles, bilk the score,
> Then kill a constable, and drink five more;
> But he can draw a pattern, make a tart,
> And has the Ladies' Etiquette by heart . . .

he was railing at puppets with an assumed violence and a laboured wit. Often his wit was more deft than this, as when he wrote of the sportsman, killed in the hunting field –

> Like a slain deer, the tumbrel brings him home,
> Unmissed but by his dogs and by his groom,

or of the squire who had done the Grand Tour –

> How much a dunce that has been sent to roam
> Excels a dunce that has been kept at home.

But in his negative strictures, as in his positive appeals, he was essentially the mild moralist attempting to frown with the severity of a Methodist upon the frivolities of the world, to

> Discern the fraud beneath the specious lure,
> Prevent the danger, or prescribe the cure. . . .

proclaiming how

> Peace follows Virtue as its sure reward,
> And Pleasure brings as surely in her train
> Remorse and Sorrow and vindictive Pain . . .

castigating the writers of the thinly-disguised 'inflammatory tales' as the 'flesh-flies of the land,' denying the

right of the Deists to criticize the Bible on the ground
that

> A lewd interpreter is never just,

urging moderation on the 'wild enthusiast,' damning 'the
free-thinkers' brutal roar' and the 'endless lies' of the
Press, and concluding with an edifying tribute to the
virtues of 'the Cross.'

'I am no preacher,' he wrote at the end of *The Progress
of Error*, and we may admit that his preaching, straining
as it did towards satire, was wholly unconvincing. The
result of trying to rant like a Methodist and flay like a
Churchill was a sort of exasperated bleat. Only the
underlying attitude was his own, the appreciation of the
moderate and the decent, the unostentatious and homely
virtues. But it was still a negative attitude. Strong feeling
he feared because it endangered his self-possession, and
so even the innocent allurements of Nature were suspect.
Even the

> harmony from yon sequestered bower,
> Sweet harmony, that soothes the midnight hour,

was considered a hindrance upon

> the rugged path, the steep ascent
> That Virtue points to. . . .

A timid and negative morality, in short, still interposed
between Cowper and the Nature in which he was to find
himself as a poet.

In *Truth*, which he wrote next, he played upon the

theme of salvation by faith, independently of works, his purpose being 'to inculcate the eleemosynary character of the Gospel, as a dispensation of mercy, in the most absolute sense of the word, to the exclusion of all claims of merit on the part of the receiver.'

We have already stressed the dangers involved in such a doctrine, since a God Who dispenses mercy independently of the individual's conduct may be supposed to dispense vengeance with as scant a regard for moral merit. And this poem, although of no more value as literature than its predecessor, has a greater personal interest. For Cowper expressed in it both the positive and negative elements of the faith to which he aspired. When he wrote –

Oh how unlike the complex works of man,
Heaven's easy, artless, unencumbered plan. . . .
Legible only by the light they give,
Stand the soul-quickening words – BELIEVE AND LIVE,

still more when he lauded the beauty of the pheasant which

Shines without desiring to be seen,

he was appreciating, however imperfectly, the fact that to reflect in your being a creative necessity is something more essential than to subscribe to any arbitrary morality; that, indeed, a morality divorced from real religious experience is barren, if it is not bigoted.

In this sense, the sense of Blake's 'whatever lives is holy,' 'BELIEVE AND LIVE' are in reality soul-quickening

words. The creative life transcends the categories of good
and evil, but it does so by understanding both so profoundly as to pass beyond them. It is for the individual,
however, to achieve this relation to life, to rise above the
merely legal restrictions of a moral code to the freedom
of pure creativeness, to discover the mercy of God beyond
the plane of rewards and punishments, by realizing the
perfect humanity which possessed Tchehov when he
wrote – 'And everything is forgiven, and it would be
strange not to forgive.'

But Cowper denounced the individual for presuming
to possess or exert faculties without which the God in
him could not be realized; he did not merely dissociate
the mercy which God dispensed from the conduct of the
individual. He urged that only by ceasing to be an
individual and approximating to a worm could he hope
to merit it.

Truth, therefore, was a polemic not only against pride
but against intelligence, a plea not only for humility but
for abject self-contempt. As he wrote –

> How readily upon the Gospel plan
> That question has its answer – What is man?
> Sinful and weak, in every sense a wretch;
> An instrument whose chords, upon the stretch,
> And strained to the last screw that he can bear,
> Yield only discord in his Maker's ear.

And so learning and wit were snares, and Voltaire's
respect for truth and humanity counted for nothing
against a cottager who knew 'her Bible true,' while

> Not many wise, rich, noble, or profound
> In science, win one inch of heavenly ground.

So far as Cowper attacked the self-conceit of a narrow rationalism, or exalted the integrity of the poor and simple above the affectation and licence of the rich, he was of course vindicating the truth which Wordsworth was later more profoundly to affirm.

But behind all his words was a penal threat, –

> Marshalling all his terrors as he came,
> Thunder and earthquake, and devouring flame,
> From Sinai's top Jehovah gave the law,
> Life for obedience, death for every flaw.
> When the great Sovereign would His will express,
> He gives a perfect rule; what can He less?
> And guards it with a sanction as severe
> As vengeance can inflict, or sinners fear.

In spite of this he could profess

> That Scripture is the only cure of woe,

and assert that

> often Unbelief, grown sick of life,
> Flies to the tempting pool, or felon knife.

With far more truth he might have testified out of his own experience that a Belief which outraged humanity and debased intelligence demoralized to the point of suicide. Instead he wrote luridly of

> the sinner, when he feels
> A growing dread of vengeance at his heels,

placating the angry tide of deity by accepting the proffered
Scriptures –

> "The book shall teach you; read, believe, and live!"
> 'Tis done – the raging storm is heard no more,
> Mercy receives him on her peaceful shore.

Such was the 'religious truth' which dominated this poem,
and the quality of the verse is sufficient proof of the
insincerity of Cowper's belief in it.

As the days, however, began to lengthen his spirits
rose, and in *Table Talk*, which he wrote next, he ex-
patiated at least as much on the art of poetry as on
the law of God, while he even invoked 'Libery' in
strains of which a later Romantic would not have been
ashamed, –

> O Liberty! the prisoner's pleasing dream,
> The poet's muse, his passion and his theme,
> Genius is thine, and thou art Fancy's nurse,
> Lost without thee the ennobling powers of verse;
> Heroic song from thy free touch acquires
> Its clearest tone, the rapture it inspires.
> Place me where Winter breathes his keenest air,
> And I will sing if Liberty be there;
> And I will sing at Liberty's dear feet
> In Afric's torrid clime or India's fiercest heat.

The dialogue form in which the poem was cast encouraged
a more impassioned style. 'B' could sing extravagantly
of Liberty, knowing that 'A' was at hand to remind him
that Freedom, grown freakish,

> Spread anarchy and terror all around,

and so compel the admission that Discipline must also 'employ her wholesome arts.'

Good-sense, however, employed thus as an alternating corrective to excess, did not reduce the whole poem to a level of tame moderation. And in the passages on the art of poetry, to which this pæan to Liberty was a prelude, Cowper attacked the conventionalized diction and sentiment of Augustan verse with an eloquence which was new to him and much of which had the ring of personal conviction.

Having 'dropped his word in favour of religion' by reprobating 'the lascivious pipe and wanton song,' he felt himself free to consider poetry as an art and as the voice of an informed humanity, writing how

> She pours a sensibility divine
> Along the nerve of every feeling line,

and how

> When remote futurity is brought
> Before the keen enquiry of her thought,
> A terrible sagacity informs
> The poet's heart. . . .
> Hence, in a Roman mouth, the graceful name
> Of prophet and of poet was the same;
> Hence British poets too the priesthood shared,
> And every hallowed Druid was a bard. . . .

> but modern taste
> Is so refined and delicate and chaste,

That verse, whatever fire the fancy warms,
Without a creamy smoothness has no charms. . . .

Give me the line that ploughs its stately course
Like a proud swan, conquering the stream by force:
That like some cottage beauty strikes the heart,
Quite unindebted to the tricks of art.
When labour and when dulness, club in hand,
Like the two figures at St. Dunstan's stand,
Beating alternately, in measured time,
The clock-work tintinnabulum of rhyme,
Exact and regular the sounds will be,
But such mere quarter-strokes are not for me . . .
Manner is all in all, whate'er is writ,
The substitute for genius, sense, and wit.

Both in what he claimed for poetry in these lines and in
what he criticized, Cowper's attitude was in a true sense
moral. The virtue which he demanded of poetry was a
creative strength and integrity, not a subservience to
religious bigotry. All that was virile and independent in
him spoke in the lines –

Nature, exerting an unwearied power,
Forms, opens, and gives scent to every flower,
Spreads the fresh verdure of the field, and leads
The dancing Naiads through the dewy meads;
She fills profuse ten thousand little throats
With music, modulating all their notes,
And charms the woodland scenes and wilds unknown
With artless airs and concerts of her own;

But seldom (as if fearful of expense)
Vouchsafes to man a poet's just pretence.
Fervency, freedom, fluency of thought,
Harmony, strength, words exquisitely sought,
Fancy that from the bow that spans the sky
Brings colours dipt in heaven that never die,
A soul exalted above earth, a mind
Skilled in the characters that form mankind . . .

The conception, like the diction, was generalized, but
it was manly and disinterested. It was not so when he
wrote of the age of Charles II that it

> Swarmed with a scribbling herd as deep inlaid
> With brutal lust as ever Circe made

or that

> 'Twere new indeed to see a bard all fire,
> Touched with a coal from heaven, assume the lyre,
> And tell the world, still kindling as he sung,
> With more than mortal music on his tongue,
> That He who died below, and reigns above,
> Inspires the song, and that his name is Love.

Christ was a poet because he was ideally creative, not
because he was edifying, and it is because Religion
has generally demanded that poets should be edifying
that it

> has so seldom found
> A skilful guide into poetic ground,

Cowper, in this poem, hovered between the true and the partisan view. In condemning decorative affectations or conventional polish, his moral judgment was also æsthetic; in urging poets to hymn the God of Orthodoxy or preach a moral lesson, he was merely a special pleader for Newton.

And it was his own humility once again which dictated his partisanship. Since, in his own words,

> no prophetic fires to me belong,
> I play with syllables and sport in song,

he could only justify himself in his own eyes by playing 'the faithful monitor's' instead of the 'poet's part.' The exercise of a creative imagination, which gives a final religious satisfaction, was beyond his powers. Yet in one passage he did visualize the intimate communion with life which was, in some measure, soon to be his —

> The nightingale may claim the topmost bough,
> While the poor grasshopper must chirp below.
> Like him unnoticed, I, and such as I,
> Spread little wings, and rather skip than fly;
> Perched on the meagre produce of the land,
> An ell or two of prospect we command,
> But never peep beyond the thorny bound,
> Or oaken fence, that hems the paddock round.

Too humble to

> Paw up against the light and do strange deeds
> Upon the clouds

he was to identify himself with 'an ell or two of prospect' as none had done before him.

But this was not yet. In his next poem, *Expostulation*, the Judaistic tone was even more pronounced, since he compared English with Jewish history and foretold

The stroke that a vindictive God intends.

Pope influenced Cowper little, but there is a curious parallel between the lines in which the laureate of Deism approved the order of the Universe –

To Him no high, no low, no great, no small;
He fills, He bounds, connects, and equals all,

and Cowper's tribute to Providence –

Know, then, that heavenly wisdom on this ball
Creates, gives birth to, guides, consummates all.

But while Pope's conception brought him serenity because, however superficial, it was concisely rational, Cowper's had all the terrors of the logical and the limitless. In him a Romantic sense of life's mystery, by which Pope was untroubled, combined with a narrow Augustan rationality to justify a God Who was at once inexplicable and judicial. Throughout this poem he proclaimed man 'as a mere instrument in hands divine' and as a criminal meet for a most undivine judgment.

As the summer advanced, however, he grew a little less sententious. *Hope*, his next poem, began with a tribute, not to God, but to Nature, to her gaiety and animation, and her concern for man's happiness. The

moral note, however, soon intervened; Nature was regarded not for herself, but only as 'handmaid to the
purposes of Grace.'

Here again Cowper approached a problem which was
to engross the minds of his Romantic successors, the
problem of how to reconcile Nature's vital but conscienceless forces with human and spiritual values; but he merely
repeated the pious truism that while to the sinner the
very sun's light was hateful, to the moral and devout
man all nature was joyous, because the same God
diffused Himself through it as was 'triumphant in his
heart.'

Yet how imperfectly this accorded with his own
experience he must have known, if he had dared to study
it disinterestedly. It was of himself, for example, that he
wrote –

> A dark importance saddens every day;
> He hears the notice of the clock perplexed,
> And cries, "Perhaps eternity strikes next";
> Sweet music is no longer music here,
> And laughter sounds like madness in his ear:
> His grief the world of all her power disarms,
> Wine has no taste, and beauty has no charms.

Thus he felt in his desolated hours, and yet the only
medicine which he could prescribe was one from which
he had derived no benefit –

> God's holy word, once trivial in his view,
> Now by the voice of his experience true,

Seems, as it is, the fountain whence alone
Must spring that hope he pants to make his own.
Now let the bright reverse be known abroad;
Say man's a worm, and power belongs to God.

By no such negative path can any man, who has become
too self-conscious to preserve a blindly instinctive relation
to life, regain his identity with her. Cowper was to
derive more virtue from Nature than from 'God's holy
word,' but he was never to learn that only by being
equally loyal to Nature and to intelligence might man
realize both his humanity and his divinity. In his next
poem, *Charity*, he wrote indeed –

Nature imprints upon whate'er we see
That has a heart and life in it, "Be free!"

But while he could hang upon this an impassioned
denunciation of slavery, he could not extend his logic
to include enslavement by outworn religious doctrine.
Reason, he urged,

unless divinely taught,
Whate'er she learns, learns nothing as she ought;

And by 'divinely taught,' he meant, of course, by 'scriptural
revelation.'

Here again he was enough of a Romantic to realize the
sterility of intellectual self-conceit, but too cowed by
Evangelicism to contemplate the creative enlargement of
reason in imagination. Pathetically he thought to cure
the malady of self-consciousness in himself and others by

abasing intelligence before a primitive faith instead of making it the guiding principle of a new and truer one.

Before, however, his next two poems were written, a new influence had entered his life which was to complete his emancipation from Newton and fertilize all the latent poetry in his nature. And already, in *Conversation* and *Retirement*, this influence had begun to exert itself. For the first time, in *Conversation*, he indulged in humour that was neither censorious nor moralistic, writing, for example, of the 'scrupulous good man' that

> He would not with a peremptory tone
> Assert the nose upon his face his own;

and that

> The emphatic speaker dearly loves to oppose
> In contact inconvenient, nose to nose;
> As if the gnomon on his neighbour's phiz,
> Touched with the magnet, had attracted his.

His description, too, of the polite inanities that pass for talk at an afternoon at-home was shrewdly comic, and although he concluded with a lengthy exposition of the superiority of religious conversation to all others, Religion had clearly ceased quite so sternly to bring 'the trifler under rigorous sway.'

And in *Retirement* the new virtue which had quickened his being is even more apparent. It is indeed, in some sort, a prelude to *The Task*, a first tentative sketch of that art of life in communion with Nature which he was to explore. 'O Nature!' he wrote,

whose Elysian scenes disclose
His bright perfections, at whose word they rose,
Next to that Power, who formed thee and sustains,
Be thou the great inspirer of my strains,
Still, as I touch the lyre, do thou expand
Thy genuine charms, and guide an artless hand. . . .

The God of Orthodoxy still interposed between him and
Nature; he still viewed her as 'the map of God's extensive
plan' and admonished the man

Who studies nature with a wanton eye
Admires the work, but slips the lesson by.

And consequently much of his diction was still conventional –

Pastoral images and still retreats,
Umbrageous walks and solitary seats,
Sweet birds in concert with harmonious streams,
Soft airs, nocturnal vigils, and day-dreams. . . .

But if Nature's streams did no more than 'tinkle sweetly
in poetic chime,' he had begun to invoke her for herself,
to seek in her not merely a confirmation of theology, but
a principle of life which would reinforce his own. He had
begun, in short, to be a poet and not a moralist.

Nature, indeed, was never to cure him of his theological
obsession. For although he could identify himself with
her through the particular, he never realized that the
secret of the universal lay in her keeping too, that the
ultimate communion with the source of life for which he

longed was to be achieved, not by submission to a faith which his intelligence refused, but by an intelligent expression of the life which, in his own words,

> Mounts from inferior beings up to God,

and which in the perfected harmony of human faculties becomes God.

For him an external Deity was always to interpose between Man and the natural life, which it should be his aim to perfect.

> Man is a harp whose chords elude the sight,
> Each yielding harmony, disposed aright;
> The screws reversed (a task which if He please
> God in a moment executes with ease),
> Ten thousand thousand strings at once go loose,
> Lost, till He tune them, all their power and use.
> Then neither heathy wilds, nor scenes as fair
> As ever recompensed the peasant's care,
> Nor soft declivities with tufted hills,
> Nor view of waters turning busy mills,
> Parks in which Art preceptress Nature weds,
> Nor gardens interspersed with flowery beds,
> Nor gales, that catch the scent of blooming groves,
> And waft it to the mourner as he roves,
> Can call up life into his faded eye
> That passes all he sees unheeded by.

This, indeed, was 'a sight for Pity to peruse' and for sympathy to lament in vain. For it was now beyond Cowper's powers to escape from the mechanic God, Who could reverse the screws of his being in a moment with ease and to Whom he had so humbly surrendered his destiny.

But if he could not escape the fixed terrors of theology, he could at least momentarily forget them in the familiar beauty of Nature. And for a few years, under the stimulus of one who had no sympathy for Evangelical tenets, he was to be happy, as he had seldom been, in such forgetfulness. The charming *Invitation into the Country* which he addressed to Newton was indeed in its Tennysonian lyricism, if not in its personal reference, an appropriate expression of the new devotion which was now, like a late spring, to succeed the winter of religious bigotry.

> Old Winter, halting o'er the mead,
>   Bids me and Mary mourn;
> But lovely Spring peeps o'er his head,
>   And whispers your return.
>
> Then April with her sister May
>   Shall chase him from the bowers,
> And weave fresh garlands every day,
>   To crown the smiling hours.

§ 5

Thin, then, as was the stream of poetry which Cowper had released during 1781, it was characteristic, and it showed an increasing inwardness. Although his diction was often as conventional as the religious sentiments which it adorned, it was recognizably his own. He claimed as one of his principal advantages, as a composer of verses, that he had not read an English poet for thirteen years and but one for twenty, and although Churchill's influence was evident in the earlier poems, it was transient.

In his attention to 'those niceties which constitute elegance of expression,' he owed something perhaps to Prior, whose ability 'to make verse speak the language of prose without being prosaic' he admired so much. But his elegance, if less convincingly than in his letters, was essentially his own. That the substance of his verse was so unreal was due to the fact that he was declaiming for the most part a faith and a morality which failed in literature as in life to evoke his creative resources. His volume might be, as he claimed, 'at the bottom a religious business,' but it was far less a transcript of his own experience than 'a summary of such truths' as Newton thought it proper to enforce.

In rhyming, however, as a kind of verbal carpentry, in polishing, and in touching and retouching with the utmost care, he had often been so totally absorbed that 'neither the past nor the future . . . had any longer a share in his contemplation'; and in *Conversation* and *Retirement*, at least, he must have begun to discover that verse-making might offer something more than a transient amusement.

Certainly he was aware of a want of fire and animation in what he had written, but he attributed it to middle-age. 'The season of the year,' he remarked, 'which generally pinches off the flowers of poetry, unfolds mine, such as they are, and crowns me with a winter garland. In this respect, therefore, I and my contemporary bards are by no means upon a par. They write when the delightful influences of fine weather, fine prospects, and a brisk motion of the animal spirits, make poetry almost the language of nature; and I, when icicles depend from all the leaves of the Parnassian laurel, and when a reasonable man would as little expect to succeed in verse as to hear a blackbird whistle.' Yet even as he wrote these words, the icicles had begun to thaw and the blackbird to whistle in his heart.

The poems, then, which we have considered, together with a score and more of occasional verses, were issued in March, 1782, by Johnson, Newton's publisher. Since the volume owed so much to Newton's influence, it was natural that Cowper should have asked him to write an explanatory preface 'in order to obviate in some measure those prejudices that will naturally erect their bristles against it.'

Eventually Newton consented; but although the preface which he wrote was dictated by genuine friendship, its sermonizing tone and its typical commendation of Cowper as an example to the faithful and a warning to the godless was far from happy. A minister's character may be, as Cowper wrote with pardonable flattery, 'more splendid than a poet's,' but to claim for poetry the virtues of a tract is hardly to do it a service. So at least thought the publisher, who advised that it should be withdrawn, as likely to recommend the volume to the religious, but to disgust the profane.

Cowper was too detached from the world to be deeply concerned with its reception by the critics and the public. He was much gratified, however, by a report of Dr. Franklin's admiration and he awaited with some eagerness the verdict of 'that critical Rhadamanthus,' the *Monthly Review*. 'Alas!' he wrote, 'when I wish for a favourable sentence from that quarter. . . . I feel myself not a little influenced by a tender regard to my reputation here, even among my neighbours at Olney. Here are watchmakers, who themselves are wits, and who at present perhaps think me one. Here is a carpenter, and a baker, and not to mention others, here is your idol Mr. Teedon, whose smile is fame. All these read the *Monthly Review*, and all these will set me down for a dunce, if those terrible critics show them the example. But oh! wherever else I am accounted dull, dear Mr. Griffiths, let me pass for a genius at Olney!'

For the most part, however, the critics were mildly appreciative, if hardly encouraging. But he needed no encouragement. For not only had verse-making become a necessary habit, but Olney itself had become a vital source of inspiration. Mrs. Unwin's appreciation had meant much to him; it had been 'a spur to diligence and a cordial to his spirits,' but it had not dissipated the fanatical shadow which Newton's religion had cast over the poetry of humanity and of Nature. For that service he was indebted to a woman, more worldly, more impulsive, and incidentally more exacting.

SECOND SPRING

SECOND SPRING

§ 1

L ooking out of his window, one day in July, 1781, Cowper noticed two ladies entering a draper's shop on the opposite side of the street. He recognized one as Mrs. Jones, the wife of a neighbouring curate. The other was unknown to him, but on inquiry he learnt that she was Mrs. Jones' sister and the widow of a Sir Robert Austen.

So impressed was he by her looks that, forgetting his shyness, he begged Mrs. Unwin to invite the ladies to tea, and although, on their arrival, his shyness returned, Lady Austen quickly put him at his ease. She did more; she so delighted him with her gay and rippling conversation that he expanded like a flower in the spring sunshine. Into the provincial religious atmosphere of Olney she brought the fresh air of a wider world. She had beauty of a refined order and just the subtle blend of sense and sensibility which awoke a kindred chord in Cowper's nature. To consider her a providential compensation for the loss of Newton was to undervalue her virtue. She was in truth Newton's antidote. And when, in the evening, Cowper conducted her and her sister home across the meadows to Clifton Rectory, a new radiance had come into his life. As he was to write later in the year —

who can tell how vast the plan
Which this day's incident began?

The attraction was mutual. To Unwin Cowper wrote that

Lady Austen 'has fallen in love with your Mother and me,' but he too, so far as he could, had fallen in love with her·

That he did not realize the fact was to prove even more embarrassing to her than to him; that his love was indistinguishable, save by a subtle shade, from warm friendship was certainly true. His friendship was, in fact, as near to love, and her love was as near to friendship, as their respective natures allowed. And ignorant as she was at this time of his sad history, and seeing him so gallantly rejuvenated in her presence, she had every excuse for falling in love with him.

He was one of the most kindly and cultivated of men, and despite the icicles of age, which he lamented, he was still young both in temper and appearance. He had hibernated rather than aged, and his light brown hair, bluish-grey eyes and fresh complexion belied his fifty years. He himself noted that the effect of mental depression was not discernible in his face and body, although it might be expected to wear out a frame of adamant. And Lady Austen inspired him to play truant from this depression and the provincial devoutness which aggravated it, to rediscover a pleasure even in social life and in the innocent worldliness which Evangelicism had so unnecessarily reprobated.

She had 'seen much of the world' and accounted it 'a great Simpleton, as it is,' but she did not account it a Sodom or brand all its manners as sins for which God would call it to terrible account. And the harmless vanity which compelled her to have her hair dressed on Saturday and, as rumour had it, to sit up all night to prevent its disarrangement, because the Olney barber refused to break his Sabbath, found, doubtless, a sympathetic response in the Cowper who was concerned that his stocks should be of the latest fashion.

For deeply as Cowper immersed himself in the country and violently as he scolded the town, he never lost his taste for the refinements of polite society. But Lady Austen, like himself, combined such tastes with an endearing naturalness. 'She has,' he wrote to Unwin, 'a degree of gratitude in her composition, so quick a sense of obligation, as is hardly to be found in any rank of life and, if report say true, is scarce indeed in the superior. Discover but a wish to please her, and she never forgets it; not only thanks you, but the tears will start into her eyes at the recollection of the smallest service. With these fine feelings she has the most, and the most harmless, vivacity you can imagine.'

Later, indeed, he was to find that her vivacity was sometimes too much for him, but for the time it refreshed and revived without exhausting. Consequently this summer was perhaps the happiest which he ever spent. Everything conspired to give him pleasure. He had his proofs to correct and his gardening, and the greenhouse was converted into a summer-parlour. Its walls were hung with mats and the floor covered with a carpet, while the myrtles made the most agreeable blind imaginable. In this, the pleasantest retreat in Olney, he spent all his leisure time, relishing the more the sound of the wind in the trees, the singing of birds and the scents from the garden, because they were exchanged for the incessant

barking of dogs, screaming of children, and putrid exhala-
tions which floated into the parlour from the Olney
market-place.

His walks too became a new adventure. For Nature
responded to his expansiveness; she too reflected the
virtue of Lady Austen, and was loved at last for herself.
And there were picnics, such as that in the spinney of
Weston Park, of which he wrote – 'Lady Austen's
lackey and a lad that waits on me in the garden drove a
wheelbarrow full of eatables and drinkables to the scene
of our *Fête Champêtre*. A board laid over the top of the
wheelbarrow served us for a table; our dining-room was a
root-house lined with moss and ivy. At six o'clock the
servants, who had dined under the great elm upon the
ground, at a little distance, boiled the kettle and the said
wheelbarrow served us for a tea table. We then took a
walk into the Wilderness, about half a mile off, and were
at home again a little after eight, having spent the day
together from noon till evening without one cross occurrence or the least weariness of each other, a happiness
few parties of pleasure can boast of.'

In all this there was just that blend of decorum and
simplicity which appealed to him, and so high were his
spirits that they danced even towards Newton, to whom
he wrote a 'Hop-o'-my-thumb' letter – 'and now I have
writ, in a rhyming fit, what will make you dance, and as
you advance, will keep you still, though against your will,
dancing away, alert and gay, till you come to an end of
what I have penn'd.'

And when Lady Austen, who had a fortune that was

'both genteel and perfectly safe,' announced her determination to settle in the portion of Orchard Side unoccupied by himself and Mrs. Unwin, it seemed indeed that
a new scene was opening, 'which, whether it perform what
it promises or not, will add fresh plumes to the wings of
time.'

In indulging in these expectations, Cowper was bliss-
fully blind to what Hayley called the dangers attending
'an intimacy, so very close, yet perfectly innocent, between
a poet and two ladies who, with very different mental
powers, had each reason to flatter herself that she could
agreeably promote the studies, and animate the fancy
of this fascinating bard.'

Indeed, he was particularly pleased with the plan upon
Mrs. Unwin's account, who, since Mrs. Newton's departure, was 'destitute of all female connexion,' and he wrote
lyrically of a friendship

> That has cemented us in one;
> And placed it in our power to prove,
> By long fidelity and love,
> That Solomon has wisely spoken, –
> "A threefold cord is not soon broken."

It was, however, Lady Austen who first disturbed his
innocent serenity. In October she returned to London.
To Cowper she had then become 'Sister Ann,' and on her
departure she proposed a regular correspondence with
'Brother William.'

Cowper was delighted and for some months their
correspondence proceeded smoothly. Judging too by the

'Poetical Epistle' which he addressed to her in December, he expressed his friendship with a charming, but possibly indiscreet, warmth. Indeed, a poet would be false to himself if in such matters he kept a watch upon his pulse. As Cowper wrote –

> But when a poet takes the pen,
> Far more alive than other men,
> He feels a gentle tingling come
> Down to his finger and his thumb,
> Derived from nature's noblest part,
> The centre of a glowing heart.

But when he went on to inform Lady Austen that such an itching and tingling particularly affected him 'when called to address myself to you,' it was hardly surprising that she was encouraged to nurse the thought of a tenderer relation than that of friendship.

Her letters, indeed, became increasingly effusive. She began to exceed Cowper himself in the expectations of felicity which she built upon their friendship and to idolize him quite extravagantly. And he became correspondingly embarrassed, the more so, perhaps, because his feelings for her were unconsciously nearer to love than he would admit.

At last he felt it his duty to warn her against indulging in too romantic notions. He wrote doubtless with great tact and with 'the most upright inoffensive intentions,' and Mrs. Unwin, we are not surprised to learn, honoured the letter with her warm approbation. But upon Lady Austen's growing warmth of sentiment it descended like a cold douche. She could not but feel it as a rebuff alike to her tenderest feelings and her pride. Her reply 'could by no means be replied to' without entering into questions which Cowper was most concerned to avoid, and the friendship which had promised so much, the

> page of Providence quite new,
> And now just opening to our view,

seemed to have been torn from the book of life before time had inscribed it with poetry.

Fortunately, however, Lady Austen relented. She sent Cowper, through her sister, a present of three pairs of ruffles, and he made the only return in his power by laying his volume of poetry at her feet.

Yet he doubted with reason whether any reconciliation could be complete when 'that unreserved confidence which belongs only to true friendship, has been once uprooted.' He needed so much a friendship which had the creative virtue of love without its disturbing demands. But before he came fully to realize the material difficulties of such a position, Lady Austen was to give him all that it was in her power to give and in his to receive.

Their relations were never perhaps as innocently and elegantly ecstatic again as in the summer of 1781. But they were easy, tender and vital enough to generate the poetry of *The Task*.

§ 2

The early months of 1782, however, found him depressed. His chief occupation during the winter had been to walk ten times a day from the fireside to his cucumber frame and back, which was hardly an inspiring routine, and the breach with Lady Austen was still un-closed. If he did nothing, he was dejeincluded; if he did any-thing, he was weary; and his weariness was best described by the word lassitude, which, as he remarked, is of all weariness in the world the most oppressive. Nature, once again, seemed to have withdrawn herself with Lady Austen and the sun, and the dread sentence of death sounded again in his ears.

To distraincet himself he began to work on a poem which, when completed more than two years later, he entitled *Tirocinium; or a Review of Schools.* Its tone was similar to the earlier poems in his published volume and he soon laid it aside. A drawing of Madame Guyon, who a cen-tury before had learnt in suffering what she taught in song, hung over the mantelpiece of his friend Bull. To Cowper it seemed the face of an angel, and after borrowing and reading her poems he found that she sang like an angel too. Her experience, indeed, and in particular her six years' loss of religious consolation, was very similar to his own, as was also the quietism and self-abasement by which she sought to turn the edge of the world's cruelty. Her simple and unaffeincted piety, too, which he found 'sweet beyond expression,' had little of the inverted violence of Newton's.

In translating her poems, however, Cowper inevitably intruded something of his own negative attitude, and by endeavouring to cure her of what might be considered an eccentric familiarity with God, by adopting, in his own

words, 'a more sober and respectful manner of expression,'
he deprived her verse of much of the *naïveté* which proved
the reality and intimacy of her faith. In the process he
also proved once again the demoralizing unreality of his
own. Only when he rendered her despair did he breathe
a personal conviction, as in the lines –

I suffer fruitless anguish day by day,
    Each moment, as it passes, marks my pain;
Scarce knowing whither, doubtfully I stray,
    And see no end of all that I sustain . . .

My peace of heart is fled, I know not where;
    My happy hours, like shadows, passed away;
Their sweet remembrance doubles all my care,
    Night darker seems, succeeding such a day . . .

Has hell a pain I would not gladly bear,
    So thy severe displeasure might subside?
Hopeless of ease, I seem already there,
    My life extinguished, and yet death denied.

From a few of the poems, however, that expressed a
gentle resignation, such as *The Love of God the End of Life*
and *Repose in God,* he must have obtained a passing
comfort. But it was a secular event which gave him the
opportunity of expressing, not his weakness, but his
strength.

The lines which he wrote later in the year *On the loss of
The Royal George* embodied just that passive heroism which
was his through long years of inward wretchedness. The

very theme of shipwreck was, in a mental and spiritual sense, his own. And when he wrote of the *Royal George* –

> It was not in the battle;
>   No tempest gave the shock;
> She sprang no fatal leak;
>   She ran upon no rock.

the weight of his own impassive foundering was behind the words. The same sense of a hopeless destiny to be manfully endured dictated, to a less degree, the fine Ode, *Boadicea*, written some years earlier. But in that Ode there is a touch of rhetoric. In *Toll for the Brave* there is none. There is a stark simplicity, more impressive perhaps than the glory and glamour which other poets have associated with active valour. In its quiet gravity is concentrated his bleak acceptance of the fact of Death in Life.

In his rendering, however, of one of Madame Guyon's poems he had written –

> The rocks replied – "To-morrow,
> "To-morrow brings thee joy."

And in July joy came with Lady Austen. Her impulsive affection overrode at once any feeling of awkwardness and compelled even an unseasonable summer to smile. And when a flooded autumn followed, and it was impossible for him, without a horse, to visit her at Clifton Rectory, she mounted an ass, as soon as the water was fordable, and visited him.

Later, when in the absence of Mrs. Jones the Rectory

was besieged during the night by roughs intent on bur-
glary, she took refuge with Mrs. Unwin. And at Orchard
Side she stayed until apartments could be prepared for her
at Olney Vicarage. Thus she came, even in point of residence, to reign in Newton's stead; the doorway in the wall
between the two houses was reopened and henceforth she
met Cowper and Mrs. Unwin daily, and they dined with
one another alternately every day, except Sunday.

She played on the harpsichord and sang songs which
Cowper wrote for her, praising domestic peace and
Nature's delights with a light-heartedness that Newton
would doubtless have contrasted most unfavourably with
the fruit of an earlier collaboration in sacred song. They
played, too, at battledore and shuttle-cock, and if the
weather forbade the regular morning walk, he 'rang a
thousand bob-majors' upon the dumb-bells. In the
afternoon he wound thread. 'Thus,' he wrote, 'did Her-
cules, and thus probably did Samson, and thus do I; and
were both these heroes living, I should not fear to challenge them to a trial of skill in that business or doubt
to beat them both. As to killing lions, and other
amusements of that kind, with which they were so
delighted, I should be their humble servant, and beg to be
excused.'

In the evenings there were no less heroic adventures.
He read aloud, generally from books of travel, and his
imagination was so captivated that, in his own words, 'I
seem to partake with the navigators in all the dangers they
encountered. I lose my anchor; my mainsail is rent into
threads; I kill a shark, and by signs converse with a

Patagonian, and all this without moving from my fireside.'
Doubtless these tales of storm-tossed navigators fascin-
ated him by offering a physical analogy with his mental
state. And by sharing imaginatively in their dangers and
the intrepid spirit which surmounted them, he forgot his
own fears.

For his joy was a little forced. His spirits could not
'bear a bustle,' and at times Lady Austen's vivacity tired
him, while her affection demanded a response which left
him uneasy. Possibly it reminded him of his position ten
years before, of his engagement to Mrs. Unwin and the
consequences. Each previous attack, he remembered, had
occurred at an interval of ten years, and he began to
despond.

Yet at this very moment, as if to prove the truth of his
contention that 'the most ludicrous lines I ever wrote have
been written in the saddest mood, and but for that saddest
mood, perhaps had never been written at all,' he achieved
the poem which by making 'all the world laugh' was to
secure his popularity as a serious poet too. Lady Austen
started the laugh of which the ripples were to spread so
far.

One evening, to cheer him, she told the droll tale of
how a certain citizen of London town rode out to celebrate
the twentieth anniversary of his wedding, how he went
further than he intended, and all his misadventures. She
told it well, and Cowper was soon convulsed with mirth.
It was the kind of tale which constantly returns upon the
memory to excite a new convulsion, and he could not
sleep for it. He began putting it into rhyme, and before

the morning *John Gilpin* had roughly materialized. After a few days, devoted to polishing and improving it in the greenhouse, the ride 'that could never have been accomplished, in a route that could never be followed,' had attained its final form.

Cowper inherited a taste for the light ballad from his father, and he even asserted that if graver matters had not called him another way, he would have addicted himself to this sort of composition more than to any other. His letters are the best proof of his aptitude for it. Indeed, it is arguable that the quality of humour revealed in *John Gilpin* is even better displayed in his prose accounts of farcical local incidents, and that the necessity of rhyme and the conscious ingenuity which it involved cramped somewhat his style without concentrating to any greater degree his humour.

His account in a letter of the upsetting of Tom Freeman, the gingerbread baker, and his gingerbread wife when returning from Hunslope fair at 10 p.m. is a typical example – 'The horse having a lively imagination, and very weak nerves, fancied he either saw or heard something, but has never been able to say what. A sudden fright will impart activity, and a momentary vigour, even to lameness itself. Accordingly, he started, and sprang from the middle of the road to the side of it with such surprising alacrity, that he dismounted the gingerbread baker and his gingerbread wife in a moment. Not contented with this effort, nor thinking himself yet out of danger, he proceeded as fast as he could to a full gallop, rushed against the gate at the bottom of the lane, and opened it for himself, without perceiving that there was any gate there. Still he galloped, and with a velocity and momentum continually increasing, till he arrived in Olney!'

Again, his description in 1780 of 'Puss' escaping and running right through the town, pursued by men, women children and dogs, compares well with the stanza –

> The dogs did bark, the children screamed,
>   Up flew the windows all;
> And every soul cried out, "Well done!"
>   As loud as he could bawl.

The droll personification of inanimate things, too, illustrated in the lines –

> "I came because your horse would come,
>   And, if I well forebode,
> My hat and wig will soon be here,–
>   They are upon the road."

was one of his habitual tricks as a letter-writer, while into the lines –

> His horse, who never in that sort
>   Had handled been before,
> What thing upon his back had got
>   Did wonder more and more,

he projected his own diffident respect for a beast 'whose walk would seem tedious, whose trot would jumble me, and whose gallop might throw me into a ditch.'

John Gilpin, however, if it lacks something of the pri-

vate flavour, the subtle gradations, of his prose facetious-
ness, has all the advantages of being perfectly adapted
for public recitation. And from the time that Henderson,
the comedian, suddenly made it all the rage by reading it
at the Freemasons' Hall, its popularity was assured.

John Gilpin revived its author. It remained an 'inex-
haustible source of merriment' and carried him through
the dead season of the year. Lady Austen wished him to
write a sequel, but he wisely refused. She then urged
him to try writing in blank verse, and in the summer of
1783 he agreed to do so, if she would give him a subject.
'Oh,' she replied, 'you can never be in want of a subject;
you can write upon any – write upon this sofa!'

Once again she had quickened him to action. With her
insight into his nature, she knew that only diffidence
cramped his faculties, that he had but to be given an
object and a preliminary push, and that then he would
gather momentum, as he did in his letters. The quiet
stream of his creative energy would flow if once the
delusive dam of self-depreciation were pierced. And with
an impulsive sentence she pierced it. 'I sing the Sofa,'
he began in obedience to her behest, and for a hundred
lines trickled indecisively along a channel of Miltonic
parody. And then suddenly the fissure widened and the
liberated waters ploughed a deeper channel. He passed
from the sententious to the sensitive, from the external
to the intimate, from the moralistic plane of Newton to
the naturalistic of Sister Ann. With the words, 'For I
have loved the rural walk,' he was embarked upon his
new adventure, had discovered that 'in our life alone does

Nature live,' and that he might relive his hours with her
with a quickening of senses and a quietness of spirit that
no sectarian devotion could give.

Yet although so early in *The Task* he had discovered
Nature as a source of pleasure and of a new poetry, he
was too dependent on his mood and too devoid of any
regular plan to cling to her. And when he deserted her,
he lost her vital support, and sank once again to the moralistic level of his earlier verse.

For his poem was not so much the harvest of his creative hours as, in literal fact, a daily task undertaken and
maintained for the good of his health. He wrote sometimes an hour a day, sometimes half a one, sometimes two,
and his verse was a barometer of his mood, which for
various reasons was particularly changeable. A damp
summer depressed him and a visit by the Newtons agitated
him. To judge, indeed, by *The Rose*, which was written
at this time, Newton had not yet learnt that the brusque
methods of a muscular Christian were unsuited to his
host's temperament. And Cowper's gentle depreciation
of his guest's rough reproof of his melancholy is as applicable to Newton's conduct in general as to the particular
incident which provoked it. He was writing of a rose,
weighted with rain-drops, which he seized too rudely and
so snapped from its stalk –

> "And such," I exclaimed, "is the pitiless part
>   Some act by the delicate mind,
>   Regardless of wringing and breaking a heart
>   Already to sorrow resigned!

"This elegant rose, had I shaken it less,
    Might have bloomed with its owner awhile;
And the tear that is wiped with a little address
    May be followed perhaps by a smile."

Such a reproof was surely more Christian than the treatment of which it complained.

Although, too, he was 'never much addicted to anxious thoughts about the future, in respect of temporals,' the humiliating peace under which England had been compelled to surrender the American Colonies grieved the patriot in him, who confessed to his Country that 'with all thy faults, I love thee still.' 'As when the sea is uncommonly agitated,' he wrote, 'the water finds its way into creeks and holes of rocks, which in its calmer state it never reaches, in like manner the effect of these turbulent times is felt even at Orchard Side.' The effect, however, was not always depressing. For, shocking as it seemed to Newton, he was politically a Whig, and the tide of emancipation which was beginning to flow in France excited his approval.

But he was himself no nearer emancipation. Before meals, when the rest of the party stood for grace, he still remained seated, taking his knife and fork in his hand to signify that he had no part in the exercise. The strange limits, too, of his good-sense are well illustrated by two passages occurring in his letters about this time. In one he wrote – 'Is it possible that the wise men of antiquity could entertain a real reverence for the fabulous rubbish which they dignified with the name of religion?' – a sentence which compares with the lines in *The Task* –

> Such dupes are men to custom, and so prone
> To reverence what is ancient. . . .

In the other, reverencing himself the 'fabulous rubbish' of a later religion, he doubted not 'that Adam on the very day of his creation was able to express himself in terms both forcible and elegant, and that he was at no loss for sublime diction, and logical combination, when he wanted to praise his Maker.'

The Task reflected not only his fluctuations of mood, but this curious conjunction of a generous freedom of mind with a credulity which could accept the Miltonic Adam as a fact and a witness to the powers of 'revelation.' But at least he wrote without intermission, even when his ink was frozen by one of the severest winters ever known, and he was attacked by rheumatism in his back.

In November he paused for a moment, stung at last to expression by Thurlow's and Colman's failure even to acknowledge the gift of his poems, and wrote in *The Valediction* an elegy to friendship, both dignified and moving. And when the year ended, he looked back 'on all the passages and occurrences of it, as a traveller looks back upon a wilderness.' Nor did the New Year at first bring new hope. 'Nature revives again,' he wrote to Newton, 'but a soul once slain lives no more. The hedge that has been apparently dead, is not so; it will burst into leaf and blossom at the appointed time; but no such time is appointed for the stake that stands in it. It is as dead as it seems, and will prove itself no dissembler. The latter end of next month will complete a period of eleven years in which I have spoken no other language. It is a long time for a man, whose eyes were once opened, to spend in darkness; long enough to make despair an inveterate habit; and such it is with me.'

To Newton, however, he inevitably confided his darkest moods. And in reality the hedges did not bud for him in vain. 'All the sounds that Nature utters,' he wrote to another, 'are delightful – at least in this country,' and he shared in the pleasure of creatures 'who seem only to please themselves.' But if spring restored him to Nature, it parted him finally from the Egeria who had released the spring of nature in his verse.

In the previous autumn his relations with her had not been quite easy. He had drifted into the habit of paying his 'devoirs to her every morning at eleven.' But the morning was his work-time, and since breakfast was seldom over before ten, only one hour in the day was left for writing. He was too polite and too anxious not to hurt Lady Austen's feelings to break with the habit, but he chafed a little at having 'to neglect the 'Task' to attend upon the Muse who had inspired the subject.'

It was, however, Mrs. Unwin's feelings which dictated the final cleavage. She was, as Cowper wrote, 'one of the sincerest of the human race', but this could hardly prevent her feeling some twinges of jealousy towards a younger woman more talented and comely than herself, and one whose vivacity was more potent than her piety, and to whom the poet she had cherished for nearly twenty years addressed the lines —

> The star that beams on Anna's breast
>   Conceals her William's hair,
> 'Twas lately severed from the rest
>   To be promoted there.
> The heart that beats beneath that breast
>   Is William's well I know,
> A nobler prize and richer far
>   Than India could bestow.

Cowper's own relation to Lady Austen was poised on a razor-edge between friendship and love; but when he realized that the happiness of Mrs. Unwin was also involved, the relation at once became too difficult to sustain. To the one he went for inspiration, to the other for sympathetic criticism. The one was his Muse, the other his 'lady chamberlain, who licenses all I write.' The one he almost loved, the other he deeply valued.

Compelled to choose between them, he was in no doubt. He wrote Lady Austen 'a very tender, yet resolute letter in which he explained and lamented the circumstances that forced him to renounce her society.' She burnt the letter in anger, and that was the end of their relationship. Early in May she had gone to Bristol, and she and Cowper never met again.

We cannot but regret the necessity. Yet Cowper could not have done otherwise. The very qualities which made Lady Austen an inspiration eventually disqualified her as a friend, and something nearer than a friend. 'A character,' as Cowper wrote, 'with which we spend all our time should be made on purpose for us; too much or too little of any single ingredient spoils all.' To one who needed peace even more than animation, who was too old and injured to adapt himself to a new way of life, this was the truth.

Lady Austen had given all that she could to Cowper, and it was as much his own nature as his fidelity to Mrs. Unwin which limited his capacity to respond. Above all, she had let light into the prison of provincial piety. And fortunately, before her departure, Cowper had made two new friends, who continued that service so long as any service could avail him anything. Sir John and Lady Throckmorton, as they later became, had recently come into residence at Weston Hall, a mile from Olney. To Weston Park Cowper and Mrs. Unwin walked almost every day of the year, when the weather would permit, and already in the first book of *The Task* he had described in intimate detail the beauty of its trees and the lovely view from its terrace, sloping down to where

> The Ouse, dividing the well-watered land,
> Now glitters in the sun and now retires,
> As bashful, yet impatient to be seen.

But even more than the 'groves, heaths, and smoking villages remote,' he loved the sylvan reaches of the park itself. He would enter it through a spinney, and, if he did not linger at the Moss House, pass through another plantation and a curving avenue of chestnuts trees to reach the Alcove, a small hexagonal structure, open on three

sides, where he would rest, while his eye travelled along
the airy roof of a magnificent avenue of limes.

Henceforth these walks were enriched by the possibility
of meeting 'Benevolus' and his wife, who soon proved
'peerless neighbours,' or of enjoying, in their absence,
the garden and its contents. The Throckmortons were
Catholics, but much more amiable, as Cowper soon discovered, than many Protestants. They were young and,
like Lady Austen, brought to Olney a breath of unpro-
vincial air.

Later Cowper became intimate enough with them to
address Lady Throckmorton as 'Mrs. Frog,' and to enjoy
much hospitality at their hands. But they met frequently
even at this time and 'entertained with the utmost polite-
ness.' And so Lady Austen's absence was less felt. He
was not unhappy to relapse with Mrs. Unwin into their
former duality. Devoted companionship was a satisfying
possession, and gratitude was a less exacting emotion than
love. As he picked strawberries at Weston or searched
the hedges for honeysuckle, he was content to forgo the
lyrical picnics that Sister Ann had inspired.

And *The Task* was nearing completion. He was no
longer distracted by any affectionate obligations. And as
he sat transcribing it in the greenhouse in September,
the gentleness of the autumnal sun and the calmness of
the season consecrated his mood of resignation. Through
the wide-open door and windows floated the scent of
every flower in a garden full of flowers of his planting, and
the incessant humming of the bees. Nothing, he felt,
must ever be allowed to break his attachment to this spot

of earth, this island, precariously secured by how many small and kind familiarities from the unfeeling sea that encircled it and even its calmest moments murmured a menace in his ears.

The very stones in the garden-walls had become his intimate acquaintance: he would miss almost the minutest object. And in one of his most charming lyrics he lamented at this time the poplars which had for so many years flanked a field at Lavendon to which he often used to walk, and which now had fallen to the woodman's axe —

> The poplars are felled; farewell to the shade
> And the whispering sound of the cool colonnade
> The winds play no longer and sing in the leaves,
> Nor Ouse on his bosom their image receives.

He never perhaps wrote a more musical line than the second in this stanza, or one in which the leafy enchantment of the country which he loved was more perfectly married to sentiment and to a classical elegance. And although sometimes the monotony weighed upon him and it seemed that no place contributed less to the catalogue of incidents, the very smallness and humbleness of his world encouraged him to magnify it in his mind and so enlarge himself. 'Great revolutions,' he wrote, 'happen in this Ant's nest of ours. One emmet of illustrious character and great abilities pushes out another; parties are formed, they range themselves in formidable opposition, they threaten each other's ruin, they cross over and are mingled together, and like the coruscations of the Northern Aurora, amuse the spectator, at the same time that by some they are supposed to be forerunners of a general dissolution.'

And just as the small details of hedge and field acquired an intimate significance for one whose relation to them was undistracted by any ulterior thought or impulse, so the postboy, poor Jenny Raban, Nathan Sample, the malt-ster, or George Bell, whose sole occupation centred in filling his glass and emptying it, acquired a weight of human verity.

Finely sympathetic as Cowper was, he viewed them for the most part as a whimsical spectator, but he forgot his own tragedy in dramatizing the comedy of their manners. How true, for example, to rustic life was the 'group of about twelve figures,' which he saw one morning from his window, 'very closely engaged in a conference. . . . The scene of consultation was a blacksmith's shed, very comfortably screened from the wind, and directly opposed to the morning sun. Some held their hands behind them, some had them folded across their bosom, and others had thrust them into their breeches pockets. Every man's posture bespoke a pacific turn of mind; but the distance being too great for their words to reach me, nothing transpired.'

The Task, however, is the lasting monument of the virtue of his local attachment. He returned the last proof of it in May 1785, the month in which for a few days his fatal obsession left him, like 'a flash in a dark night, during which the heavens seemed opened only to shut again.' Yet he was sufficiently emancipated from Newton to refuse 'absolutely, though civilly' the request made in a 'fretful and peevish letter' that the proofs should be sent to him, and he even informed Unwin that 'if he says more on the subject, I shall speak freely, and perhaps please him less than I have done already.' Lady Austen had at least deposed the vice-regent, if not the Regent himself. And he was quietly satisfied with *The Task*. He had not lounged over it, but on the contrary found it a severe exercise to mould and fashion it to his mind: and he was persuaded that he would not forfeit anything by this volume that he had gained by the last. Although at one time he determined not to include *John Gilpin*, as out of harmony with the seriousness of the rest, he yielded to his publisher's wish. And when the book appeared at the end of June, the 'knight of the stone-bottle' ensured its popularity. The public were ready to listen to a moralist who had proved himself a humorist. And in so doing they discovered also a naturalist.

§ 3

The Task is rather a companionable than a great poem, because it lacks any deep organic unity. Cowper himself admitted that his work could not boast a regular plan, while claiming 'that the reflections are naturally suggested always by the preceding passage, and that except the fifth book, which is rather of a political aspect, the whole has one tendency: to discountenance the modern enthusiasm after a London life, and to recommend rural ease and leisure, as friendly to the cause of piety and virtue.'

So far, however, as this tendency dominated the poem, it depressed its vitality. Cowper emphasized it because he

was anxious to prove the moral usefulness of his activity.
But his explicit moral aim was in fact a confession and
proof of creative weakness. For the moral impulse of a
great poem is implicit, as is its thought, in an act of pure
expression and its unity is something far more inward
and necessary than 'that sort of light connection which
poetry demands' or a general tendency to be edifying.

We find in *The Task* the same accidental association of
reflections, interspersed with more vivid descriptions of
life, which we find in his letters. One thing led to another
with little more necessity than in some ruminating ramble
with a friendly listener. Such unexacting thought was
indeed a necessity of his nature. 'I can assert with the
strictest truth,' he wrote, 'that I not only do not think
with connexion, but that I frequently do not think at all.'
At most he strove only for 'the stamp and clear impression
of good sense,' and so prudent an aim, as Mr. Lascelles
Abercrombie has finely written in a too little-known
poem –

> refuses faith in the unknown powers
> Within man's nature; shrewdly bringeth all
> Their inspiration of strange eagerness
> To a judgment bought by safe experience;
> Narrows desire into the scope of thought.
> But it is written in the heart of man,
> Thou shalt no larger be than thy desire.
> Thou must not therefore stoop thy spirit's sight
> To pore only within the candle-gleam
> Of conscious wit and reasonable brain;

> But search into the sacred darkness lying
> Outside thy knowledge of thyself, the vast
> Measureless fate, full of the power of stars,
> The outer noiseless heavens of thy soul.

Cowper's inability to do this, a deficiency which he shared
with most of his contemporaries, limited him as a poet
and maimed him as a man. His reflections in *The Task*
were often just, as when he wrote –

> But not to understand a treasure's worth
> Till time has stolen away the slighted good,
> Is cause of half the poverty we feel,
> And makes the world the wilderness it is.

But if such reflections

> meliorate the heart,
> Compose the passions, and exalt the mind,

they would do the same in prose, and are in essence
prosaic. The lack of inward vitality, the desultory and
discursive impulse, is also revealed in the quality of his
blank-verse. He found it the most difficult species of
poetry that he had ever meddled with, and he paid as
close attention to the pause and the cadence as to clarity.
There was, as he wrote, a pleasure in such poetic pains –

> Which only poets know. The shifts and turns,
> The expedients and inventions multiform
> To which the mind resorts, in chase of terms
> Thought apt, yet coy, and difficult to win. . . .

But if such labour and the skill it demanded proved useful in stealing away the thought 'from themes of sad import,' it does not necessarily exhilarate the reader. And the careful and sensitive industry of the craftsman, as his translation of Homer was to show even more damagingly, could not conceal an inherent languor.

In his earlier couplet-writing he had improved on Churchill as a craftsman who appreciated the flexible possibilities of enjambement, but rhythmically he was inferior, and often the sound of his verse was as emptily pompous as the sense. In his blank-verse, as in many of his shorter poems, he came far nearer achieving an individual rhythm within a conventional pattern. But his devotion to Milton, from whom his age had to some extent derived the deadening syllabic regularity of their verse, together with his own defect of will and energy, prevented him from realizing the possibilities of that counterpoint of subjective impulse and regular prosody, which Blake discovered. Only in the passages in which real feeling restored 'the tone of languid nature,' did his rhythm possess an inward necessity; elsewhere his blank-verse was as skilfully conventional as the thought which it dressed, or as soberly flat as the lines –

> Knowledge and wisdom, far from being one,
> Have ofttimes no connexion. Knowledge dwells
> In heads replete with thoughts of other men,
> Wisdom in minds attentive to their own.

Even more depressing however than the dullness of uninspired sobriety is the moral violence by which he consoled himself for a want of real moral energy. The passages in which he raved against 'the lewd vain world' are unrelieved, for the most part, even by satirical wit. When he wrote of cities –

> Thither flow
> As to a common and most noisome sewer,
> The dregs and feculence of every land.
> In cities foul example on most minds
> Begets its likeness;

or extended his indictment to the world at large –

> Pass where we may, through city or through town,
> Village or hamlet, of this merry land,
> Though lean and beggared, every twentieth pace
> Conducts the unguarded nose to such a whiff
> Of stale debauch, forth issuing from the styes
> That law has licensed, as makes temperance reel,

we realize from another standpoint how far a narrow good-sense can distort the mind from truth.

When Cowper came into personal contact with a drunkard he was never rabid. The drunkards of the village were no less a source of humour than of head-shaking. But his mind was the slave of a ranting morality, when he deser ed the concrete. He could not project his humanity imaginatively into the unknown. He became then merely a biassed generalizer and saw in London, with a sick distaste for what his nerves could not endure –

> The fairest capital of all the world,
> By riot and incontinence the worst.

The best then of his moral strictures in *The Task* were those based on his own immediate experience, as, for example, the attack, in its second book, on clerical affectations in the pulpit, which was suggested by the vulgar rhetoric indulged in by a local preacher.

He himself, however, realized occasionally that he was doing violence both to his nature and to the truth in his worst tirades against 'vice, vanity, and folly,' or in stooping to the lurid banality of the story of 'young Misagathus,' which might be entitled, after the kind of tract that it resembles, 'God Scorned or the Atheist's End.'

'But hush!', he wrote,

> – the Muse perhaps is too severe,
> And, with a gravity beyond the size
> And measure of the offence, rebukes a deed
> Less impious than absurd. . . .

And in fact he only became a poet when he forgot that his principal purpose was 'to allure the reader by . . . poetical embellishments, to the reading of what may profit him.'

Fortunately he forgot this at once when his heart yielded to the 'soft and secret power' of Nature. At once his mind became the servant of his sympathies. Its good-sense survived as just observation, its elegance as selective taste, and its moral judgment as an appreciation of peace, gentleness, and all kinds of humble integrity.

To Nature's power to reinforce and unify his faculties he testified later, when he remarked that he had, though not a good memory, a good local memory, and could recollect by the help of a tree or a stile what was said at a particular spot. Similarly, we may say that his thought was only good when it was local, when its roots were in concrete experience.

Deficient in animal energy, he required this inflowing from the physical world to release a self-centred intelligence. And in describing nature he revived his sense of pleasure and was to some extent absorbed in a life larger than his own. 'Everything,' he wrote, 'I see in the fields is to me an object, and I can look at the same rivulet or at a handsome tree, every day of my life, with new pleasure.' And it is perhaps significant of his objective vision that he excelled particularly in describing the countryside in winter, when its form was most classical.

In this surrender of himself to an object his very deficiency was a virtue. No restless personal energy, no distracting thoughts, had to be subdued. The 'wise passiveness' which Wordsworth had so patiently to cultivate was a necessity of his being. He claimed with justice that not one of his descriptions from Nature was second-handed nor one of his delineations of the heart borrowed from books, or in the least degree conjectural. His feeling was wholly personal, and if his good-sense restricted its range and depth, it ensured its humble sincerity.

Nature did not quicken him to ideas. Of metaphysics he admitted he knew little, and *The Task* has little, if any, metaphysical reality. At most he generalized on Nature's processes, as in the lines –

By ceaseless action all that is subsists.
Constant rotation of the unwearied wheel
That Nature rides upon, maintains her health,
Her beauty, her fertility.

And, as we shall see, it was his failure to apprehend
Nature ideally, to enter into her being by realizing both
her discord and her harmony, that compelled him to
attach a Creator to her, with powers of arbitrary intervention, and to reverence in Him the fierce combative
qualities, which he went to Nature to forget.

His abstract conceptions were thus embodied in a
theological formula, while his personal attachment to
Nature remained sensitively concrete. The landscape had
his discriminating praise, 'its Author' his theoretical and
undiscriminating reverence, and the two were never
brought either into a confusing or a necessary relation.
As he wrote –

But trees, and rivulets whose rapid course
Defies the check of winter, haunts of deer,
And sheepwalks populous with bleating lambs,
And lanes in which the primrose ere her time
Peeps through the moss that clothes the hawthorn root,
Deceive no student. Wisdom there, and Truth,
Not shy as in the world, and to be won
By slow solicitation, seize at once
The roving thought, and fix it on themselves.

This patient loyalty to fact explains his limited perfection
as a poet of Nature, often exquisite in the truth and sym-

pathy of his descriptions, but without depth of vision or any intense imaginative or evocative power. As he wrote –

> Thou knowest my praise of nature most sincere,
> And that my raptures are not conjured up
> To serve occasions of poetic pomp.

Only occasionally the lover of Milton mastered the lover of nature, as in the lines on the avenue of limes and chestnut trees in the park at Weston, where he loved to walk –

> How airy and how light the graceful arch,
> Yet awful as the consecrated roof
> Re-echoing pious anthems!

For the most part his observation was as exaćt as his thought was discursive, and even when his eye

> posted on this speculative height
> Exults in its command,

he paints the distance with the same fidelity to detail as the foreground, and his details have the reality of a clinging personal interest. When he writes, –

> I fed on scarlet hips and stony haws,
> Or blushing crabs, or berries that emboss
> The bramble, black as jet, or sloes austere,

it is as if he picked them again and set them in his verse; and elsewhere he communicates his experience, not so much by distilling it, as by reporting it with the minutest exactitude. In such lines as the following, for example, he discovered the life that resides in simple fact, –

> Hence, ankle-deep in moss and flowery thyme,
> We mount again, and feel at every step
> Our foot half sunk in hillocks green and soft,
> Raised by the mole, the miner of the soil.

or

>   rills that slip
> Through the cleft rock, and chiming as they fall
> Upon loose pebbles, lose themselves at length
> In matted grass, that with a livelier green
> Betrays the secret of their silent course.

or

> I saw the woods and fields at close of day
> A variegated show; the meadows green
> Though faded; and the lands, where lately waved
> The golden harvest, of a mellow brown,
> Upturned so lately by the forceful share:
> I saw far off the weedy fallows smile
> With verdure not unprofitable, grazed
> By flocks, fast feeding, and selecting each
> His favourite herb; while all the leafless groves
> That skirt the horizon, wore a sable hue,
> Scarce noticed in the kindred dusk of eve.

There is in such writing no fevered searching for distinctive or evocative epithets. But the eye is finely enough focussed to achieve at almost every step 'new discoveries' in the familiar, and not only in nature herself, but in the creatures and the countrymen who depend upon her. How perspicuously true, for example, are the following two pictures, –

> He from the stack carves out the accustomed load,
> Deep-plunging, and again deep-plunging oft,
> His broad keen knife into the solid mass;
> Smooth as a wall the upright remnant stands,
> With such undeviating and even force
> He severs it away.

or, of the woodman's dog –

> Shaggy, and lean, and shrewd, with pointed ears
> And tail cropped short, half lurcher and half cur,
> His dog attends him. Close behind his heel
> Now creeps he slow; and now with many a frisk
> Wide scampering, snatches up the drifted snow
> With ivory teeth, or ploughs it with his snout;
> Then shakes his powdered coat, and barks for joy.

Sometimes, indeed, his facts are dead, because not quickened by

> admiration feeding at the eye
> And still unsated.

This is particularly true of the book entitled *The Garden*, in which his horticultural knowledge serves rather for a florist's catalogue than a poem, and his song, to quote his own words, is

> Cold as its theme, and, like its theme, the fruit
> Of too much labour, worthless when produced.

Nature's wildness too was outside his sympathy and beyond his powers to express. He loved her

> in her cultivated trim
> Dressed to his taste.

And although he came far nearer than his contemporaries to her rural reality, he viewed her, if not as a classical estate, as a kind of garden with 'the mild and genial soil of cultivated life,' a pastoral enclosure, snug and sheltered from the rank forces of chaos. Moreover, like many of his contemporaries, like John Armstrong, for example, who discussed the influence of nature in a poem entitled *The Art of Preserving Health*, or Matthew Green in his *A Cure for the Spleen*, he viewed her somewhat as a convalescent from the disease of the town and its over-refinement, grateful that

> The spleen is seldom felt where Flora reigns.

It was typical too of his sober taste and of the 'coddled poet' which Byron named him, to write of the gypsies –

> Strange! that a creature rational, and cast
> In human mould, should brutalize by choice
> His nature, and, though capable of arts
> By which the world might profit and himself,
> Self banished from society, prefer
> Such squalid sloth to honourable toil!

Equally typical of his plain good-sense was his subsequent
admission that

> Such wealth and gaiety of heart enjoy
> The houseless rovers of the sylvan world;

or his refutation elsewhere of

> those golden times
> And those Arcadian scenes that Maro sings . . .
> . . . those days were never: airy dreams
> Sat for the picture; and the poet's hand,
> Imparting substance to an empty shade,
> Imposed a gay delirium for a truth.

It is then chiefly by his fidelity to fact that he stands as
the intermediary between Thomson and Wordsworth.
Indeed, like Wordsworth, he at times attributed a poetical
virtue to the mere chronicling of fact which it did not
possess. But, unlike him, he could seldom feel himself
at any depth into inanimate things, despite his claim that, –

> The man to solitude accustomed long
> Perceives in every thing that lives a tongue;
> Not animals alone, but shrubs and trees
> Have speech for him, and understood with ease.

His intuition was comparatively superficial, if disinterested, because he never strove to discipline ideas to facts
or to interpret facts ideally, but only to invest them with
sentiment or reflect upon them.

Yet many of his sentiments and reflections were kindred
to Wordsworth's. The contrast he drew, for example,

between the ancient virtue and modern laxness of the Universities anticipated a passage in *The Prelude,* and when he wrote of the seaman, –

> his very heart athirst
> To gaze at Nature in her green array,
> Upon the ship's tall side he stands, possessed
> With visions prompted by intense desire:
> Fair fields appear below, such as he left
> Far distant, such as he would die to find,

he forestalled the sentiment of 'The Reverie of Poor Susan.' The theme too, of the betrayed or deserted woman, so dear to the Romantic poets, emerges in the story of 'crazed Kate,' –

> There often wanders one, whom better days
> Saw better clad, in cloak of satin trimmed
> With lace, and hat with splendid riband bound.
> A serving-maid was she, and fell in love
> With one who left her, went to sea, and died.
> Her fancy followed him through foaming waves
> To distant shores, and she would sit and weep
> At what a sailor suffers; fancy too,
> Delusive most where warmest wishes are,
> Would oft anticipate his glad return,
> And dream of transports she was not to know.
> She heard the doleful tidings of his death,
> And never smiled again. And now she roams
> The dreary waste; there spends the livelong day,
> And there, unless when charity forbids,

The livelong night. A tattered apron hides,
Worn as a cloak, and hardly hides, a gown
More tattered still; and both but ill conceal
A bosom heaved with never-ceasing sighs.

Above all in his appreciation of the hard life and humble virtues of the poor, he was Wordsworth's forerunner. And his sympathy, even more perhaps than Wordsworth's, had the veracity of fact, –

The frugal housewife trembles when she lights
Her scanty store of brushwood, blazing clear,
But dying soon, like all terrestrial joys.
The few small embers left she nurses well,
And while her infant race, with outspread hands,
And crowded knees, sit cowering o'er the sparks,
Retires content to quake, so they be warmed. . . .
The taper soon extinguished, which I saw
Dangled along at the cold finger's end
Just when the day declined, and the brown loaf
Lodged on the shelf, half eaten without sauce
Of savoury cheese, or butter costlier still,
Sleep seems their only refuge: for, alas!
Where penury is felt the thought is chained,
And sweet colloquial pleasures are but few . . .

The same blend of human sympathy and realistic logic characterized his attacks on war, on the cruelty of sport, and on the conscienceless industrialism which was spreading like an ugly growth about him. And at times, as in the opening lines of the second book, his humanitarianism

was fired by a fine impatience which approaches the
revolutionary passion of his successors, –

> Oh for a lodge in some vast wilderness,
> Some boundless contiguity of shade,
> Where rumour of oppression and deceit,
> Of unsuccessful or successful war,
> Might never reach me more! My ear is pained,
> My soul is sick with every day's report
> Of wrong and outrage with which earth is filled.
> There is no flesh in man's obdurate heart,
> It does not feel for man. The natural bond
> Of brotherhood is severed as the flax
> That falls asunder at the touch of fire.

And elsewhere he wrote of this 'natural bond', –

> I was born of woman and drew milk,
> As sweet as charity, from human breasts.
> I think, articulate, I laugh and weep,
> And exercise all functions of a man.
> How then should I and any man that lives
> Be strangers to each other?

Lastly he championed freedom with a warmth for which
he hoped he would not be censured and denounced the
'horrid towers' of the Bastille as fervently as Wordsworth
later acclaimed their fall. His sympathy for the prisoner
compelled to wear out time in a comfortless existence was
indeed more real, perhaps, than Wordsworth's, because
for so many years he himself had been a prisoner

> with a sickly hope
> By dint of change to give his tasteless task
> Some relish.

But his romanticism was fundamentally restricted compared with that of his successors because, while attacking the tyranny of men, he continued to accept the tyranny of a Biblical God.

The later Romantics strove to humanize both God and man. They realized however subconsciously that man's God, no less than man himself, had become divorced from the natural life in which He had originated. Originally He had symbolized the natural forces which man feared and imperfectly understood. But He had in time become invested with all the arbitrary and calculating sovereignty of an Oriental potentate. Similarly man had once lived the instinctive life with the instinctive virtue of the creature, but in growing self-conscious he had, like his God, become a hybrid, a mixture of instinctive impulse and calculating self-interest.

Behind the return to Nature, therefore, of the Romantic movement, and developing out of it, was, however vaguely and sentimentally, a demand that man should rediscover not only his own unity with life, but his God's.

The dualism between man's self-centred intelligence and his creative instincts was felt to correspond with the dualism between an external individualistic Deity and the impersonal forces of Nature. And by humanizing and spiritualisting his instincts man sought also to humanize and spiritualize his God. He too was conceived as a mind and a force striving after perfe&t and harmonious expression in the matter of life, and He was both dethroned as a supernatural tyrant and distinguished from a mere embodiment of natural necessity.

Cowper's gentle naturalism, however, was far too humble and provincial to extend to God. He did not even credit Him with the human virtue of justice –

> God may choose His mark,
> May punish, if He please, the less, to warn
> The more malignant.

Such a conception corresponded indeed with Nature's carelessness of the individual, and of the finer moral values in her perpetuation of the type. But Cowper attributed sele&tive purpose to it. He invested God, in short, with man's calculating self-interest and Nature's crude, but disinterested, will to perpetuate life. And to this component of force and unscrupulousness he entrusted man's destiny, consoling himself with the Biblical promise of a New Jerusalem descending miraculously out of heaven, –

> Six thousand years of sorrow have well nigh
> Fulfilled their tardy and disastrous course
> Over a sinful world; and what remains
> Of this tempestuous state of human things
> Is merely as the working of a sea
> Before a calm, that rocks itself to rest:
> For He, whose car the winds are, and the clouds
> The dust that waits upon His sultry march,

When sin hath moved Him, and His wrath is hot,
Shall visit earth in mercy; shall descend
Propitious in His chariot paved with love;
And what His storms have blasted and defaced
For man's revolt, shall with a smile repair.

The Biblical Utopia, which he went on to sketch, was similar in its gentle innocence to the Naturalistic Utopia which the Romantics derived from Rousseau; but while theirs may have been sentimental in its disregard of man's original savagery, it had at least its roots in the natural life from which alone man by his own efforts can achieve the God-like. Cowper's Utopia on the other hand was conceived as a miracle imposed on life in a sudden conciliatory mood by an external Deity.

In its naturalism therefore, as in its moral and reflective passages, *The Task* was a curious mixture of the conventional and the true, of humane insight and reactionary absurdity. Cowper described nature with perfect truth, but he emphasized only her pacific aspect, referring all that was subhuman and superhuman in her to an omnipotent 'Lord of all.' By so doing he excluded from her province everything which might have disquieted him, her dark rapacity or her elemental force. He made her minister to that 'domestic happiness,' with its closed shutters and drawn curtains and snug warmth, of which he sang so endearingly the charm.

But by shutting Nature's discord out he shut his own theological discord in. Until the dark figure of an irresponsible God had been resolved into its elements in

Nature, had been realized as a confused embodiment by man of Nature's law and Nature's savagery, He continued to tyrannize over the mind and to prevent the emergence of a truer and more human conception.

Thus Cowper, by concentrating on Nature's gentle aspect, perpetuated his God's ferocity. She served him only as a soothing narcotic, and it remained for the Romantics to discover in her a creative meaning that strengthened the will of man by identifying him with the conflict of force and intelligence in the universe, which it was for him as a responsible being to resolve into harmony.

Cowper was born too early and was too inherently timid to take the necessary step forward, to disown the God of destruction, who leaves in his wake, as Professor Whitehead has written, 'the loss of the greater reality.' It required both inspiration and audacity, as his Romantic successors showed, to reject the idea, rooted in man's primitive instinct, of a catastrophic intervention of the supernatural into the natural order, and to substitute for it the idea of spirit as immanent in physical life. And one who wrote, –

> To combat may be glorious and success
> Perhaps may crown us, but to fly is safe,

was too cautious to realize that there could be no safety in clinging to a creed which he had outgrown, while his feeling was never urgent enough to override his caution. He wished to enjoy even nature 'with propriety' and when, in writing the Common-Scene in *The Task*, he had 'a

strong poetical desire' to describe a peculiar scent in the
fields about Olney, he suppressed it because he 'feared lest
the unfrequency of such a singular property in the earth
should have tempted the reader to ascribe it to a fanciful nose, at least to have suspected it for a deliberate
fiction.'

The suppression was typical of his taste, and certainly
we owe the representative quality of *The Task* to it. But it
reveals also the fear of extravagance which depressed his
faculties and divided him from the Romantics who cap-
tured a new reality by daring a divine excess. The reproof
which he administered to Science was also of course
dictated by his enslavement to theology. As he wrote, –

> Full often too
> Our wayward intellect, the more we learn
> Of nature, overlooks her Author more.

To inquire into Nature's causes was to him an affront to
'revelation' instead of the necessary process by which
'revelation' might be tested, purged, and verified.

Over *The Task* then, as over its author's life, the same
dread Deity lowered. He might forget Him in the peace
of the countryside or in pleading for humanitarian reform,
but the enslavement which he lacked the will to challenge
persisted.

> Scripture is still a trumpet to his fears:
> What none can prove a forgery, may be true:
> What none but bad men wish exploded, must.
> That scruple checks him.

And that scruple reduces almost all that Cowper wrote of God to emptiness in modern ears. Such lines as

> To walk with God, to be divinely free,

or

> He is the freeman whom the truth makes free
> And all are slaves beside,

mean nothing, because 'Scripture is still a trumpet to his fears,' and, to his own destruction, his intelligence is fettered by it.

But the Olney fields and woods were a scripture which he could read without fear and transcribe with a truth which time does not outdate. Here he could overlook the Author in his absorption in the work, could identify himself with animate and inanimate things and become, if not a living soul, a living sense.

'There is in souls a sympathy with sounds,' he wrote in a passage which more than any other breathes the music of his yielding nature,

> And as the mind is pitched the ear is pleased
> With melting airs or martial, brisk or grave:
> Some chord in unison with what we hear
> Is touched within us, and the heart replies.
> How soft the music of those village bells
> Falling at intervals upon the ear
> In cadence sweet! now dying all away,
> Now pealing loud again, and louder still,
> Clear and sonorous, as the gale comes on.

> With easy force it opens all the cells
> Where memory slept. Wherever I have heard
> A kindred melody, the scene recurs,
> And with it all its pleasures and its pains.

Such poetry, the language of a heart that longed to resolve
discord in peace, sounded a new note in English literature
and speaks no less persuasively to our modern sensibility.
And so long as men walk the countryside with a 'wise
passiveness,' loving the humble things of earth for themselves, so long will they appreciate Cowper's stream of
panegyric down

> The vale of nature, where it creeps and winds
> Among her lovely works with a secure
> And unambitious course. . . .

He is the perfect companion on a country walk so long as
he feeds with heart and eye on the world immediately
about him, or delicately explores the gradations of a landscape. He engages our interest too and our sympathy
when he pleads, 'a stricken deer' himself, for kindness to
animals and laments the cruelty of man to man. And
when he lifts his eyes to evoke the evening in the tones of
a domesticated Milton –

> Come, evening, once again, season of peace:
> Return, sweet evening, and continue long!
> Methinks I see thee in the streaky west,
> With matron step slow moving, while the Night
> Treads on thy sweeping train; one hand employed

In letting fall the curtain of repose
On bird and beast, the other charged for man
With sweet oblivion of the cares of day;

we feel, despite the literary reminiscence, the magic and the largeness of the hour.

It is only when he begins to scold the vices of the town, to be sententious or uneasily devout, that he wearies us. Doubtless the fruit 'picked from the thorns and briars of reproof' satisfied his serious-minded contemporaries, who frowned with much justice upon the corrupt materialism of their age. His piety, too, harmonized with and contributed much to the revival of religious feeling, while his romanticism was tempered and devout enough to attract, without alarming, his contemporaries.

But poetry is not born of moral acerbity or the embellishment of a creed. Cowper wrote of the vices of the town without real knowledge, as he bowed to the omnipotence of God without real faith. And the portions of *The Task* devoted to these subjects are dead. It lives, not by virtue of imaginative force, but of local concentration. It is a desultory poem, strewn with passages of fine and personal definition, a poem steeped in a sympathy for simple things that too often curdles into provincial prejudice. It voices the social instincts of a solitary, the sentiment of a man of good-sense, and the romanticism of a moralist.

From a personal standpoint it reflects the changing moods, the interrelation of liberating impulse and crippling inhibition, which affected Cowper from day to day.

And it ended with a cry for peace, for an end to the theological anxiety which drained away his vitality and divided him from the fields and woods where life fulfilled its purpose with no uneasy questioning and glided through the twilight 'by stealth away.'

> So glide my life away! and so at last,
> My share of duties decently fulfilled,
> May some disease, not tardy to perform
> Its destined office, yet with gentle stroke,
> Dismiss me weary to a safe retreat,
> Beneath the turf that I have often trod.

It was not much to ask of life or of death, and Cowper had come so near to nature in *The Task* that there seemed a hope of his request being granted. If he could but perpetuate his tender interest in her and deepen his attachment, the trumpets of the day of judgment might cease to sound. His supernatural terrors might subside in the placid stream of organic life.

But, in truth, as the sensitive materialism of *The Task* suggested, his tender and absorbing interest in nature could never be deepened and extended to include his whole being. He loved her for her charm, her graces, and even her prettinesses, as a sympathetic and finely appreciative friend; he lacked the passion to lose and find himself in her embrace. In *The Task* he had turned from her to moralize or to prostrate himself before a supernatural deity; and while he did so, her virtue left him. For in her lay the secret of the moral and the supernatural; in her, as Wordsworth was to discover, was 'The soul of Beauty and enduring Life,' the spiritual reality of which her form was the plastic image.

But in Nature's presence Cowper stood 'a sensitive being,' but not a '*creative* soul.' She eased the tension of his nerves, but she could not liberate his mind, warped by theology and fettered by good-sense. She could not reveal her meaning to one who, when he ceased to scrutinize her features with a tender interest, feared to enjoy her save

> With a propriety that none can feel
> But who, with filial confidence inspired,
> Can lift to heaven an unpresumptuous eye,
> And smiling say – "My Father made them all!"

And so the busy quiet of the fields and woods was to prove at last as ineffectual a medicine to his melancholy as the snug warmth of the parlour. From the God who tormented him there could be no secure retreat. Only by going out boldly to meet Him could he have proved his fears to be the delusion that they were, and by quelling a Tyrant discovered a Friend. But the peace which succeeds the victory of understanding, so different from a fugitive quietism, was beyond his powers to achieve.

'The heart is a nest of serpents,' he wrote to Newton at this time, sinking back into self-hating isolation, 'and will be such while it continues to beat. If God cover the mouth of the nest with his hand, they are hush and snug; but if he withdraw his hand, the whole family lift up their heads and hiss, and are as active and venomous as ever. This I always professed to believe from the time that I had embraced the truth, but never knew it as I know it now.'

Once again, however, for a short while, a woman was to uncover the mouth of the nest, and disclose, not the serpents of sin, but the singing birds of hope.

¶ PART FIVE

ST. LUKE'S SUMMER

F. Haskell.

ST. LUKE'S SUMMER

§ I

THREE months after the appearance of *The Task*,
Cowper, on coming down to breakfast, found on the
table a letter from his cousin Lady Hesketh, which bridged
in a moment the gulf which Evangelicism had dug between them. 'This is just as it should be,' he said within
himself. 'We are all grown young again, and the days that
I thought I should see no more, are actually returned. . . .
I have laughed with you at the *Arabian Nights' Entertain-
ments*. . . . I have walked with you to Netley Abbey, and
have scrambled with you over hedges in every direction,
and many other feats we have performed together, upon
the field of my remembrance, and all within these few
years. . . . The hours that I have spent with you were
among the pleasantest of my former days, and are therefore chronicled in my mind so deeply, as to feel no
erasure.'

And now he was no longer compelled to find what
comfort he could in looking backward. The hope of better
days seemed again to dawn upon him, and he even had
occasionally an intimation, though slight and transient,
that God had not abandoned him for ever.

The success which *The Task* immediately achieved with
the public counted for little as a tonic to his spirits compared with the renewal which it brought of a correspondence with one whose letters were the joy of his heart and
contained 'nothing but what was comfortable.'

Cowper was attached to Lady Hesketh by the tenderest

associations, and although he never mentioned her sister, Theodora, in writing to her, he loved her 'as a sister' and the more for her sister's sake. In her he found at last a vent for the impulsive affeɛtion which he had stifled for so many years. He wrote to her with an impetuous ardour, found nowhere else in his letters. No longer was he at a loss for a subjeɛt. He had so much to say that he hardly knew where to begin, and his wit and humour were caught up in a childlike exultation.

'I am glad that I always loved you as I did,' he wrote. 'It releases me from any occasion to suspeɛt that my present affeɛtion for you is indebted for its existence to any selfish considerations. . . . I perceive myself in a state of mind similar to that of the traveller, described in Pope's *Messiah*, who, as he passes through a sandy desert, starts at the sudden and unsuspeɛted sound of a waterfall.' And again, – 'My dearest Cousin, – whose last most affeɛtionate letter has run in my head ever since I received it. . . . I do not seek *new* friends, not being altogether sure that I should find them, but have unspeakable pleasure in being still beloved by an old one. I hope that now our correspondence has suffered its last interruption, and that we shall go down together to the grave, chatting and chirping as merrily as such a scene of things as this will permit. . . . I cannot believe but that I should know you, notwithstanding all that time may have done: there is not a feature of your face, could I meet it on the road, by itself, that I should not instantly recolleɛt. I should say, that is my cousin's nose, or those are her lips and her chin, and no woman upon earth can claim them but herself. As for

me, I am a very smart youth of my years; I am not indeed
grown grey so much as I am grown bald. No matter:
there was more hair in the world than ever had the honour
to belong to me; accordingly having found just enough to
curl a little at my ears, and to intermix with a little of my
own, that still hangs behind, I appear, if you see me in an
afternoon, to have a very decent head-dress, not easily distinguished from my natural growth, which being worn
with a small bag, and a black ribband about my neck,
continues to me the charms of my youth, even on the
verge of age.'

Lady Hesketh, like Lady Austen, was of the world
without being worldly, and while she delighted Cowper
by the peculiar quickness of taste with which she relished
what she liked, her temperament was far more equable
than Lady Austen's. She confessed in one of her letters
that 'that passive spirit which is often honour'd by the
name of good-nature . . . is not a sort of goodness which
suits my taste,' yet her own good-nature was as consistent
as her good-sense.

Very early in their correspondence she begged Cowper
to tell her if she could help him financially, and it was
doubtless with her knowledge that he began to receive
anonymous gifts, including a yearly annuity of £50, from
her sister, Theodora. Cowper seems to have attributed
them to her father, Ashley Cowper, but he constituted
her as his 'Thank-receiver-general.'

The necessity, as he remarked, of writing all his letters
in the same terms, always thanks – thanks at the beginning and thanks at the end, was a pleasant employment

when those thanks were indeed the language of the heart. And her gifts were as valuable for breaking the monotony of his days as for gratifying in small ways his sense of elegance. They were events eagerly anticipated both for themselves and as a tangible token of affection. 'Neither can I at all doubt,' he wrote, 'that if you were to tell me that all the men in London of any fashion at all wore black velvet shoes with white roses, and should also tell me that you would send me such, I should dance with impatience till they arrived. Not because I care one farthing of what materials my shoes are made, but because any shoes of your sending would interest me from head to foot.'

And when he received a writing-desk of cedar, beautifully lacquered, mounted with silver and inlaid with ivory, his delight knew no bounds. 'Oh, that my letter,' he exclaimed, 'had wings, that it might fly to tell you that my desk, the most elegant, the compactest, the most commodious desk in the world, and of all the desks that ever were or ever shall be, the desk that I love the most is safe arrived. . . . My precious cousin, you have bestowed too much upon me. I have nothing to render you in return, but the affectionate feelings of a heart most truly sensible of your kindness. How pleasant it is to write upon such a green bank!'

Nature might be wintry without, but summer was in his heart, and the dark and dangerous months passed more happily than for many a year. His gratitude even flowed out beyond the person of his cousin to life itself. 'Mine has been a life of wonders for many years,' he wrote, 'and a life of wonders I in my heart believe it will be to the end. Wonders I have seen in the great deeps, and wonders I shall see in the paths of mercy also.' A new earth was overarched by a new heaven.

And when in February, 1786, Lady Hesketh promised to visit Olney, he hugged the prospect of his felicity with a glee which fully bore out his assertion that 'I am neither young nor superannuated, yet am I a child.' 'I shall see you again,' he told her. 'I shall hear your voice. We shall take walks together. I will show you my prospects, the hovel, the alcove, the Ouse, and its banks, everything that I have described. I anticipate the pleasure of those days not very far distant, and feel a part of it at this moment. Talk not of an inn! Mention it not for your life! We have never had so many visitors, but we could easily accommodate them all. . . . My dear, I will not let you come till the end of May or beginning of June, because before that time my greenhouse will not be ready to receive us, and it is the only pleasant room belonging to us. When the plants go out we go in. I line it with mats; and there you shall sit with a bed of mignonette at your side, and a hedge of honey-suckle, roses, and jasmine; and I will make you a bouquet of myrtle every day.'

And now all his thoughts were set upon finding a house for her and counting the days of separation, which had for so long seemed permanent that the prospect of meeting her was as miraculous as a resurrection from the dead. His cousin even invaded the dark province of his dreams. He dreamed that, sitting in the summer-house, he saw her coming towards him, sprang up with inexpressible pleasure, caught her in his arms, and said, 'Oh my precious,

precious cousin, may God make me thankful that I see thy face again!' And the satisfactory part of this dream, as he remarked, was that it promised to be realized.

After much house-hunting the Vicarage was once more secured as a residence, all anxiety seemed at an end, and he could write, with a side-glance it may be at a former occupant as well as at a popular song, – 'Come then, my beloved cousin, for I am determined that, whatsoever king shall reign, you shall be *Vicar* of Olney.' And he added the assurance that she need not fear 'religious conversation,' that pulpits were for preaching and the parlour, the garden and the walk abroad for friendly and agreeable talk.

April brought fears of a two months' delay, and he confessed that with very little encouragement he could actually have cried, but a week later he was easy in his mind again. 'That's my good cousin!' he wrote, 'now I love you! now I will think of June as you do, that it is the pleasantest of all months, unless you should happen to be here in November too, and make it equally delightful.'

The grass, he remarked, was beginning to grow, the leaves to bud, and everything was preparing to be beautiful against she came. And he vowed that he would be beautiful too, that no fit of dejection could seize him with one in whose company he had never been unhappy a whole day in his life.

Another month ran by, and every day he thought of her, and almost all the day long, and the imminence of what had grown by expectation to be one of the most

extraordinary eras of his extraordinary life excited flutter-
ings and tumults and a mixture of something painful at
the heart of his delight. He had determined to meet his
cousin at Newport, and as he pictured himself setting out,
heard the wheels of the carriage eating up the miles, and
visualized the ecstatic crisis of their meeting, he felt that
the pleasure and the pain together would be as much as
he would be able to support.

Lady Hesketh wisely advised him to await her at Olney,
and so Kitch, the gardener, was deputed to meet her
at the Swan in Newport, clothed, the better to play the
part of proxy, in a smart blue coat with white buttons that
had once belonged to his master.

Cowper promised to be as philosophically careful as
possible of his fine nerves, and to ease his anxiety and anticipate the moment of arrival he sketched in detail what
would meet his cousin's eye as she entered the house.
Nature, too, was an aid to self-forgetfulness. The grass
under the windows of his summer-house was all be-
spangled with dew-drops as he wrote early in the morning, and the birds were singing in the apple-trees, among
the blossoms.

Hope sang with them in his heart. If the letters of his
cousin had wrought such a change in him for the better,
surely her presence might heal even a wound so deep-
seated as his.

§ 2

In mid-June Lady Hesketh arrived and the church
bells were rung in her honour. Twenty years had passed

since she had left Cowper speechless in his chambers in the Temple, and he had said in his heart – 'Farewell! there will be no more intercourse between us for ever.' Ten more years were to run before he was to repeat that farewell with an anguish heightened by the remembrance of new joys which he had shared with her. Much, indeed, of the happiness which he did experience during these years he owed to Lady Hesketh, and the five months which immediately followed her arrival rank with the first summer which Lady Austen spent at Olney, as perhaps the happiest in his life.

Her first appearance was too much for him; his spirits broke down under the pressure of too much joy and left him flat and melancholy. But he quickly recovered. His expectations seemed fully realized. She was the kindest relation that ever man was blessed with, pleased everybody and was pleased in her turn with everything, was always cheerful and sweet-tempered, and knew no pleasure equal to that of communicating pleasure to all around her. In short, she was, as ever, his pride and his joy, and he was convinced that her presence was a cordial of which he would feel the effect, not only while her visit lasted, but while he lived.

Lady Hesketh's carriage, too, helped to enlarge his world and she encouraged him to be more social. She wished him particularly to see as much of the Throckmortons as possible with ease to himself, being sure that a little variety of company and a little cheerful society were necessary to him. And soon Cowper could write that their reserve and his was wearing off.

To drive out in a carriage, however, or take tea at the Hall was a sign of sin among the strict Evangelicals of Olney, and when rumour informed Newton that Cowper was becoming a gentleman of fashion, he made a last effort to assert his clerical authority. He wrote accusing Cowper directly, and Mrs. Unwin by implication, of deviating into forbidden paths and leading a life unbecoming the Gospel, of conversing too much with people of the world, and finding too much pleasure in doing so. He added that he never so much doubted of his restoration to Christian privileges as now, and ended with a baleful reminder that there was still an intercourse between London and Olney, and that Cowper could not offend against the decorum, which he was bound to observe, but the news of it would most certainly be conveyed to him.

Doubtless Newton wrote, as Cowper acknowledged, with the best motives, but the letter is a further proof of his bigoted blindness to the needs of natures which differed from his own. Stated crudely, he preferred Cowper to be a mad Evangelical, than a sane and social gentleman. For ten years he had received assurance of his unhappiness with sympathetic equanimity; but a mere rumour of his enjoyment provoked an immediate remonstrance. He wished him to be cured, but only by his prescriptions, which, in fact, perpetuated the disease. To the end of his days he believed that the years in which Cowper served Evangelicism as 'a burning and a shining light' were 'a life of heaven upon earth,' and that he had never 'had a comfortable hour since the last day of his attendance upon public worship.'

Fortunately, however, he could no longer enforce his view. Cowper in a letter, perfect in temper and dignity, refuted his desire for 'a prudish abstinence' from the mild dissipation of taking tea at the Throckmortons or at Gayhurst or of driving to Bozeat turnpike and back again, and he added that the two families with which they had 'kicked up this astonishing intercourse' were as harmless in their conversation and manners as could be found anywhere. And when, in November, 1786, he moved from Orchard Side to Weston Lodge, a house belonging to the Throckmortons and within easy reach of the Hall, the intimacy upon which Newton frowned was sealed by a constant interchange of hospitality.

He left his old prison with something like heartache and with tears in his eyes, but the new house which Lady Hesketh had furnished, which stood on higher and healthier ground, and was as commodious as Orchard Side had been cramped, more than reconciled him to the change.

He had a neat, warm and silent study which looked out on an orchard of trees and a pretty village. Here he installed his linnets and his cats, hung two landscapes by Vernet on the walls, and two by Rubens, with some engravings illustrating Homer and an engraving of Homer himself, arranged his few books in the chiffonnier, and seated at his lacquered desk in one of the cambric muslin caps made for him by Lady Hesketh, wrote to her, – 'You must always understand, my dear, that when poets talk of cottages, hermitages, and such-like things, they mean a house with six sashes in front, two comfortable parlours, a smart staircase, and three bedchambers of convenient dimensions; in short, exactly such a house as this.'

For Lady Hesketh had left Olney in the same month that the move to Weston was made. She had satisfied all her cousin's expectations except the ultimate one. He had begun to hope that, having walked the whole breadth of the Red Sea, he was beginning to climb the opposite shore; he had even prepared to sing the song of Moses. But now he confessed his disappointment. The miracle had not occurred.

Indeed, it was so far from having occurred that two months after her going, his spirits were once more eclipsed. In the interval William Unwin had died suddenly of typhus. But although the loss of so cheerful a friend and correspondent must have depressed him, he loved life too little, and envied the dead, who could no longer be forsaken, too much to sorrow unduly. Yet it is plain that the habitual acquiescence in the dispensations of Providence which supported Mrs. Unwin in her loss commanded more than ever from him a mere lip-service. He had to admit that Unwin had been taken at the very moment in his life when there seemed to be more urgent want of him than ever before, at an age when he was pre-eminently useful to his family, his friends and the world. 'These are mysteries,' he wrote to Lady Hesketh, 'that we cannot contemplate without astonishment,' and although he insisted that they 'must be revered in silence,' his silence was increasingly uneasy.

Indeed very soon after, for almost the only time in his life and actually in a letter to Newton, he confessed to

doubts of the perfect justice of Providence, 'though conscious that such questions ought to be suppressed.' He
was writing of the wretched lot of slaves before Emancipation. 'Is it essential,' he inquired, 'to the perfection of a
plan concerted by infinite wisdom, that such wretches
should exist at all, who from the beginning of their being,
through all its endless duration, can experience nothing
for which they should say, It is good for us that we were
created? These reasonings, and such as these engage me
often. . . . I know . . . that the answer to which it lies
open is this, or somewhat like it, – God is sovereign. All
are His, and He may do what He will with His own. . . .
And lastly – All these things will be accounted for and
explained hereafter. An answer like this would have satisfied me once, when I was myself happy. . . . But in
the school of affliction I have learned to cavil and to
question . . .?'

Doubtless Newton regarded such questions as a logical
by-product of Lady Hesketh's carriage and tea at the
Throckmortons. But if Cowper could have pressed them
resolutely, he might have emancipated himself alike from
meaningless optimism and meaningless pessimism. As
Keats was to write, – 'Until we are sick, we understand
not . . . we see not the balance of good and evil; we are
in a mist . . . we feel the "Burden of the Mystery". . . .
Now if we live, and go on thinking, we . . . shall explore
them.' Had Cowper been capable of exploring those
dark Passages, of a 'stepping of the imagination towards
new Truth,' he might, even now, have emerged into
the light.

But his mind did not 'perfectly recover its tone' after the shock of Unwin's death. He missed his cousin and the dreaded months were upon him. The 'uncontrollable sovereignty' which he had dared to question reasserted its sway, and on the 24th of January, 1787, he was once more deranged. The attack was preceded and accompanied, to a greater extent than its predecessors, by positive physical symptoms. He suffered from giddiness and headache, 'jarrings,' as he wrote, 'that made my scull feel like a broken egg-shell.' But the basic cause was, once again, an efflux of vitality. The whole complaint, as his doctor told him, 'was owing to relaxation,' and he himself defined the same condition in mental terms when he wrote, – 'The mind of man is not a fountain, but a cistern; and mine, God knows, a broken one.'

He was drained of life for six months, during which time the sight of anyone but Mrs. Unwin was intolerable, and he tried twice to hang himself. And then suddenly he recovered. But now more than ever the past was a pledge for the future. He could enjoy the society of the Throckmortons, could drive over to Chicheley to visit 'the most companionable and domestic Mr. Chester' and his multitudinous family, could make a gravel walk for winter use under a warm hedge in the orchard, look forward to his cousin's return, and, to all appearance, be as full of fun as ever.

But never again could he pretend to hope. He was at the mercy of incalculable forces. 'It is a sort of April-weather life,' he wrote, 'that we lead in this world. A little sunshine is generally the prelude to a storm.' Life flattered him for the moment; it would spurn him when it chose and when he least expected it. He had ceased to cherish any elusion. He knew that he had put out new leaf, only to wither again.

§ 3

Behind the hope and disillusionment of these four years lay a routine of industry. After the completion of *The Task* Cowper had tried for some time to proceed in the same track, but found it impossible. It may be that he had exhausted the vein of originality which he possessed as a poet of nature, or rather that he had made all the 'new discoveries' in the Olney landscape which he could. The limits of his temperament and of his province worked together to suggest that a continuation on these lines could only involve repetition. Later, indeed, in *Yardley Oak*, he was to combine, as he had never quite succeeded in doing in *The Task*, fidelity to the fact of nature with personal reflection. But he needed to leave nature as a poet before he could return to her with a difference.

Meanwhile his incapacity depressed him as much as his idleness. He took up the *Iliad* and, merely to divert attention and with no preconception of what he was entering upon, translated the first twelve lines. Thus in typical fashion he began a labour which was to occupy him with some intermission for the rest of his life. That for some years it proved an agreeable and salutary diversion is certain, but there came a time when he began to wonder why it pleased God that he should be hunted into so enormous and laborious a business. And although in his

last melancholy days he derived some faint comfort from
revising his revisions of Homer, the weight of the undertaking, before it was finished, was to press hard upon his
spirits.

To some extent he owed his impulse as a translator to
Lady Austen. For he had read her Pope's translation, and
when he grumbled at it, she suggested that he himself
should make the simpler version for which he clamoured.
But Lady Austen only revived an ancient project, dating
from the days when Cowper read the *Iliad* and *Odyssey*
with his friend Alston at Westminster, comparing them
with Pope's translation, while his love and admiration for
the original increased in proportion to his distaste for a
version which so thoroughly disguised it.

It was, indeed, as much a distaste for Pope's bedizening
as an admiration of the original which inclined him to the
venture. And in a letter, signed 'Alethes,' to the *Gentleman's Magazine* in August, 1795, he prepared the way for
his own translation by a reasoned criticism of Pope's,
which he described as 'Homer in a strait-waistcoat.' More
intimately he wrote to Lady Hesketh, – 'Homer, in point
of purity, is a most blameless writer; and, though he was
not an enlightened man, has interpreted many great and
valuable truths throughout both his poems. In short, he
is in all respects a most venerable old gentleman, by an
acquaintance with whom no man can disgrace himself.
The literati are all agreed to a man, that although Pope
has given us two pretty poems under Homer's titles, there
is not to be found in them the least portion of Homer's
spirit, nor the least resemblance of his manner. I will try,

therefore, whether I cannot copy him somewhat more
happily myself.'

And in a sense other than humorous Homer was for
Cowper something of a 'venerable old gentleman.' Later,
in excusing to Newton his absorption in a pagan poet, he
remarked that Homer might suggest reflections service-
able in a sermon, and that he inculcated constantly 'the
belief of a Providence.' At the same time he rejected
the theory that 'under Homer's narrative lay concealed a
mystic sense, sometimes philosophical, sometimes religious, sometimes moral,' confessing that he himself, except
here and there, discerned nothing more than the letter.

To Homer, in short, as a mythopoeic poet, as the
dynamic source of Greek religion and art, he was almost
wholly insensitive. He appreciated the natural simplicity
of the original enough to know the meretriciousness of
Pope's translation, but he lacked the natural energy which
dictated the simplicity. In this creative zest Pope was
indeed his superior. Even more so was Chapman, although
Cowper supposed that a man with so little taste for Homer
could only have undertaken the task for pecuniary advantage. Yet Chapman clearly derived more enjoyment from
translating the 13th book of the *Iliad* than Cowper, who
wrote, – 'Is it possible for a man to be calm, who for three
weeks past has been perpetually occupied in slaughter –
letting out one man's bowels, smiting another through the
gullet, transfixing the liver of another, and lodging an
arrow in the buttock of a fourth? . . . In order to interest
myself in it, and to catch the spirit of it, I had need discard
all humanity. It is woeful work.'

Any modern writer who has outgrown the aggressively primitive must sympathize with his feeling. But Cowper had nothing of the primitive in him. He lacked the staunch earthliness which underlay both the pagan virtues and vices, and which is the very sap of Homer. And so if Pope reduced some of Homer's characters 'to the perfect standard of French good-breeding,' he reduced them to that of a well-bred English gentleman, with a cultivated taste for the classics, a dislike of affectation and an appreciation of the simple elegances of life.

As he wrote, – 'There can be no dignity in simplicity unless it have elegance also, and that is the point at which I drive continually.' He drove at it industriously enough, although elegance seemed sometimes woefully out of place. He found it difficult, for example, 'to dignify in our language and in our measure the exact process of slaying a sheep and dressing it.' But he was 'careful to the utmost line of all possible caution, both with respect to language and versification.' Single lines cost him the labour of hours, so anxious was he to make it all 'smooth turnpike,' and true to his age's ideal of moderation, he strove to make his translation 'close, but not so close as to be servile; free, but not so free as to be licentious.'

And inevitably in the process only a shadow survived of the Homer whose poetry was governed by no such prudent considerations, but flowed from an organic fount of being. Homer never sacrificed beauty to embellishment, because he obeyed a creative impulse. But Cowper, in avoiding the decorative on conscious principle and from a merely verbal standpoint, sacrificed the beauty of life itself, its richness, strength and variety, to a prosaic smoothness. He tried to conceal its tedium by ingenious manipulation, as he tried to conceal its flatness by a gentle pomp. But his attempt to 'plough the fields of Troy' was foredoomed to failure, because he was too innately cultivated to plough the soils of life.

In this literary venture more than any other a lack of animal spirits was a fatal defect, which taste, judgment and industry could do little to supply. It was the least fertile, as it was the most laborious, of his diversions.

But at least it made him oblivious for many hours of the day to his surroundings. As soon as breakfast was over he retired to his 'verse manufactory,' and the afternoon, except for a walk, was devoted to the same daily self-imposed task of forty lines. It trespassed even upon his walks, during which he would set his foot on a molehill, place his hat, with the crown upward, on his knee, and pencil on scraps of paper some fragment upon which his mind had been working. Before the end of January, 1786, he had completed the *Iliad* and decided, after revision, to advance upon the *Odyssey*. Meanwhile he submitted specimens of his translation, and in one case the whole manuscript, to various critics, and was more teased than encouraged by their remarks, hints, suggestions and objections.

Vowing, however, with Lady Hesketh to hang all these critics together, he pushed doggedly on. The derangement of 1787 compelled a stoppage, but he resumed in November. Physically, however, he was far from recovered. Like Coleridge, he was 'so well admonished of

every change in the atmosphere by his bodily feelings,
as hardly to have any need of a weather-glass to mark
them,' and he complained of a stomach that would digest
nothing and of a fever which was only 'not worth a
thought,' because he had had more or less of it almost all
his life.

Transcribing Homer under such conditions was heavy
work. 'As when an ass,' he wrote, 'being harnessed with
ropes to a sand-cart, drags with hanging ears his heavy
burden, neither filling the long echoing streets with his
harmonious bray, nor throwing up his heels behind,
frolicksome and airy, as asses less engaged are wont to do,
so I . . . seldom allow myself those pretty little vagaries,
in which I should otherwise delight.'

Yet in a braver moment he compared himself with
perfect impropriety to 'one of those flaming steeds harnessed to the chariot of Apollo, of which we read in the
works of the ancients,' and the *Odyssey*, begun in September, 1788, was finished by the end of November, 1789.

He began it in the mellow trance of late summer.
'Here is no noise,' he wrote, '*save* (as the poets always
express it) that of the birds hopping on their perches and
playing with their wives, while the sun glimmering
through the elm opposite the window falls on my desk
with all the softness of moonshine. There is not a cloud
in the sky, nor a leaf that moves.' And a dry winter,
pleasant for walking, and Lady Hesketh's return favoured
his progress. His nights were no longer troubled by fantastic anxieties because she had not written for a fortnight.
The winter glided merrily away while she was with him,

annihilating the difference between cold and heat, gloomy skies and cloudless.

Nevertheless, he approached the end of the *Odyssey* with flagging spirits. The muse of fire which he invoked did not descend from heaven, and although he felt some pride in his accomplishment, it had become a weary business. Lady Hesketh's cheerfulness, however, sustained him through a wet summer and autumn, and without a break he applied himself to a final revision, like a prisoner in the Bastille 'counting the nails in the door for variety's sake in all directions.' His revision was so thorough that it occupied him for more than a year, and it was not until July, 1791, that his Homer at last appeared.

He was happy in his release from an oppressive labour, and sufficiently pleased with his application to think that he had 'licked the clumsy cub into a shape that will secure to it the favourable notice of the public.' For the rest of his life he was to try intermittently to improve its shape, clinging to this dead monument of patient industry with a pathetic appreciation of its sheer bulk. Happily, too, the five hundred subscribers collected by zealous friends and the qualified praise of Thurlow, Mrs. Montague, and others went far to persuade him that the monument was not as dead as time was soon to prove it.

§ 4

Meanwhile the dark cloud which was to banish finally the sun from Cowper's life had begun to gather. In January, 1789, Mrs. Unwin, who had long been troubled with pain in her side, got a terrible fall on the ice-covered gravel. She was partially crippled for three months, and Cowper feared that she must have received some greater hurt than he was at first aware of.

Certainly she never from this time recovered her normal health, and she began to suffer from constant headaches. The pain in her side, which no one understood, continued, and her lameness showed little improvement. She tried to conceal her indispositions to avoid worrying Cowper, and thereby only increased his anxiety. Others might enhance his sense of life, but to her he clung in his hours of living death. She was the one stable principle in an incalculable universe, the plank which had enabled him to regain the shore after successive shipwrecks. A threat to her well-being shook, as nothing else could, the ever quaking foundations of his world.

Fortunately there was little need yet to visualize the double desertion which awaited him, and for the time his world was peopled as never before. The fame which *The Task* had earned him continued to add to the number of his friends and correspondents, some of whom had the additional charm of youth.

Early in 1787, for example, a young student, Samuel Rose, paid the first of many visits, bringing the thanks of some of the Scotch professors to the poet of *The Task*. He was soon christened 'the Rosebud,' and his love of walking led his host to Kilwick Wood and Yardley Chase, where they discovered a fine old hollow oak, which was to evoke perhaps the deepest harmonies which Cowper wrung from nature.

But it was within his own family that he discovered the

most devoted and appreciative of friends. In January, 1790, a young kinsman on his mother's side, John Johnson, arrived with some poetry which he asked Cowper to criticize, pretending at first that it came from Lord Howard, but later confessing that it was his own. Cowper was suffering at the time from his usual fears of the full moon and the fatal month, numbering the nights as they passed and in the morning blessing himself that another had gone and no harm had happened. The incursion of an impulsive, bashful and scatter-brained undergraduate was therefore very welcome, and he at once conceived a great affection for the 'wild boy,' who had his mother's blood in his veins.

'Johnny of Norfolk,' as he soon came to be called, charmed by his simplicity of character and a most agreeable kind of humour. He played the fiddle and disported himself like a good-natured puppy. 'Yours, my dear Johnny,' wrote his gratified cousin, 'are vagaries that I shall never see practised by any other; and whether you slap your ancle, or reel as if you were fuddled, or dance in the path before me, all is characteristic of yourself, and therefore to me delightful. . . . Continue to take your walks, if walks they may be called, exactly in their present fashion, till you have taken orders. Then, indeed, for as much as a skipping, curvetting, bounding divine might be a spectacle not altogether seemly, I shall consent to your adoption of a more grave demeanour.'

Soon Cowper treated him as a son, and he was to serve him with truly filial devotion. Fate, indeed, which had robbed him in childhood of a mother, made some tardy amends by consoling his old age with the affection of members of his mother's family. Among these was his cousin, Mrs. Bodham, who now became one of his correspondents and sent him a portrait of his mother which he received 'with a trepidation of nerves and spirits somewhat akin to what I should have felt, had the dear original presented herself to my embraces. I kissed it and hung it where it is the last object that I see at night, and, of course, the first on which I open my eyes in the morning.'

The lines which it evoked were written not without tears, but tears of pleasure as well as of sorrow, and nowhere else perhaps did he subdue the rhymed couplet so completely to the needs of his nature. All its hard conceit is dissolved in warmth and softness. It has ceased to be the medium of Pope and awaits the ardent indolence of the young Keats.

And so, although he felt at times that his day was beginning to shut in, as every man's must who is on the verge of sixty, Johnny and his sister Catherine, 'with a smile so like my mother's that in this cousin she seems almost restored to me again,' and other Norfolk relatives encouraged a backward rather than a forward glance, and one that leapt the imprisoned years.

Age lost its sting and youth revived in a heart which time might wound but could never harden. As he wrote with playful tenderness to one of his newly discovered cousins, – 'Do you consider, child, that when you call yourself an old woman, you make it impossible for me to be young? Know you not that it is forty years since we saw each other; that I was at that time at least two years

older than you and consequently, I continue to be so still?
How then can you be old, when I, who am so much your
elder, have still, as Falstaff says, a smatch of my youth, and
am almost as active as ever? Oh, when shall we ride in
a whiskum snivel again, and laugh as we have done
heretofore?'

And the spirit of youth was alive in the world. On the
14th of July, 1789, the Bastille had been stormed, and on
the 5th of October the King and his family had been
compelled to move from Versailles to Paris. Cowper was
too old and cautious to share the bliss which a young poet,
who was so greatly to transcend him, felt merely 'in that
dawn to be alive.' But he had denounced the Bastille in
The Task, and the news of its fall must have gratified him.
He was sympathetic, too, to the early Revolutionary demands, remarking that 'the French, who like all lively
folks are extreme in everything, are such in their zeal for
freedom. . . . Perhaps it deserves not much to be wondered at, that at their first escape from tyrannic shackles
they should act extravagantly and treat their Kings as they
sometimes treated their idols. . . . They want nothing
now but a little English sobriety, and that they want
extremely.'

He boldly denounced, too, the riots against Priestley by
supporters of the Church and King, considering that never
was religious zeal more terribly manifested or more to the
prejudice of its own cause, and he read in events a lesson
for his own country, being convinced that the hour was
come when power founded in patronage and corrupt
majorities must govern the land no longer.

But while he condemned the interference of Austria and Prussia, its consequences inevitably shocked him into a violent antipathy. His daily toast had been 'Sobriety and Freedom to the French,' but they were proved too destitute of the former to justify it any longer; and when news came of the execution of Louis XVI, the 'old Whig' which he claimed to be was finally outraged. 'I will tell you,' he wrote, 'what the French have done. They have made me weep for a King of France, which I never thought to do, and they have made me sick of the very name of liberty, which I never thought to be. Oh, how I detest them!'

Of all worldly events, however, he was no more than a detached spectator. He had not, like Wordsworth, ventured a faith in the French Revolution, and so he had not to suffer its loss. The arrival of a periwig, 'the very perfection of all periwigs,' apart from the fact that his head would only go into the first half of it, was a more engrossing topic; or a farmer's dog by which he was in danger of being devoured, until he warned its owner that when he went forth to ramble in the fields, he did not sally like Don Quixote with a purpose of encountering monsters.

For the honours of the world, too, he had as little taste as for its infamies. When in May, 1790, by the death of Thomas Warton, the laureateship fell vacant, Cowper was named as a possible successor. But at the first rumour of it he drew back. 'Heaven guard my brows from the wreath you mention,' he wrote to Lady Hesketh, who had offered her best services in his cause; 'it would make me miserable.' The necessity of going to Court or kissing hands was in itself prohibitive.

And so for more than two years the threatening cloud still but hovered upon the horizon. Sometimes events reminded him of it and he cast a fearful glance into the future. 'To a greater trial no man can be called,' he wrote in August, 1790, to Newton, whose wife was seriously ill, 'than that of being a helpless eye-witness of the sufferings of one he loves.' And two months later he remarked, – 'What would become of me on a similar occasion? I have one comfort and only one; bereft of that, I should have nothing left to lean on; for my spiritual props have long since been struck from under me.'

But through 1791 the sort of April-weather life continued. With Homer completed, he found himself, after five years of perpetual versification, a vacant man. And in spite of Johnson's diverting company and some trouble with his eyes, he could not afford the luxury of idleness. He tried to revert to original verse, but could write nothing that would satisfy, although 'The Four Ages of Man,' which was suggested as a subject, appealed to him.

'The Four Ages,' however, was to remain 'a brief fragment of an extensive projected poem.' For his publisher now invited him to supervise an edition of Milton which was to be illustrated by Fuseli and to rival, and if possible exceed in splendour, Boydell's Shakespeare. His proposed duties were to translate the Latin and Italian poems, settle the text, select notes from others and writes notes of his own.

It happened that a few months before he had been re-

reading Milton's Latin poems with particular attention.
He was, too, as his own poetry shows, a devout admirer of
Milton, but his immobility was a grievous handicap to
research and he had had no experience of annotation. A
sense, however, of his own bankruptcy as a poet inclined
him 'to drudge, in descant dry, on others' lays,' and a similar sense of bankruptcy as a man dictated the manner in
which he came to a decision. For it was not his scholarly
equipment which he considered in the last resort, but
whether he was providentially called. And the oracle
which he consulted was an omen of the darkness which
was descending upon his days.

§ 5

For ten years at least Cowper had made occasional
reference in his letters to Samuel Teedon, the village
schoolmaster. His visits were described as more tedious
than entertaining, and his habit of discoursing with an
eloquence peculiar to himself 'on the many providential
interpositions that had taken place in his favour' was
ridiculed in *Conversation*. Cowper admitted that with all
his foibles he was a deserving man, but he accounted him
the prince of all bores. 'At Olney,' he wrote in 1785,
'I have a Mr. Teedon to dread, who in his single person
includes the disagreeables of them all. He is the most
obsequious, the most formal, the most pedantic of all
creatures, so civil that it would be cruel to affront him, and
so troublesome that it is impossible to bear him. Being
possessed of a little Latin, he seldom uses a word that is
not derived from that language, and being a bigot to

propriety of pronunciation, studiously and constantly lays
the accent upon the wrong syllable. I think that Sheridan
would adore him.'

When *The Task* was published, Mr. Teedon read it with
care and, as if fearful that its author had overlooked some
of them himself, pointed out to him all its beauties. 'I do
assure you,' wrote Cowper of the incident, 'the man has
a very acute discernment, and a taste that I have no fault
to find with.' After the derangement of 1787 Cowper
softened a little towards him, but he still knew him for
what he was. 'Poor Teedon,' he wrote, 'has never missed
calling here once, and generally twice a week since
January last. The poor man has gratitude, if he has not
wit. . . . I blame myself often for finding him tiresome,
but cannot help it.'

Now, however, this pompous and eccentric schoolmaster was suddenly elevated to the office of private
confessor. His claims to be heaven's special favourite and
a medium for God's messages were accepted without a
smile. He was to receive £20 a year for being 'fervently
engaged in prayer' on Cowper's behalf, a stipend which
he called '*Dona Dei*,' while betraying considerable anxiety
each quarter lest it should be discontinued. The vanity
which he had indulged in persistent calls upon a poet and
a social superior was henceforth gratified beyond his
wildest hopes. For it lay with him now even to sanction
his patron's literary activities.

After earnest prayer he reported that Heaven approved
the editing of Milton, and Mrs. Unwin wrote in acknow-
ledgment, – 'Mr. Cowper desires Mrs. Unwin to acquaint

Mr. Teedon that his anxiety did not arise from any
difficulties he apprehended in the performance of the
work, but in uncertainty whether he was providentially
called to it or not. He is now clearly persuaded, by Mr.
Teedon's experience and gracious notices, that he is called
to it, and is therefore perfectly easy.'

Events were to disprove Mr. Teedon's inspiration in
this as in all other matters, but Cowper clung to the
delusion of his infallibility as long as he could. He made
Mr. Teedon the interpreter of his dreams, and from
October, 1791, to February, 1794, he saw, wrote, or heard
from him almost every day. Teedon, as the diary which
he kept shows, was as much deluded by self-importance
as his victim by self-despair. He played the oracle quite
sincerely, with a solemn unction which veiled, if it did
not remove, the embarrassing inconsistency between his
claims and his performance.

For Cowper had soon to complain that 'your experiences and mine make a series of exact contradictions.'
And like all who resort to drugs, whether spiritual or
physical, he found eventually that the narcotic aggravated
the disease. Doubtless at first it afforded him some relief
to confide his terrors to another, but he was in fact
entering upon a course of morbid indulgence which
sapped the little independence of mind which remained
to him.

Even more ominous was Mrs. Unwin's collaboration.
She had ceased to be a prop on which he could lean. Her
mental and moral strength was failing with her bodily.
She was sinking into the stagnant pool of fictitious piety

which had always threatened, but never before submerged, her good-sense.

And then on December 17, 1791, the cloud that had so long hung upon the horizon darkened the sky. As Cowper was sitting at his desk near the window and Mrs. Unwin at the fireside, he heard her suddenly exclaim, 'Oh, Mr. Cowper, don't let me fall!' He turned and saw her actually falling, together with her chair, and started to her side just in time to prevent her.

It was a stroke, which for a time deprived her of the use of her legs and attacked her sight and speech. Fortunately Lady Hesketh was with them, and the patient recovered rapidly enough to suggest that Teedon's prayers were answered. But the blow had fallen on Cowper with all the refinements of mental torture, and although he could forget himself a little in tending Mrs. Unwin and take pleasure in marking her daily improvement, he felt the shock, as he wrote, in every nerve. It was not so much the event itself, as what it portended which appalled him. Another such stroke, he was convinced, would completely overset him, and the dread of it was to darken every day and almost every hour of reasonable life which remained to him.

'She has been,' he wrote, 'my faithful and affectionate nurse for many years, and consequently has a claim on all my attentions. She has them, and will have them as long as she wants them.'

Nobly he honoured his vow, and at a pathetic cost to his own well-being. For increasingly, as Mrs. Unwin became more dependent and exacting, it prevented him

from exercising the two activities, country walks and
literary labour, which had reinforced his sanity. Instead,
he was tied to the side of one whose very feebleness was
a perpetual reminder of the doom which awaited him,
and for consolation he could only turn to Mr. Teedon,
whose assurance of overwhelming grief and sorrow on the
receipt of mournful letters was as ineffectual a restorative
as his oracular promises.

'My experience,' Cowper wrote to him in February,
1792, 'is such as it is very difficult to reconcile with the
promises imparted to you on my behalf. My days are
spent without one symptom of spiritual life, and my nights
not seldom under a constant sense of God's contempt and
abhorrence.' And from this time his daily reports to the
quack consultant, whom Lady Hesketh named 'that Everlasting Persecutor,' were one long wail of despair inter-
ceding for reassurance, rising in a crescendo of bitterness
to sink at last in the grey silence of an exhausted credulity.

But before the creeping paralysis had reduced him as
well as Mrs. Unwin to impotence, he was to embark on
a first and last adventure. As if to shake off the spectres
that whispered in his ears and to taste liberty before the
prison gates finally closed, he was to defy the immobility
of twenty years and make a triumphant progress to the
south of Sussex.

§ 6

Three months after Mrs. Unwin's stroke Cowper received a letter and a sonnet from the poet Hayley. Hayley
had been engaged to write a life of Milton for a sumptuous

edition planned by the publisher Boydell, and the news-
papers represented him and Cowper as rivals. He wrote
to disclaim all competition, observing that the two works
were not of a character to clash, and expressing his
admiration of Cowper's poetry.

Cowper acknowledged the letter the same evening on
which he received it, assuring Hayley that every remark
of his on Milton would be highly valued. Within a month
the two poets were on such terms of intimacy that Cowper
could write, 'God grant that this friendship of ours may
be a comfort to us all the rest of our days,' and when
Hayley expressed some doubt of his ability to satisfy the
high moral standards of the poet of *The Task*, he replied, –
'No, my friend, fear not that I shall ever treat a mayflower,
as you, like a loathsome weed; if I know myself at all,
I am neither cruel nor capricious, and now I will be a fool
and tell you my dream. I dreamed last night that a beautiful red-breast, while I sat in the open air, flew to me and
perched on my knee. There it stood quietly awhile to be
stroked, and then crept into my bosom. I never in my
waking hours felt a tenderer love for anything than I felt
for the little animal in my sleep, and were it possible that
I could ever actually meet with such an incident, I could
as soon reject poor Bob and trample him under my foot,
for which I should deserve death, as I could show
unkindness to a certain William of Sussex.'

Such a letter is further proof of the readiness with
which Cowper 'felt a disposition of heart' towards anyone
who showed him sympathy. And Hayley's heart was
effusively warm. Lady Hesketh feared that his known

indifference to 'religious principles' would prove fatal to friendship. But Cowper was not the man to reject a friend because he had settled a mistress, who bore him a son, in his gardener's cottage when his marriage had proved a failure. And of Hayley's writings he only knew enough to say with perfect tact that he was greatly struck with the evident facility with which they were written.

But although Hayley was nearly fifteen years his junior, and lacked the qualities which linked Cowper with the coming age, the two poets had much in common. Both embraced through delicate health a life of retirement, and both professed a moral purpose. There was no acerbity in Hayley, as there was no depth. His morality was mildly hedonistic. He desired simply to 'promote the cultivation of good humour,' of which he was an agreeable example. His observation, he had said, of the various effects of spleen on the female character induced him to believe that he might render an important service to social life, if his poetry could induce his young and fair readers to cultivate the gentle qualities of the heart, and maintain a constant flow of good humour. With this view he composed his *Triumphs of Temper*, and he had once the gratification to hear from 'the very good and sensible mother of a large family, that she was indebted to that poem for a complete reformation in the character of her eldest daughter, who, from being perverse and intractable, was rendered by her ambition to imitate Serena, the most docile and dutiful of children.'

A friend who could maintain so potent a flow of good humour was a very valuable acquisition. And although

Hayley's reputation as a poet, based chiefly on his epistles in verse on Painting, History and Epic poetry, was in fact a tinsel one, it was considerable at the time. Cowper's life had been devoid of literary friendship, and even

> An English Sparrow, pert and free,
> Who chirps beneath his native tree,

enhanced his sense of the value of letters. And when Hayley arrived on a visit in the middle of May, and his face, far from paralysing friendly intentions, as his host had feared, proved as handsome as his disposition was amiable, it seemed possible that the poet in Cowper might take new heart.

Three days later, however, the two returned from a walk to find that Mrs. Unwin had had another seizure. This disaster put to the severest possible test the virtue of Hayley's buoyant nature and notably confirmed it. He took command of the household, procured an electrical machine for treatment, and, in Cowper's words, was 'all in all to us on this very afflictive occasion.' He not only softened the blow which Cowper had been convinced would completely overset him, but he minimized its seriousness by making his host promise to visit him with Mrs. Unwin at Eartham.

So successful were his efforts that within a few weeks Cowper could write to Lady Hesketh, – 'yet once again, I am willing and desirous to believe, we shall be a happy trio at Weston.' And when in a month Mrs. Unwin could walk with assistance upstairs and down, when she told him at his first visit in the morning that she had entirely forgoten her illness, it seemed as if he had been living in a dream.

Inevitably, however, after Hayley's departure, the dream tended to assume again the nature of a nightmare. For the more ambitious Mrs. Unwin became of independence, the more perpetual was the need of watchfulness. Even if she wished to move round the room, he had to travel with her. She had to be fed too, and since she could neither knit nor read, it seemed a cruelty to leave her for a moment unattended. Each new little feat which she accomplished was encouraging, but each served also to remind him of her feebleness, of the pitiful contractions of her muscles and the thickness of her speech. Little wonder was it that he felt that, had we eyes sharp enough, we should see the arrows of Death flying in all directions, or that he proclaimed a sable thread intermixed now with the very thread of his existence.

And there was a collateral anxiety. For his work on Milton was inevitably at a standstill and he chafed at the thought of failing his publisher in an expensive undertaking. Bitterly he wrote to Teedon, – 'Unbelief on my part in my present circumstances is unavoidable. In all my concerns I feel and see an express contradiction to every promise that you have ever received on my account, and particularly in the affair of Milton.'

Yet he continued to beg Teedon to accommodate his prayers to his condition. And how hopeless that condition was when his invalid had a bad day or night, Teedon only knew. 'I can attain . . . to no settled hope of her recovery,' he wrote to him after one such night. 'Every paralytic stroke exposes a person more to the danger of another, and I am in constant fear of a repetition. . . . My nocturnal experiences are all of the most terrible kind. Death, churchyards, and carcasses, or else thunder-storms and lightnings, God angry, and myself wishing that I had never been born. Such are my dreams; and when I wake it is only to hear something terrible, of which she is generally the subject. Who can hope for peace amid such trouble? I cannot. I live a life of terror. My prospects respecting this life as well as another seem all intercepted; I am incapable of proceeding in the work I have begun. . . .'

That his sufferings wanted the dignity and defiance of tragedy only adds to their pitifulness. The writhings of a gentle being in the torture-chamber offer us no catharsis, and when the torturers are phantoms of a fear-haunted mind, we are deprived even of the relief of hatred. For it was the poet in Cowper, the image-maker, that in the uncontrolled province of sleep translated the anxiety of the day into the terrible forms of nightmare, while the shuddering pietist in him seized upon any chance sentence that rose to the surface of consciousness at the moment of waking and proclaimed it a message from on high. Thus a simple line from *Comus*, 'the wonted roar is up amid the woods,' running in his head on waking, could poison a whole day with a conviction of fatality to come.

Laudanum, however, eased his nights, Johnson came and cheered his days, and when by the end of June Mrs.

Unwin could walk with support forty-two times the length of the gravel walk in the orchard, the journey to Eartham seemed possible. Teedon was asked to invoke the Lord for a word of direction and was informed somewhat ungrammatically, – 'Go, and I will be with him.'

To one who had 'seen no bustle, and made none, for twenty years together,' the mere prospect of travelling supplied a tonic excitement, so that in the midst of all his solicitudes he laughed to think what they were made of. 'Other men,' he wrote, 'steal away from their homes silently, and make no disturbance; but when I move, houses are turned upside down, maids are turned out of their beds, all the counties through which I pass appear to be in an uproar.'

Fortunately, too, Mrs. Unwin had no fears of the journey, and he began to hope that at Eartham he might recover the habit of study and that the sea air would restore them both. And when on August 1, attended by Johnson and accompanied by Beau, the dog, they set out on their three days' journey in a coach ordered for them by Abbot, who had just painted Cowper's portrait, the terrors by the way, which he had so agonizingly envisaged, failed to materialize.

Mrs. Unwin, despite the heat, was cheerful from beginning to end. Samuel Rose mitigated the halt at Barnet, and although Cowper was a little daunted 'by the tremendous height of the Sussex hills,' which they crossed by moonlight, they reached Eartham between nine and ten at night in excellent spirits.

Hayley proved a perfect host, and he did not exaggerate when he claimed for the 'elegant mansion' which he had enlarged from a summer-house that it was 'a little temple consecrated to Liberty and Friendship, where difference of opinion produces no hatred, and similarity of pursuit no jealousy.'

Surrounded by what Cowper called the most delightful pleasure grounds that he had ever seen, it stood on rising land overlooking a flat plain, patterned with fields, trees and hedges, finely pencilled or swimming in haze, which reached to the sea, upon the curve of which on clear days the Isle of Wight hung like a cloud. Behind the house the ground dipped into a deep well-cultivated valley enclosed by wooded downs.

At first Cowper found it, like Gibbon, a little Paradise. He was as happy as it was in the power of terrestrial good to make him. In the morning, before Mrs. Unwin came down, he studied Milton with Hayley and docilely accepted all his host's tinsel emendations. To be at work again was in itself a restorative, and his publisher put him at ease by assuring him that the edition would in any case be delayed. His fellow-guests, Mrs. Charlotte Smith, the novelist, and Romney, the painter, who insisted on drawing him in crayons, were unexacting, although he confessed that his long separation from the world had disabled him as a conversationalist.

Mrs. Unwin too was gaining strength; she crossed a room for the first time unassisted, and sunned herself in a Bath-chair which Hayley's son pushed about the grounds. Cowper's days were happy again; he seemed

to Johnson younger than he had ever known him
and to be laughing from morning to night. And he
remarked of the portrait in crayons which Romney drew
of him –

> that symptoms none of woe
> In thy incomparable work appear.
> Well; I am satisfied it should be so,
> Since, on maturer thought, the cause is clear;
> For in my looks what sorrow couldst thou see
> When I was Hayley's guest, and sat to thee?

But there was less truth in the nicely-turned compliment
than Romney guessed. For at night the remembrance of
his laughter did but deepen his gloom. He measured his
recovered youth against Mrs. Unwin's enfeeblement and
trembled for the solitude in which a few years must place
him.

And as the novelty of change wore off, he began
secretly to hunger for Weston. He confessed himself un-
accountably local in the use of his pen, and that, like the
man in the fable, who could leap well nowhere but at
Rhodes, he seemed incapable of writing at all, except at
Weston. At heart he was homesick for the countryside
which had become a part of his being. Its genius, he
wrote, 'suits me better, – it has an air of snug conceal-
ment, in which a disposition like mine feels itself
peculiarly gratified; whereas here I see from every
window woods like forests, and hills like mountains, – a
wilderness, in short, that rather increases my natural
melancholy, and which, were it not for the agreeables I

find within, would soon convince me that mere change of place can avail me little.'

Anything approaching the elemental was more than his spirits could bear. It seemed in league with those supernatural forces which hated his human identity and would plunge it in an abyss of nothingness.

And so, refusing Hayley's pressing invitation to prolong their visit into the New Year, he left Eartham on September 17, with tears, indeed, at parting, but rejoicing both for his own sake and Mrs. Unwin's at every turn of the wheel that brought them nearer home. A storm was raging when they reached it, and in the darkness Mrs. Unwin nearly slipped from the chair on which she was being carried in. It was a dismal home-coming, in keeping with the gloom which was now to hang over all his days until the last landmark of sanity was obliterated.

¶ PART SIX

WINTER'S WITHERING

WINTER'S WITHERING

§ I

THE inevitable reaction from excitement, the approach of winter and incessant rain, were but auxiliaries to the eternal nightmare of fear on Mrs. Unwin's account. Within a week all his sprightly chords were broken; soon he felt himself 'the most unpitied, the most unprotected, the most unacknowledged outcast of the human race.' And Mrs. Unwin was dejected like himself, dejected both on his account and on her own. Unable to amuse herself either with work or reading, she too looked forward to a new day with despondence, weary of it before it began, and longing for the return of night.

To trace the course of his sufferings through the year which followed would be but to perpetuate his torture. Yet never, perhaps, did a man show more heroism of a passive kind. He was deprived of all the weapons by which for twenty years he had fended despair. His walks were restricted to the orchard, and Mrs. Unwin hung upon his arm. It was hard to find time even to write a letter, since to hold a pen in his hand while she sat silent and looking at the fire too painfully emphasized her isolation. As to Milton, he exclaimed that he might almost as well be haunted by his ghost, as goaded with such continual reproaches for neglecting him. 'How often,' he wrote later, 'do I wish, in the course of the day, that I could be employed once more in poetry, and how often, of course, that this Miltonic trap had never caught me!'

Every kind of positive diversion was forbidden him, and

Teedon, James's powders, and laudanum were his only
resource. Yet during the day, and so long as he could be
of service to Mrs. Unwin, he held on to sanity. He was
helped to some extent by the nature of his weakness,
the afternoon and evening being, as he said, his best
times, not because he was more spiritual, but because
the animal in him had been recruited by eating and
drinking.

But he paid terribly at night for the heroic tension of
the day. Then he was plunged in deeps, unvisited, he
was convinced, by any human soul but his, or seemed to
be scrambling always in the dark among rocks and preci-
pices, without a guide, but with an enemy ever at his
heels, prepared to push him headlong. And often his very
finger-ends tingled with terror.

The enemy was God or Satan, he knew not which. And
this robbed him of any possible comfort which he might
have derived from the accidental words which he heard
on waking and attributed to a supernatural voice. For
even when he heard such a sentence as 'I love thee even
more than many who see thee daily,' he could not tell
'whether the dream was from a good source or not . . .
for it was accompanied with little or no sensation of a
spiritual kind.'

Yet while admitting that these phenomena were 'words
articulated merely, and unaccompanied with any power,'
he credited them with a profound import. He was driven,
therefore, to interpret their triviality as a sign of God's
derision, as he interpreted the encouraging answers which
Teedon professed to have received to his prayers as but

biting sarcasms, sharp strokes of irony, on the part of the Almighty.

Once again his very logic served to fix and aggravate his fearful delusions, and a typical example of calculating reason working within irrational experience is afforded by one of his dreams. He dreamed that he was taking a final leave of his dwelling, and of every object with which he had been most familiar, on the evening before execution. 'I felt,' he wrote, 'the tenderest regret at the separation, and looked about for something durable to carry with me as a memorial. The iron hasp of the garden-door presenting itself, I was on the point of taking that, but recollecting that the heat of the fire in which I was going to be tormented would fuse the metal, and that it would therefore only serve to increase my insupportable misery, I left it.'

The prudence which he practised in this dream was indeed the corollary of the panic which created the image of hell-fire. And it was because his logic was too narrow to inform either sub-rational or super-rational experiences, that he was imprisoned equally by both. His poetry attests this no less than his life. It was never wholly creative, in the sense that all his faculties, all the resources of his nature, were fused in an act of expression. The best of his lyrics survive by virtue of their simple tenderness, but the finest essence of poetry is not in them because his reason played a too conscious part in the process. Of the union and transformation of reason and feeling in imagination he was incapable. Yet only by such imagination could he have liberated and given true meaning to the feelings which, when they transcended gentle sentiment, attached themselves, for want of an inner reason of their own, to the dark forms of Calvinism or the fantastic and accidental images of sleep.

The occasional poems which he had continued to write ever since the completion of *The Task* were devoid of imagination. The majority of them were admittedly mere impromptus, always graceful and ingenious, but with little creative necessity. Yet even when he wrote of the misery which gnawed at his heart, he did so with a cool correctness –

> To me the waves that ceaseless broke
> Upon the dangerous coast,
> Hoarsely and ominously spoke
> Of all my treasure lost.
>
> Your sea of troubles you have past,
> And found the peaceful shore;
> I, tempest-tossed, and wrecked at last,
> Come home to port no more.

In writing thus, he stood as a rational being outside his suffering little less than he did in the conventional verses which he supplied for several successive years to the parish of All Saints', Northampton, to be annexed to its bill of Mortality. And it was because his reason had no inward share in the experience that it has so little reality as poetry, and was beyond his reach either to understand or to remedy.

Yardley Oak is indeed the only poem of his later life,

except the one into which he was to pour in a final
desperation something of dark ecstasy, which has any real
inwardness. It differs, indeed, from all his other verse, both
in its rhythmic sonorousness and its degree of reflective
imagination.

Yet we have only to compare it with the *Lines written
above Tintern Abbey*, which were to appear within but a few
years, to realize that although Cowper did something
more here than play the organ of Milton with a wholly
personal touch, the music has no overtones or undertones;
it is personal in idiom and arrangement, not in essence.
The vision is still external, and thought and feeling are
attached to the thing observed rather than identified
with it.

And even in the sonnet which he addressed to Mrs.
Unwin, when his sun was setting behind thickening
clouds through which only the faintest beams could penetrate, Milton was more evident than himself. Deeply
as he felt, he could not quite transcend a literary formality.

Mary! I want a lyre with other strings,
Such aid from Heaven as some have feigned they drew,
An eloquence scarce given to mortals, new
And undebased by praise of meaner things,
That, ere through age or woe I shed my wings,
I may record thy worth with honour due
In verse as musical as thou art true,
And that immortalizes whom it sings.
But thou hast little need. There is a book
By seraphs writ with beams of heavenly light,

On which the eyes of God not rarely look,
A chronicle of actions just and bright:
There all thy deeds, my faithful Mary, shine,
And, since thou own'st that praise, I spare thee mine.

It is a fine sonnet, but we never forget that its austerities
were borrowed from Milton and a little domesticated by
the borrower. Absolutely sincere as the feeling is, from
the first line, in which he disclaims truly enough a com-
pulsive inspiration, to the last, in which he deprecates the
value of his tribute, it is no more than tenderly judicial
throughout.

The lines *To Mary*, however, written six months later,
are of a far more personal quality. Only the refrain at the
end of each stanza fatigues the ear and suggests a literary
artifice. When sentiment is so true as it is in these lines,
we hardly feel the want of passion. Here, as in the best
passages in *The Task*, Cowper distilled poetry out of
fact, tenderly and delicately recorded. The affection and
gratitude of years, and a compassionate and self-reproach-
ful resignation to the ruin which the years had brought,
are in the lines, but they never overflow them. They are
simply stated, and their reality is known by the precise
fidelity of the statement. Never perhaps did human
affection prove its humble, unassertive, and permanent
worth more poignantly in the hour of time's defeat.

The twentieth year is well-nigh past
Since first our sky was overcast;
Ah, would that this might be the last,
                    My Mary!

Thy spirits have a fainter flow,
I see thee daily weaker grow;
'Twas my distress that brought thee low,
    My Mary!

Thy needles, once a shining store,
For my sake restless heretofore,
Now rust disused and shine no more,
    My Mary!

For though thou gladly wouldst fulfil
The same kind office for me still,
Thy sight now seconds not thy will,
    My Mary!

But well thou playedst the housewife's part,
And all thy threads with magic art
Have wound themselves about this heart,
    My Mary!

Thy indistinct expressions seem
Like language uttered in a dream;
Yet me they charm, whate'er the theme,
    My Mary!

Thy silver locks, once auburn bright,
Are still more lovely in my sight
Than golden beams of orient light,
    My Mary!

For, could I view nor them nor thee,
What sight worth seeing could I see?
The sun would rise in vain for me,
    My Mary!

Partakers of the sad decline,
Thy hands their little force resign:
Yet, gently prest, press gently mine,
                    My Mary!

And then I feel that still I hold
A richer store ten thousandfold
Than misers fancy in their gold,
                    My Mary!

Such feebleness of limbs thou provest,
That now at every step thou movest
Upheld by two, yet still thou lovest,
                    My Mary!

And still to love, though prest with ill,
In wintry age to feel no chill,
With me is to be lovely still,
                    My Mary!

But ah! by constant heed I know,
How oft the sadness that I show
Transforms thy smiles to looks of woe,
                    My Mary!

And should my future lot be cast
With much resemblance of the past,
Thy worn-out heart will break at last,
                    My Mary!

But, in fact, his heart was nearer breaking-point than hers. For one who could feel so tenderly and yet see so dispassionately as these lines show him to have done, no escape from the daily ordeal of pity and fear was possible. He had struggled hard against a deepening demoralization. He had risen at six in the morning to cut short the melancholy of his early hours and buried himself in Greek commentators, 'playing at push-pin with Homer . . . fingering and polishing, as Paris did his armour.' He had busied himself with the building of two summer-houses and a garden shed, and tried to forget himself in little spurts of humour.

But after Hayley's visit in November, 1793, he could struggle no more. His conviction that his next plunge would be into madness grew more intense. And when Lady Hesketh arrived at the end of the year she saw at once that he was at the end of his resources and must be rescued from a situation which was indeed terrible.

But although during the next few months both Johnson and Hayley came to her assistance, Cowper had then sunk into deeps of melancholy from which no human hand could rescue him. Sitting silent or walking incessantly backwards and forwards like a tiger in a cage, eating little and with 'something indescribable in his appearance,' he had ceased to hope or believe anything. Sane on all other subjects but that of God's anger towards him, he was equally at the mercy of poor Mrs. Unwin's disabled body and his own disabled mind.

And when in April, 1794, she was reduced to 'a dreadful spectacle' by another stroke, she became so irritable and exacting as to hinder all Lady Hesketh's attempts for his relief. 'If the Angel Gabriel,' Lady Hesketh wrote in despair, 'was to persuade her to let him leave her, she would not comply.' She dragged him round the garden, though even a strong man could scarce support her, and the weight of her upon his arm was as nothing compared to the weight upon his spirits. For he felt now not merely pity on her behalf and anxiety on his own, but self-contempt for having failed her and so alienated, as he thought, her affection. As the fragmentary diary, which he kept at this time, shows, he even interpreted the facial distortions of her paralysis as an undisguised expression of aversion from himself.

To a mind so stricken with self-hatred, the news that Hayley's efforts had at last succeeded and that he had been granted a pension, or the letters of appreciation which a number of prominent people wrote him at Hayley's instigation, could bring no comfort. They affected him as little as if he had been insensible. Clearly the only hope of restoring him lay in combating this insensibility by change of scene, and, in the process, weakening Mrs. Unwin's hold upon him.

A year before, Lady Hesketh had urged him in vain to leave Weston for Norfolk. But now he was too indifferent to resist. Home there could be for him nowhere so long as he was an outcast from life, who felt all the veins of his heart to be ossified. And even fields and woods, endeared by long association, were no more than scenic properties to one who could never 'take an interest in green leaves again.'

Yet homeless at heart as he now was, the thought of leaving Weston, if only for a time, as was at first suggested, could not but deepen his sense of isolation. And it was

as he sat brooding listlessly over this prospective sunder-
ing with everything in life to which he had clung for comfort that he received a message that a poor creature like
himself wished to see him. It was a good Quaker, William
Crotch, who, passing near Weston, felt a religious concern
to pay the stricken poet a visit, and who, on entering,
walked up to him and, without any other greeting, took
him by the hand and sat down by his side. For a whole
hour they thus sat hand in hand, without speaking a word.
And then Crotch said farewell and took his leave.

The scene haunts the memory like some benignant
rift in a lowering evening sky. Amid all the religious men
who were zealous on Cowper's behalf, how few of them
had the unpretentious humanity of this kindly Quaker.
How few could invoke the help and express the reality
of God through the hand of simple friendship.

Cowper had demanded so little of life, and life had punished his humility. His, if any man's, had been the charity which 'suffereth long and is kind, vaunteth not itself,
is not puffed up.' And it would seem as if fate and his religious counsellors had conspired to offer up his essentially Christian virtue on the altar of a semi-pagan Deity.

Had he but been encouraged in the days of his first distress to accept a God in his own image rather than one who
was his moral inferior, he might not now have crouched
before Him like 'a hunted hare,' or 'a poor Fly entangled
in a thousand webs from the beginning.' In good
Crotch's trust in the inner light he might have discovered
God as a creative spirit and been saved from that alien and
confused embodiment of creative and destructive natural-

ism to which Madan and Newton had bid him bow. For if his weakness was inherent, the theology which inflamed it was acquired. And in favourable circumstances he might as easily have gone forward to the conception of God the friend as sunk at the feet of God the enemy, might have come to hold that other creed which Helen Burns professes in *Jane Eyre*, which 'makes Eternity a rest – a mighty home, not a terror and an abyss; . . . with this creed revenge never worries my heart, degradation never too deeply disgusts me, injustice never crushes me too low; I live in calm, looking to the end.'

But all his inner light was now quenched. Two days before he left Weston for ever, he wrote in his diary, – 'My Despair is infinite, my entanglements are infinite, my doom is sure. Awoke this morning and lay awake 4 hours Oh in what agonizing terrours! I have, I can have no faith in this Norfolk journey, but am sure that either I shall never begin it, or shall never reach the place. Could ye spare me, what mercy should I account it.' And on the next day he wrote, – 'To-morrow to the intolerable torments prepared for me. See now, O God, if this be a doom, if this a condition such as a creature of thine could have deserved to be exposed to. I know that thou thyself wast not without thy fears that I should incur it. But thou wouldst set me on the slippery brink of this horrible pit in a state of infatuation little short of idiotism, and wouldst in effeᵭt say to me – Die this moment or fall into it, and if you fall into it, be it your portion for ever. Such was not the mercy I expeᵭted from Thee, nor that horror and over-whelming misery should be the only means of deliver-

ance left me in a moment so important! Farewell to the
remembrance of Thee for ever. I must now suffer thy
wrath, but forget that I ever heard thy name. Oh horrible!
and still more horrible, that I write these last lines with a
hand that is not permitted to tremble!'

To be compelled to pen his own death-sentence with all
the logical self-possession of a casuist, to revolt against the
inhumanity of a God Who could exact such punishment
and yet accept it as right and inevitable – therein lay the
particular horror of his situation. Never was a sense of
lifelessness so tragically translated by reason into a command from God Himself to commit suicide, or a failure
to do so haunted by more terrible imaginations of punishment to come.

For henceforth he was to live in daily anticipation of
being confronted with the choice either of destroying himself in some dreadful way to be revealed when the time
came, or of being literally torn in pieces by the diabolic
minions of a God whose inhumanity outraged human
decency, but whose claim to human reverence was nevertheless blindly upheld.

Never did an outgrown faith, a religion which was 'the
last refuge of human savagery,' work worse havoc in a
being too sensitive and rational to need or profit by its
taboos. And if his hand did not tremble when he wrote on
the window-shutter of his bedroom on his last morning at
Weston,

> Farewell, dear scenes, forever closed to me;
> Oh, for what sorrows must I now exchange ye!

it was because a universe, accepted as heartless, had numbed it. Just as positive experience culminates in a sense of identity with everything, so negative experience ends in a sense of utter nonentity. And he whose nerves have quivered long in an agony of fear is reduced at last to nerveless impotence.

§ 2

Five years of a posthumous existence still remained to him. He spent them all in Norfolk, at North Tuddenham, at Mundsley, on the coast, where he had played as a boy, at Dunham Lodge, near Swaffham, and at East Dereham. Johnson, who was as optimistic as he was assiduous in his attentions, still hoped to quicken life in him again by constant changes of scene. And at the outset his optimism seemed for the moment justified.

The travellers stopped the first night at Eton Socon, and as he walked up and down the moonlit churchyard with 'the little man' whose gambols had once provoked so many smiles, Cowper recovered a little spirit and talked of Thomson's *Seasons*. There was a sad propriety in the fact that the last gleam of cheerfulness which ever lit up his face should have occurred in such a place. For life in Cowper henceforth was eclipsed by death. He was a cistern which leaked too badly for the springs of life ever to fill to the level where a sense of pleasure in existence begins. He was the victim of a condition, which some of his romantic successors were to experience with a difference, the condition which Coleridge, for example, lamented in his *Dejection Ode*.

But Coleridge could still see, if he could not feel, how beautiful the heavens were, while Cowper, with his narrower mind and his weaker flow of animal spirits, could neither see nor feel. And superimposed upon his physical stagnation was a metaphysical dread. This dread was to some extent inherent, and it too was known to his romantic successors, having direct affinities with Wordsworth's

> Blank misgivings of a Creature
> Moving about in worlds not realized,
> High instincts before which our mortal Nature
> Did tremble like a guilty Thing surprised.

But here again his narrower mind, warped by an acquired Calvinism, converted these transcendent instincts from which Wordsworth drew a creative inspiration into a self-destructive obsession. His mind could not enlarge itself, could not achieve that new dimension in which the particular self is no longer terrified by the universal sea which it feels in moments of weakness and abasement to wash about it, but by fearlessly plunging into it becomes one with the eternal mind and forgets the trembling Creature in the fulfilled Creator.

The melancholy and the madness of several of Cowper's contemporaries were traceable to the same cause. Thinking to secure themselves by good-sense against the sensational forces of life, they had lost vital touch with its spirit. Their rational self-sufficiency failed to satisfy their emotional nature which hungered for self-enlargement, and they could not bring the two into harmony.

When Cowper longed unavailingly for a conviction of

God's forgiveness towards him, he longed, had he known it, that his nature might be brought into creative unity. God was his enemy because he felt a reality outside himself which threatened his narrow personal identity; and it remained external to him, and therefore terrifying, because his mind could not assimilate it, at once giving it meaning and receiving meaning from it.

He was mad because he was too negatively sane to extend his thought into regions of super-rational experience. He was dispossessed because he was too self-possessed. He was a moralist who could only have achieved moral well-being by becoming a mystic. How much his constitutional lack of animal spirits was the cause and how much the consequence of this spiritual impotence, it is impossible to say. Nor does the undoubted interaction of the two make it easier to answer his pathetic question – 'Why was existence given to a creature that might possibly, and would probably, become wretched in the degree that I have been so?'

During his last years his impotence was complete. To Lady Hesketh alone he wrote by stealth, finding some slight diversion in describing in detail such things as the structure of a lighthouse. But although he was soothed by the waves' monotony, the Furies were always at his back. He watched every vessel that approached the coast with an eye of jealousy and fear, lest it arrived with a commission to seize him, and he found in a solitary pillar of rock, left by the crumbling cliff, an emblem of himself. He, too, torn from his natural connections, stood alone and expected the storm that should displace him.

And numbed though he was, he inevitably thought often of Weston with a deeper sense of homelessness. 'I have been tossed,' he wrote, 'like a ball into a far country, from which there is no rebound for me'; and, – 'Tell me if my poor birds are living! I never see the herbs I used to give them without a recollection of them.'

Johnson, however, had not yet abandoned hope. He even introduced a tube into Cowper's bedroom near the bed's head and had words of comfort spoken through it; but a tube could hardly succeed where Teedon had failed, and like all who are self-tortured, Cowper was ingenious in converting even the affectionate intentions of friends into supposed insults and so extracting pain from what was meant to give pleasure.

When, however, Johnson read novels to him, and in particular those of Richardson, he showed a certain interest, a fact which, as might be expected, brought no pleasure to Newton. 'Nothing surprises or indeed grieves me more,' he wrote, 'than what you intimate of his attachment to novels. *O quam dispar sibi!*' And he added that things were very different when he was at Olney and before Cowper had begun to associate 'with gay people' and to give in to many things of which he once thought him incapable, and of which he doubted not that he would have been incapable to that day had he continued in his right mind.

It was perhaps fitting that Newton should close his connection with the poet whose mind he had done nothing to strengthen with this last example of insensitive bigotry.

More and more now Cowper feared to be left alone and

was very wretched at week-ends when Johnson was called away by his Sunday duties, listening on the steps of the hall door for the barking of dogs two miles distant which announced his return. Each of the letters, too, which he wrote to Lady Hesketh he described as his last; and yet although he believed a summary execution to be imminent, he feared equally that death was impossible to him. Such was his alienation from life that he could not conceive of death in the ordinary course of nature. It would come by some unexampled supernatural seizure or it would not come at all. The one delusion reflected his nervous distraction, the other his nerveless state.

But at least he had now so faint a recollection of his past life and so slight an attachment to life at all that Mrs. Unwin's death in December, 1796, added little to his sufferings. He gazed on her dead face, gave one poignant cry, and never spoke of her again. He believed that he was the occasion of all that she ever did or could suffer, but his self-hatred was such that he assumed an equal responsibility for the sufferings of any other creature upon earth. And what was one among so many?

Two years later Johnson persuaded him to take up his Homer again, and he began to revise it, with a clear sense, however, now of his inadequacy and of the 'unforeseen impossibility of doing justice to a poet of such great antiquity in a modern language.' He completed his revision in the following spring, and in the same month he wrote his last two poems. Both were suggested by Anson's *Voyages*, which he was reading, and in both he expressed with a bitter self-possession his own abandoned state.

The first was composed in Latin and then translated
into English under the title *On the Ice Islands*. He too was
an island of ice launched into a deep where he was doomed
to waste away and sink. He too looked back upon a
Delos which bore 'herb, fruit, and flower,' and

> crowned with laurel, wore
> Even under wintry skies, a summer smile;
> And Delos was Apollo's favourite isle.

But now, broken off from the earth which nurtured him,
he was one of these 'horrid wanderers of the deep' to
whom the Creator of life

> deems Cimmerian darkness only due.
> Your hated birth he deigned not to survey,
> But, scornful, turned his glorious eyes away.

And in *The Castaway*, since

> misery still delights to trace
> Its semblance in another's case,

he described his own pitiful struggle in the deeps of
despair.

> Obscurest night involved the sky,
> The Atlantic billows roared,
> When such a destined wretch as I,
> Washed headlong from on board,
> Of friends, of hope, of all bereft,
> His floating home for ever left. . . .

Not long beneath the whelming brine,
　Expert to swim, he lay;
Nor soon he felt his strength decline,
　Or courage die away;
But waged with death a lasting strife,
Supported by despair of life. . . .

He long survives, who lives an hour
　In ocean, self-upheld;
And so long he, with unspent power,
　His destiny repelled;
And even, as the minutes flew,
Entreated help, or cried "Adieu!" . . .

No voice divine the storm allayed,
　No light propitious shone,
When, snatched from all effectual aid,
　We perished, each alone:
But I beneath a rougher sea,
And whelmed in deeper gulfs than he.

Cowper more nearly expressed the elemental in this poem
than in any other, but even here his experience was
physical; the concrete facts are not fully transformed by
imagination into symbols. The detailed account of the
sailor's struggles and of his shipmates' attempt at succour,
no less than the demands of rhyme made by the stanza-
form, show that it was written with absolute self-possession. His utter wretchedness was not relieved by any dark
ecstasy. The power and intensity of the poem resides in
its bleak statement. He described the final shipwreck of

his reason with the direct economy, the external precision, of classical sanity.

It was written in March, 1799, and for one more year he continued to repel his destiny. In the following January he could still write in a clear hand an improved version of a passage from the *Iliad* for which Hayley had asked. But life had deserted his body as God his spirit. He had become thin and yellow, and early in 1800 he began to fail. As the end drew near, Johnson tried to give him religious consolation, but he begged him to desist. His last words to the nurse who offered him some refreshment were, 'What can it signify?' Nothing, indeed, had signified for five weary years, and on April 25th he abandoned a life which he had tried so humbly to placate and sustain.

§ 3

Nearly twenty years earlier Cowper had written, – 'An operation is often performed within the curtains of a dying bed . . . that the nurse and the doctor have no suspicion of. The soul makes but one step out of darkness into light and makes that step without a witness.' And it would be comforting to suppose that the look of 'calmness and composure mingled, as it were, with holy surprise,' which Johnson read upon his countenance after death, betokened some such transformation.

Death, at least, could hardly prove less kind to Cowper than the life which it superseded. For extinction is preferable to a living death. And if we believed in the Providence which Newton upheld, the fate of one so lovable and so afflicted could only lead us to despise it as the workings of a callous tyrant. Then, indeed,

> As flies to wanton boys, are we to the gods;
> They kill us for their sport.

For Cowper had not even any 'pleasant vices,' of which just gods 'make instruments to scourge us.' He was the most innocent, as he was the most kindly, of men.

Yet if we cannot forgive life for its treatment of him, we can at least, by narrowing the scope of Providence and admitting the fact of chance, acquit the Creator of malice.

Cowper's life was a series of misfortunes, all of which contributed to his sad destiny. He was born with a constitutional weakness, a slender store of vitality and a trembling sensibility. He lost his mother when he most needed her. His native timidity was fatally aggravated by a schoolboy bully. He was forbidden to love when his nature first awoke to and might have found a lasting satisfaction in love. He was warm-hearted in an age of which the climate was still chilly with good-sense, and so was compelled to compromise between his heart and his head. And he fell under the influence of a religious movement which excited his nerves without satisfying his reason, and by divorcing his religious instinct from his poetical made it impossible for him to harmonize his nature in creative experience.

The qualities, indeed, which made Cowper a precursor of the Romantic Movement were his undoing. For there comes a time in human experience when man must dare a forward step, sacrificing old props and rediscovering the truth of life for himself. Cowper had reached that point, but he lacked the power to do more than compromise. He compromised in poetry with some success by blending a new warmth of sentiment with his century's sobriety. But his sensibility exposed him to feelings too intense to be reconciled with a contemporary good-sense, feelings which demanded a new language and a new extension of mind. And because he could not express these feelings in poetry, in the pure religious activity of the imagination, he came to attach them to a religious creed which inflamed, without liberating, them.

We do not, of course, claim that if he had been able to express his neuroticism imaginatively, he would have cured it. But his neuroticism would at least have become significant. The case of the Brontë family is in this respect peculiarly suggestive. The appeal which *The Castaway* made to them is well known. Charlotte at one time suffered an attack of morbid religious mania very similar to Cowper's, while Emily struggled all her life against a satanic force of self-destructive and isolating pride which at last completely possessed her. Their neuroticism, too, would seem to have had its roots in the early loss of a mother's protective affection, aggravated by a stern father and a dour environment. But both triumphed over their neurosis by sublimating it in art. And although Emily could no more achieve happiness by embodying the protest of her pride and her stifled love in Heathcliff than Melville by doing the same in Captain Ahab, each achieved reality. Shut out, as they were, by the wounds which circumstance had prematurely in-

flicted on their sensibility, from the Heaven of harmonious
self-affirmation which they desired, they at least created
their own Hell, and by projecting their fanatical frustration into an imaginative being, they starkly preserved
at once their identity and their sanity.

But Cowper surrendered his identity to the Hell of
Calvin. He did not deny life: he accepted life's denial of
him. And he attached to this periodic feeling that life
was meaningless the crude and terrible meaning of Calvinistic dogma. Certainly Evangelicism was as much the
consequence as the cause of his self-depreciation, but as
a cause it was more ruinous than any other. As Ibsen's
Mrs. Alving says, – 'It is not only what we have inherited
from our father and mother that "walks" in us. It is all
sorts of dead ideas, and lifeless old beliefs. . . . They
have no vitality, but they cling to us all the same, and we
can't get rid of them. . . . And then we are, one and all,
so pitifully afraid of the light.'

In Cowper's day Calvinistic beliefs were not lifeless.
They had still a fanatical and destructive vitality. His
tragedy was to have outgrown them rationally, but to have
been tied to them by the fears and dissatisfactions of a
sensibility too generous to accept the narrow province of
contemporary good-sense.

'There can be no peace,' he wrote at the end of his life,
'where there is no freedom; and he is a wretch indeed who
is a necessitarian by experience.'

And it was Evangelicism which, by compelling him to
abase his reason and his free-will before an omnipotent
Providence, made him a necessitarian, converting an

innate timidity and one sadly aggravated by early circumstance into a fixed delusion of unpardonable sin. If a poet is enslaved by a fixed dogma, he is indeed lost. For his imagination invests it with a fantastic reality.

Cowper must always have felt his frailty in a world less human, but more physically assured and assertive than himself. Periodic melancholy and lassitude must inevitably have been his. For he lacked the energy either to compel a meaning out of his existence or to forget in some concentrated activity the need of one. 'To reach the goal,' he wrote, 'a man must have eyes to see it; but as for me I have no prospect.' And indeed all the goals which he reached were achieved by simply moving on in an attempt to forget, by patience and perseverance in the act of motion, the want of purpose in his steps.

But he had in full measure the qualities of his defects, the humour, the capacity for simple pleasures, the equableness and the tender, if prescribed, sympathy with natural life. These qualities and the devoted friends whom they attracted might surely have sustained him, even through his later years, if Evangelicism had not hung above his head the sword of a tribal God.

It was that sword which wounded him beyond the hope of healing, and like the flaming sword at the east of the Garden of Eden, 'which turned every way,' denied him access either by earth or heaven to 'the tree of life.'

DATE DUE
